Annuals
for the
Plains and Prairies

Edgar W. Toop

D0520806

Copyright © 1997
University of Alberta

Printed in Canada

Lone Pine Publishing
1901 Raymond Avenue S.W., Suite C
Renton, Washington 98055

Lone Pine Publishing
#206, 10426 - 81 Avenue
Edmonton, Alberta T6E 1X5

University of Alberta
Faculty of Extension
Edmonton, Alberta T6G 2J7

University of Saskatchewan
Extension Division
Saskatoon, Saskatchewan S7N 0W0

All rights reserved. No part of this publication may be reproduced, stored in a retrieval system, or transmitted in any form or by any means whatsoever without prior permission of the copyright owners.

Distributed by Lone Pine Publishing.

Canadian Cataloguing in Publication Data

Toop, Edgar W., 1932–
  Annuals for the plains and prairies

Includes biographical references.
Co-published by the University of Alberta Faculty of Extension, the University of Saskatchewan Extension Division, and Lone Pine Publishing.

ISBN: 1-55091-027-2

1. Annuals (Plants) – Prairie Provinces. 2. Annuals (Plants) – Great Plains.
I. University of Alberta. Faculty of Extension. II. University of Saskatchewan.
Extension Division. III. Title.
SB422.T658 1997   635.9'312'09712   C97-910471-8

Production Team

Managing Editor:	Thom Shaw
Page Design and Layout:	Melanie Eastley
Illustrations:	Melanie Eastley
Page Composition:	Lu Ziola
Copy Editor:	Lois Hameister
Cover Photos:	All-America Selections Gail Rankin
Technical Reviewers:	Brendan Casement Buck Godwin Brian Porter Sara Williams

Preface

Annual flowers do not pose the same problems for the prairie gardener as herbaceous perennials since their life cycle is completed in one growing season. Therefore, survival through our long cold winters is not a factor. However, not all the plants that we grow as annuals or bedding-out plants are true annuals. Many are tender perennials that will flower the first year from seed if started early enough. Others are tender perennials with an underground storage organ such as a tuber, tuberous root, or corm that can be planted in the spring to produce a flowering plant in the summer. Plants which fall into these categories and can be successfully grown in northern climates are included in this book.

The list of common and well known annual flowers is relatively short including favorites such as Petunias, Marigolds and Bedding Geraniums. There is a multitude of cultivars of these popular kinds on the market and plant breeders are developing new ones every year. However, there are as many kinds of annual flowers as there are perennial flowers, if not more, that can be grown in our region. This book includes a vast array of species rather than focusing on the cultivars of the better known kinds. Not all the plants included are easy to grow, but hopefully, all can be successfully grown if given tender loving care. Species and cultivars that do well one year may not give a repeat performance the next because of the vagaries of our continental climate. But if at first you do not succeed, try again at least once.

Annuals are well adapted to producing brilliant splashes of color that will last throughout the summer once flowering begins. Since annuals survive only the one season, flower beds can be changed each year, permitting a complete change in color scheme if so desired. Many annuals make excellent cut flowers and several are capable of being dried for use in winter bouquets and arrangements. The wide range of plant size and plant form among annuals allows them to be used not only in beds, borders, and planters but also in window boxes and hanging baskets. Some are also adapted for use as ground covers, hedges, screens (climbers), and "shrubs".

E. Toop

Foreword

Annuals provide unabashed, bold garden color better than any other class of plants. Annuals complete their life cycle in one season and so "flower" their heads off for our enjoyment. Requiring little garden care, these dwarf or towering plants can flower continuously. There is a trend back to annuals for their reliable garden color and low maintenance.

Annuals for the Plains and Prairies will greatly assist any novice or experienced gardener find the right annuals for any location. The Plant Descriptions are detailed, accurate and attractive, not boring like a textbook. The illustrations and photography are excellent for educational purposes and providing garden ideas. This book will help gardeners learn about the diversity of annual plants and then select from this increasingly diverse group.

I commend Ed Toop for his research and writing ability to present information on annuals in an enchanting and alluring book. He is eminently qualified to author this reference book for gardeners in the United States and Canada. It is both an idea and reference book for all gardeners.

Noria Wolfram Kolvula
Executive Director
All-American Selections

Acknowledgements

The author wishes to thank his colleagues who have encouraged him in the writing of this book. Particular thanks go to: Brian Porter, Horticulture Specialist, Soils and Crops Branch, Saskatchewan Agriculture and Food, Regina, Saskatchewan; Brendan Casement, Nursery Crop Development Section Head, Alberta Tree Nursery & Horticultural Centre, Alberta Agriculture, Edmonton, Alberta; Buck Godwin, retired Olds College Instructor, Olds, Alberta; and Sara Williams, Horticulture Specialist, Extension Division, University of Saskatchewan, Saskatoon, Saskatchewan, for their generous constructive criticism as technical reviewers.

Thanks are also extended to Valerie Hole of Hole's Greenhouses & Gardens Limited of St. Albert, Alberta, for her valuable assistance.

Thanks are also offered to the institutions and individuals who contributed photographic materials. I am indebted to: Donna Balzer, Airdrie; John Beedle, St. Albert, Alberta; Gabe Botar, Edmonton; Brendan Casement, Edmonton; Ed Carmen, Carmen's Nursery, Los Gatos, California; Buck Godwin, Olds, Alberta; Louis Lenz, Winnipeg; Brian Porter, Regina; Gail Rankin, Edmonton; All-America Selections, Downers Grove, IL; Calgary Zoo, Calgary; Olds College, Olds, Alberta; Stokes Seeds Ltd., St. Catharines, Ontario; T & T Seeds Ltd, Winnipeg; University of Alberta Department of Plant Science, Edmonton.

Special thanks are given to my wife, Muriel, for her encouragement and support and especially for helping with the hours of proof reading that are required for a book of this nature.

It is the sincere dedication of the production team and their tremendous talent that has made this book a beautiful reality.

Edgar Toop

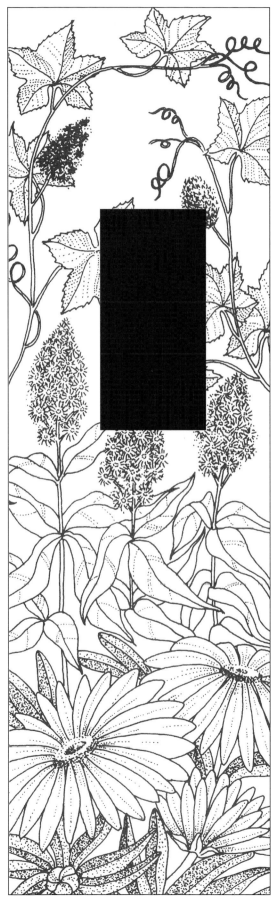

Contents

How to Use This Book

Chapter one of *Annuals for the Plains and Prairies* gives a thumbnail sketch of the historic background of gardens and gardening. Chapters three, four, and five deal with the general aspects of propagation, culture, and use of annuals and bedding plants in the home landscape. The sixth chapter deals with plants that are not normally grown from seed but are used as annual flowers in our northern gardens. More specifically, these are plants that produce an underground storage organ that can be harvested and stored over winter for replanting in the spring.

The second section of the book includes an alphabetical listing by Latin names of annuals and bedding plants, excluding those covered in Chapter six, giving descriptive details and specific hints on propagation, culture, and use. At the end of this section is a master reference chart that summarizes the pertinent information, including shortcomings, about the individual plants or of closely-related plants dealt with in the book. This chart also identifies plants that are native to the Plains and Prairies or have escaped from gardens and established themselves in the wild. Any plants so identified are obviously well adapted to prairie climatic and soil conditions.

Several plants are known in the trade by Latin names that are no longer considered correct. These invalid names (synonyms) have been included in parentheses as an aid in identification. The authority used for correct Latin names is *Hortus Third*. For each plant described, all the well-known common names have been listed. A common name index has been included on page 207 to facilitate rapid access to information on a given plant.

Color plates and illustrative drawings occur throughout the book to enhance the printed word.

Use of technical terms has been avoided as much as possible; however, a glossary for those words which may be unfamiliar to the reader has been included. Words appearing in bold type in the text will be found in the glossary.

Annual Flowers: Splashes of Summer Color

INTRODUCTION

A true annual is defined botanically as an herbaceous plant that grows from seed, produces flowers and seeds, and then dies, all in one growing season. However, many of the "annual flowers" that we grow in our gardens are not true annuals but rather tender **herbaceous perennials** that are unable to survive the winters in colder climates.

In order for a tender perennial to qualify as an annual flower, it must be capable of flowering the first year from seed or be easy to propagate from cuttings that will produce flowering plants during the summer season. This expanded definition of annuals, therefore, will cover the wide range of ornamental plants that can be grown in our northern gardens by sowing seeds or by bedding out young plants each spring.

HISTORY OF GARDENING

The development of gardens throughout the evolution of human society is a fascinating study. To define "garden" and "gardening", it is necessary to go back to the beginnings of agriculture. The earliest agriculture was carried out in areas around villages. The fields where food and fibre crops were cultivated developed either concentrically or occasionally in triangular segments, expanding from the hub, the village itself. At some point in the evolution of villages, houses came to have walled or fenced enclosures, probably initially to pen goats and sheep. These enclosures later included grape vines, fig trees, herbs, and vegetables, and came to be known as a garden. The word "garden" **etymologically** means an "enclosed space" and gardening is historically distinguished from agriculture by being within an enclosure of some kind instead of in open fields. The Latin term *horti* was the name given to these gardens or enclosures. The present day word, horticulture, was derived from this Latin term.

It is this combination of enclosure, shade, trained vines, vegetables in rows, and water, which first constituted a garden, although it is impossible to give any accurate date for the origin of this elementary stage. Communities must raise themselves above the subsistence level of existence before they can really afford to grow, or even appreciate, plants for decoration that have no utilitarian attributes. It was in Egypt by about 1500 BC that civilization first made the utility garden decorative with flower beds, pools and planted trees.

The Romans, with their advanced technology, elaborate architecture, and high standard of living, had developed farming, market gardening, and decorative gardening to new levels by the second century BC. This laid the foundations of the gardening ideals which were built up in Renaissance Europe (14th to 16th centuries) after the intervening centuries of strife and ignorance.

It was the monks in the monasteries, more than the lords in the castles, who maintained the gardening traditions through the Middle Ages. Perhaps more importantly, they also kept many plants in cultivation that would otherwise have been lost. These monastic gardens included medieval herb collections in both **apothecary** and **culinary** gardens, as well as flowers grown for church decoration.

A direct line can be traced from the monastery garden to the early gardens of English university colleges. This is hardly surprising since the buildings were also architecturally derived from the cloistered courtyards of monastic foundations.

The final development of the garden is its use for pleasure rather than plain utility. As mentioned earlier, this develops only when the culture concerned has some excess of wealth and time. Usually these surpluses are limited to the royal families, nobles, and aristocracies, while the peasants toil for their basic essentials, paying taxes to their rulers. This pattern has been repeated in vastly different epochs as civilizations have risen and fallen. Gardening, therefore, in its widest sense, is an expression of a civilization maturing. Hopefully it is not also a symbol of the beginnings of its decadence.

The design of gardens dates back to ancient symbolism. Chinese and Japanese gardens were very formal and symbolic. Gardens of ancient Egypt and Persia tended to combine symbolism and relaxation. Many garden designs were based on the cosmic

Figure 1

The Châteaux, Angers, France, an example of formal knot garden flower beds

Ed Toop

cross whose first literary appearance is in the second chapter of Genesis: "And a river went out of Eden to water the garden; and from thence it was parted, and became into four heads." A garden divided into four parts by water became a recurring theme. The Persians made carpets depicting such gardens, with a river or canals forming a cross. The four-square Tudor garden appears to be a direct descendent of this concept. Four is a basic number in the symbolism of numbers – it is the number of creation, there are four corners of the earth, there are four seasons, there are four winds of heaven, and so on.

One of the most common bed patterns to be used within early gardens was the chessboard of squares. This recurred again and again in almost every culture, no doubt an extension of the cosmic cross concept. Also common were oblong beds placed in strict alignment, somewhat more pleasant to the eye but still somewhat rigid. Gradually some variation began to appear with squares and rectangles being placed in a less regimented, but still formal, manner. Gradually less and less regimentation was imposed, allowing beds of different proportions to be placed together. Eventually the rectangle was abandoned in favor of shaped beds forming intricate patterns.

The Romans often used stones for edging their plant beds. Much later in Europe, edgings once again became common, but the favorite materials used were wood or metal. Such wooden and metal edgings were often painted in bright colors. The alternative to using these inert materials, of course, was the use of living plants as edgings. Thrift, Cotton Lavender, Germander, and Boxwood were among the favored choices – plants that either grew very compact naturally or were capable of being trimmed to shape. This use of plant edgings led to more and more elaborate designs or beds, culminating in what were referred to as knot or knott gardens (first

Figure 2

Willet-Holthuysen House, Amsterdam, an example of a knot garden

Ed Toop

Figure 3

Palace of Versailles gardens, an example of *parterre*

Ed Toop

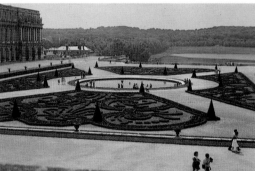

Figure 4

Small formal garden, Castle Ammersoyen, Ammerzoden, Holland

Ed Toop

recorded in 1494), where pattern was created by the use of clipped edging plants. The term originated because the patterns developed had the appearance of a knotted cord. These patterns were originally filled in with flowers or vegetables (Figure 1), but later the knots became so elaborate that they were made solely for the patterns alone (Figure 2). Sometimes plain earth was left between the clipped plants; at other times they were filled with colored earth, sand, gravel, or turf. Materials also included coal, broken bricks, powdered tiles, or coal dust mixed with chalk (to produce a blue color).

Figures 5 and 6

Capability Brown's legacy of naturalized landscaping

Ed Toop

Such knots, often designed to represent a coat-of-arms or other heraldic device, were usually placed to be looked down upon from the upper floors of the house or castle.

The word *parterre*, first used in France in 1549 and in England almost a century later, denoted any level garden area containing ornamental flower beds of any shape or size. The *parterre*, which was first developed in Italy actually, was usually a separate unit in a garden design, typically rectangular in shape and separated from other parts of the landscape layout by stone balustrades or clipped hedges. Its individual beds were often laid out as knots with some part of the pattern reserved for flowers and possibly an appropriately shaped pool. The large gardens of the 16th and 17th centuries might have a whole series of knot or parterre areas separated from each other by hedges, often part of a huge plan that included hedge mazes.

Figure 7

Picturesque setting

At the height of the classical Renaissance culture with its very ordered and formal gardens, a movement began that would convert gardens and estates into landscapes of natural informal beauty. The estates of Britain today show the legacy of "Capability" Brown, a born improver. He got the name of Capability because each time he was asked for an opinion on a property, he remarked that it had great capabilities. Some of the things that were considered important attributes to the ideal English estate garden of his day were ruins, haystacks, obelisks, precipices, wood piles, rabbit warrens, and serpentine meanders. Brown swept away all trace of the old formal avenues and garden terraces in scores of parks and estates. He destroyed a great deal of beauty with the introduction of his ideas. By the beginning of the 19th century, the classic ideal of rigid formality had changed to the picturesque. The picturesque began with the sweeping away of all formality in favor of the naturalistic but ended in the Victorian era by reinstating it to a considerable degree.

Although the earliest evidence of beds or borders being planted exclusively to herbaceous perennial flowers comes from ancient Persia, the term "herbaceous perennial border" was apparently coined by George Nicholson, curator of Kew Gardens, in 1890. It appears that perennials were favored over annual flowers in both Europe and North America at that time. During the early 1900s, tender bedding plants gained favor in the United States and reached a peak in popularity by the 1960s to the virtual exclusion of hardy herbaceous perennial flowers. In recent decades, perennials have made a return in popularity, but annuals continue to hold their own in the competition for the gardener's attention.

2 Propagating Annuals

There are many keen gardeners who prefer to grow their own bedding plants from seed or cuttings or, where practical, to direct seed into the garden where the plants are to flower, rather than purchase started plants. This gives you the opportunity of watching the plants develop through their whole life cycle and also permits you to grow rare or unusual plants that are not available for sale as bedding-out plants. Many of the plants listed in this book are not available as plants for sale for a number of reasons. Some grow so quickly from seed that there is no advantage to starting them as bedding-out plants. In fact, some will readily self-seed and require only thinning and transplanting each spring once they become established. Others do not transplant well and develop quickly from seed sown directly in the garden. Still others can be interesting and challenging for the avid gardener or botanist but require so much care that the average gardener is not interested in dealing with them.

HOME PRODUCTION

Buy seed from reputable seed companies. Companies that have been in business for many years have a reputation to maintain and will make every effort to produce and market seed that is true to type and correctly named.

SOWING SEEDS

Direct Seeding Outdoors

There are two approaches to direct seeding in the garden. One approach is to plant the seed in the bed or border where you wish to have the seedlings develop into mature flowering plants; the other approach is to sow the seed in a small, specially prepared seed bed in a protected, warm, sunny spot in the yard.

The first approach works well for those kinds of plants that germinate and develop quickly to the flowering stage and can be seeded relatively early in the spring. Some examples are California Poppies, Scarlet Runner Beans, Calendulas, and Ornamental Grasses. Sweet Peas, although slow to develop, are also direct seeded and can be sown as early in the spring as the soil can be worked into a suitable tilth for seeding. In most cases, broadcast the seed and rake it into the fine-particled surface layer of soil. Cover larger seeds to a depth of about one and a half to two times the seed diameter. Deeper seeding is recommended if the soil is light and sandy, or the bed is exposed to drying winds. Once the seedlings have developed their first set of leaves, thin them to the proper spacing required for full mature development of the plants. Seedlings can also be transplanted to fill in bare spots or to expand the size of the planting.

The second approach, using a special seed bed, works well for those kinds that require more warmth and general care in their early stages of growth or respond well to transplanting. Such a seed bed could in fact become a cold frame by building a temporary clear plastic or glass-covered structure over it. Plans for constructing a conventional cold frame are illustrated in diagram 13, but a simple sheet of plastic secured over a framework of wire arches or hoops will work. It is very important, however, that the structure be designed so that it can be readily opened and closed to control ventilation. This added protection of a cold frame greatly expands the capabilities of this special outdoor seed bed, allowing you to sow seeds even earlier in the spring than would be possible without this added protection. If the covering material is made easily portable, then it can be completely removed after all danger of cold night temperatures and the danger of frost has passed. This will allow the young plants to become acclimatized to the weather conditions before they are transplanted to the beds, borders, or planter boxes.

Figure 8

Cold Frame

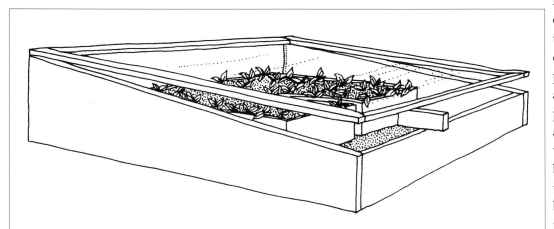

This special outdoor seed bed, whether or not it involves a covering of glass or plastic, should be well drained, well cultivated, preferably raised, and located in a sunny, wind-protected area. The incorporation of peat and sand to a good garden loam soil in the proportions of 1 part peat, 1 part sand, and 2 parts soil should make a suitable medium. If the soil has a high clay content, use equal parts of the three ingredients. Raising the bed above the level of the surrounding soil areas will ensure improved drainage and will also help in trapping solar radiation to warm the seed bed. The incorporation of chemical fertilizer or even compost or well-rotted manure is not necessary or even recommended since high fertility is not a requirement for seed germination. Once seedlings develop, however, they will require nutrients which can easily be supplied by the periodic application of a dilute solution of a complete soluble fertilizer such as 20-20-20. It is important not to have high amounts of nitrogen available since it will encourage soft, lush, or even spindly growth which is very susceptible to frost or even low-temperature injury. A rich compost or a chemical nitrogen fertilizer could result in too much nitrogen for young seedlings and germinating seeds.

The surface of the seed bed should be smooth and composed of finely divided particles, especially for sowing small-sized seed. The seed may be broadcast, but it is easier to **"prick-out"** the young seedlings for transplanting if the seed is sown in defined rows that are spaced about 1.5 to 2 in. (3 to 5 cm) apart. The depth of the groove or trench made for each row will depend on the size of the seeds to be planted. Large seeds can be individually placed about 1 to 1.5 in. (2 to 3 cm) apart so that the seedlings have more room to develop, thus delaying or even eliminating the pricking-out operation. Smaller seeds should be sown thinly enough that the

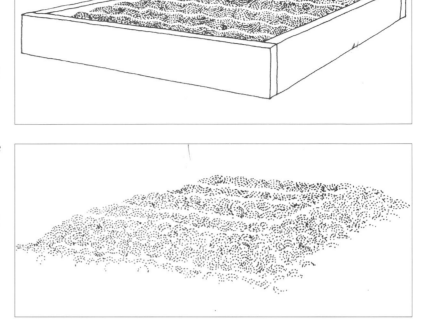

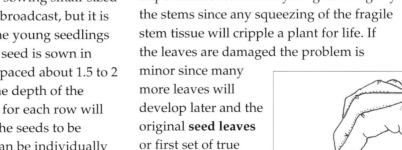

young seedlings can be easily pulled apart when they are pricked-out for transplanting.

Pricking-out involves lifting out a clump of seedlings from a seed row or patch of "broadcast" seedlings by digging in beneath their roots with a dibber (piece of doweling, pencil, or popsicle stick) and gently dropping the clump onto the ground. This action should cause the soil mixture to fall away from the roots and allow you to tease the individual seedlings apart by holding them by the leaves between your thumb and index finger. It is important not to handle young seedlings by the stems since any squeezing of the fragile stem tissue will cripple a plant for life. If the leaves are damaged the problem is minor since many more leaves will develop later and the original **seed leaves** or first set of true leaves usually die at an early age. Each little separated seedling can be replanted using the

Figure 9 and 10

Raised beds

Figure 11

Correct method of holding pricked-out seedlings

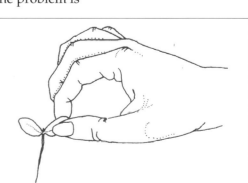

dibber to make a small hole to accommodate the tiny root and to gently push soil over and around it. This pricking-out operation is merely a transplanting procedure to space the plants far enough apart to allow them to develop as strong, bushy individuals for transplanting to the garden later. Regardless of the ultimate size and spread of the mature plants, seedlings of all kinds of plants can be spaced about 2 to 3 in. (5 to 7 cm) apart for this growing-on phase.

Starting Seedlings Indoors

For each of the plants included in the reference or plant descriptions section of this book, information is given on the suitability of starting the plant from seed indoors and, if appropriate, approximately when such seeding should take place. Timing is expressed in most instances in terms of "weeks before the last spring frost is expected." This date, of course, can vary considerably from year to year across the plains region, so the best guide is the long-term average for your particular area. For much of the northern plains region, this date occurs during the month of May through the first week of June. Information printed on the seed packets will also tell you when seeding should be done. Any quality seed package (or catalogue) should include such information as "days required from seeding to flowering" or "days required for germination."

Figures 12

Containers

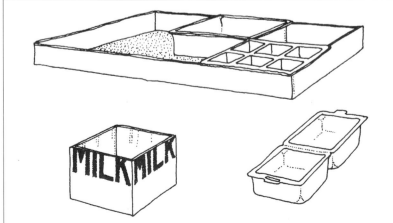

- **Containers**
  The choice of containers that can be used for seeding and **growing-on** plants for bedding-out varies from traditional plastic flats and "cell paks" to fast-food containers, milk cartons, and egg cartons. Whatever you choose should have holes for drainage. For seed germination and growth to the pricking-out stage, the container should be at least 1 in. (2.5 cm) deep; for growing-on to bedding-out size, it should be at least 3 in. (8 cm) deep.

- **Potting Mixture**
  Of more importance than the container is a suitable growing mix or medium. There are many mixes to choose from containing soil, peat, sand, perlite, and vermiculite. If soil is used, either alone or in a mixture, it is important that it be **sterile (pasteurized)** to ensure that no plant pathogens are present.

  Garden soil is not sterile and usually contains a host of micro-organisms, including those which cause **Damping-off.** Heating the soil to 180°F (82°C) will destroy the offending fungi. If you use a non-combustible container (peat pots or clay pots), the soil and the container can be placed in an oven and heated to 180°F (82°C) (the internal soil temperature) for 30 minutes. It is important that the soil be wet when put in the oven as the steam produced by the water penetrates the air spaces. Dry soil takes longer to heat and produces more odor. Use a meat thermometer to determine when the soil has reached 180°F (82°C).

  A temperature of 180°F (82°C) will also kill insect larvae and eggs and some weed seeds. Use the heat treatment prior to sowing seeds. It is a great preventative for Damping off. Avoid heating the soil above 180°F (82°C). At higher temperatures, beneficial organisms are killed and dissolved salts are released from the soil which may be toxic to plants. Alternatively, soil may be heated in a pressure cooker for 20 minutes at 5 pounds of pressure.

For germinating, and even growing-on of most kinds of plants, a commercial soil-less mix works well. For example, a mixture of peat and vermiculite, peat and perlite, or a combination of peat, vermiculite, and perlite, provides a sterile, uniform, well-aerated medium that holds moisture and has good drainage qualities as well. Each gardener tends to have a preference for a particular soil-less mix. The ingredients and proportions of a potting mixture recipe are less important that the qualities that the mix possesses. For germination, the medium should be fine-textured (small particles). It should also hold water well but have good drainage to ensure good aeration. For growing-on, the medium should be coarser but still retain the other attributes of a good growing medium. The demand for nutrients will need to be met for the growing-on phase. This can be done by incorporating pasteurized soil in the growing-on mix or incorporating a slow release fertilizer to keep the plants healthy and growing until they are transplanted to the garden. The alternative procedure is to water-in the young transplants (pricked-out seedlings) with a starter solution (10-52-10 or 10-52-17 fertilizer) and to give a weekly application of a general soluble fertilizer such as 20-20-20 thereafter. All three of these fertilizers are available in crystalline form with instructions for preparing appropriate strength solutions to be watered-in.

The planting medium, which should be moist at the time of filling, should be lightly pressed into the containers using the finger tips. Settling and leveling is also enhanced by tapping the filled containers on the table or potting bench a few times. Fill containers to within about 0.5 in. (1 to 1.5 cm) of the rim. If containers are filled to the very top, it makes watering very difficult. Keep the surface level to ensure the even distribution of water when watering is done from the top.

- **Sowing Techniques**
Seed may either be broadcast across the surface of the medium or placed in neat rows which are about 1 in. (2.0 to 2.5 cm) apart. The advantage of planting in rows is two-fold: it makes lifting out the clumps of seedlings for transplanting (pricking-out) easier, and secondly, it slows down the spread of the fungal disease Damping-off if it should get started. Damping-off is the name given to a disease caused by several types of fungi which attack young seedlings at soil level and rot the stems. It is characterized by the blackening and shrivelling of the stem while the leaves above appear healthy. Then the entire young seedling topples over.

Damping-off is highly contagious and will spread rapidly from plant to plant. If the seedlings are growing in rows, the initial spread of the disease will travel along the affected row before spreading to adjoining rows. Early detection of disease symptoms allows you to take measures to destroy the infected plants and treat the remainder of the container to halt the spread of the disease.

The depth of seeding depends on the size of the seed. Very fine seed should barely be covered and is best placed or sprinkled on the surface of the medium. It is then covered by rubbing some of the medium mix, or possibly vermiculite alone, between the palms of your hands to allow a light dusting of fine particles to fall on the seeded area. A small sieve made from window screen also works well for shaking a thin layer of fine material over the seeded area. Small trenches of varying depths can be made

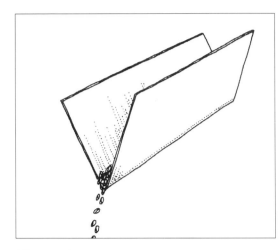

Figure 13

V-shaped paper for seeding

Figure 14

Coverings for seed flats

to define the rows when you seed larger seeds. One of the techniques for placing seed evenly along the row is to place the seed on a piece of note paper that has been folded in half to provide a v-shaped crevice. Individual seeds can then be jiggled toward the edge of the paper at the fold and allowed to fall in succession along the length of the row. Small battery-operated devices using this same principle are also available. Seeds large enough to pick up with the fingers can be individually placed by hand.

After sowing is complete and the seeds have been covered to the appropriate depth (1.5 to 2.0 times the diameter of the seed), mist the surface of the medium with sufficient water to settle the medium particles around the seeds, and thoroughly wet the seeds. Then cover the containers with plastic to prevent evaporation and keep the surface medium from drying out. Kitchen plastic wrap works well. For seeds that require darkness, lay

newspaper on top of the plastic wrap. The container can then be placed in a bright, warm area but not in direct sunlight. Check containers regularly to ensure that the medium stays moist, especially at and near the surface where the seeds are located. Wipe away any heavy condensation that may develop on the plastic cover. Once sprouting is evident, remove the covering and mist or gently water as often as is necessary to keep the surface layer moist. Good air circulation around the containers and among the developing seedlings is very important. If condensation is allowed to occur on the seedlings, or the medium is kept too moist and soggy, the young plants will be prime candidates for Damping-off.

If Damping-off should occur, remove all plants showing symptoms as well as a few of the apparently healthy ones next to them. Discard all the growing medium around and below the roots of these plants as well and replace it with fresh uncontaminated potting mixture. Then the entire flat or container should be drenched with a fungicide solution such as No-Damp, following directions on the label. No-Damp is registered for domestic (home garden) use, has no systemic effect and little residue. It should be used within 24 hours of mixing, after which it is broken down by hydrolysis.

Most seeds germinate best around room temperature (68°F, 20°C), but some have rather specific temperature requirements either below or above this level. Others have a different optimal temperature for seedling development than they do for germination. Plants that have these special requirements will often have this information provided on their seed packets.

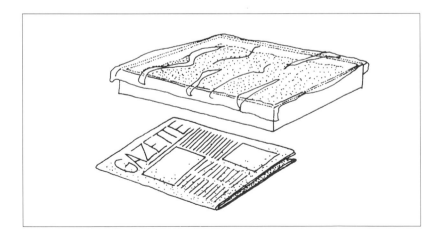

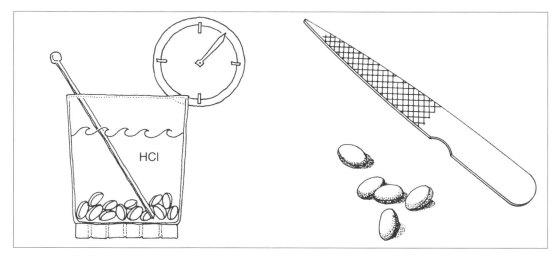

Figure 15

Scarification tools

Special Treatments

Seeds of a few kinds of annuals exhibit **dormancy** which means they require special treatment before they will germinate. This dormancy is caused by various factors or combinations of factors. The most common cause among annuals is a hard, impervious seed coat. Such seeds must have the coat cracked open or eroded away by mechanical, chemical or biological agents so that water and air can enter the seed to initiate growth processes. A second cause for dormancy is seed immaturity. Seeds of some plants are shed before the **embryo** is fully developed. A sequence of specific temperature changes is usually required to trigger this maturation or after-ripening process. A third cause for seed dormancy is the presence of growth suppressing compounds in the seed or the absence of growth promoters. Manipulation of temperature and moisture conditions provides the key for unlocking this form of dormancy.

- **Scarification**
  Scarification is the term used to describe the breaking or softening of hard seed coats. This is done by scarring individual seeds with a sharp file, rubbing the seed between two sheets of sandpaper, or tumbling seeds in a container with an abrasive agent such as carborundum. A short exposure of seeds to concentrated sulphuric or hydrochloric acid is a common commercial chemical scarification treatment. Examples of seeds that benefit from scarification to hasten germination are Moonflower *(Ipomea alba)* and Morning Glory *(Ipomea* spp. and *Convolvulus* spp.).

- **Stratification**
  To hasten the breaking of internal dormancy, seeds are alternately layered (hence the term **stratification**) within a moist medium such as clean sand, sand-peat mixture, or peat. Temperature control (level and duration) provides the necessary treatment to break the internal dormancy of the stratified seed. Some examples of annuals that require stratification are Bachelors Button *(Centaurea cyanus)* which benefits from cold stratification (32 to 41°F, 0 to 5°C) for a period of 1 week and Strawflower *(Helichrysum bracteatum)* which benefits from cold stratification for a period of 1 to 2 months.

Figure 16

Stratification

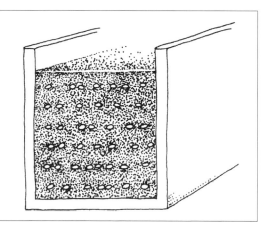

Figure 17

Soaking

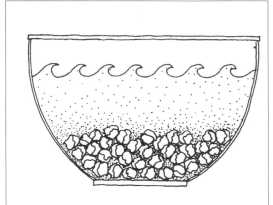

• Soaking

Seeds with hard seed coats usually benefit from being soaked in tepid water from 6 to 36 hours before planting. Some kinds, such as Morning Glories, require scarification as well. Examples of seeds that benefit from soaking alone are Sweet Peas *(Lathyrus odoratus),* Job's Tears *(Coix lacryma-jobi),* and Lupines *(Lupinus* spp.)

Artificial Lighting

For the gardeners who are interested in starting their own plants from seed every spring, it is well worth the money to invest in fluorescent light fixtures. For raising young seedlings, an irradiance level of 6,000 to 10,000 (micro)w/sq. yd. (/m^2) is required for about 16 hours each

Figure 18

Plants under fluorescent lights

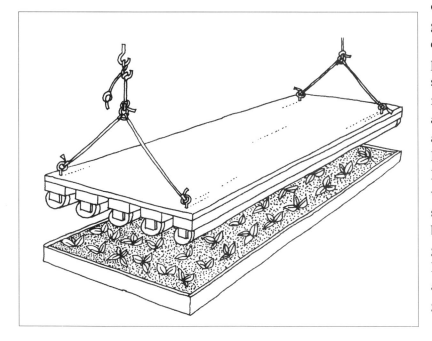

24-hour day. This can be achieved by keeping the tops of plants 1 to 2 in. (2 to 5 cm) below fluorescent tubes. Ordinary cool white or natural white fluorescent works very well, so it is not necessary to use the more expensive tubes designed for optimal plant growth and development, especially if the lighting is set up where the plants will receive some natural sunlight during the daylight hours. The closer the individual tubes are lined up together, the more the radiant energy available to the plants per unit of surface area. With a close spacing of the tubes (approximately 2.5 in (6.5 cm)), rather than the more standard setting (4.5 in. (11.5 cm)), the lights can be kept further above the plants (4 to 5 in. (10 to 12 cm)). The radiant energy falls off exponentially as distance increases. In other words, the level of energy 2 yd. (2 m) from a light bulb is not half but rather one-quarter of what it is 1 yd. (1 m) away.

With fluorescent lamps, heat is not produced along with the light in the tube as it is with ordinary incandescent bulbs. This is why they can be placed so close to the plants. However, heat is generated in the ballast built into the fixture itself, so it is important that this heat be allowed to dissipate and not be directed onto the plants. Specially designed carts or portable tray units for growing plants are available, but you can easily build a serviceable support frame to place on a table or bench and install as many single or double tube fixtures as are required. Standard units come in approximately 24-in. (60-cm), 48-in. (120-cm) and 96-in. (240-cm) lengths. Using such a lighting setup in January, February, and March for starting bedding plants from seed will greatly enhance the quality of the seedlings and the vigor of the subsequent bedding-out plants, even if you have a greenhouse. Daylength is short and light levels are low from mid-winter until the approach of the spring equinox so that plant growth is restricted, even in greenhouses.

STARTING PLANTS FROM CUTTINGS

When plants do not "come true" from seeds, as in the case of certain hybrids, some means of vegetative reproduction must be used. **Vegetative** reproduction **(asexual propagation)** is the use of plant parts other than seeds to produce a population of new plants. Cuttings may consist of portions of stems, entire leaves or portions of leaves, a leaf plus the node of the stem to which it is attached, or portions of roots. The size of cuttings and the age or maturity of the plant organs used for cuttings vary with the kind of plant being propagated and the amount of material available for use.

Figure 19

Terminal Stem Cutting

Terminal Stem Cuttings

Terminal stem cuttings or "slips" are an easy way to start new plants. Once roots develop at or near the cut surface of the cuttings you have new complete plants. Such cuttings can be made from new growth in the spring from plants that have been kept overwinter in a greenhouse or possibly as house plants. Examples are Bedding Geraniums, Show Geraniums, or Scented Geraniums as well as *Impatiens, Fuschia,* and others. Cuttings of 3 to 4 in. (8 to 10 cm) in length can be removed when vigorous shoots are about 6 in. (15 cm) or more in length. Make the cuts at, or just below, a node, remove the bottom leaves, and stick the cuttings in a suitable medium in flats or pots. Sand-peat or perlite-peat mixes are commonly used for rooting.

Leaf-Bud Cuttings

Leaf-bud cuttings are handled in a similar fashion to stem cuttings but consist of only a short piece of stem with a leaf attached. Leaves are attached to stems only at nodes and in the axils of those leaves will be one or more buds. These buds may or may not be visible. Once such a cutting

roots and the bud develops into a shoot a new complete plant has been created. It takes longer to get a good-sized plant from a leaf-bud cutting than from a stem cutting, but many more plants can be developed from the same amount of cutting material. If a plant has opposite leaf arrangement (two leaves at a node), you can make two cuttings from each node by cutting through the center of the stem segment. Leaf-bud cuttings work best, however, on plants with fairly thick or sturdy stems such as Bedding Geraniums.

Leaf Cuttings

Leaf cuttings involve an entire leaf (blade and petiole), the blade only, or a portion of the blade. Leaf cuttings are popular for propagating African Violets, Begonias, and other house plants. However, there are few annuals or bedding plants that are propagated by means of leaf cuttings. For leaf cuttings to be successful, not only do roots have to be initiated, but a bud must form as well. Not all plants have the genetic capability for initiating buds in tissues other than that at stem nodes.

Figure 20

Leaf-Bud Cutting

Figure 21

Division of Dahlia roots

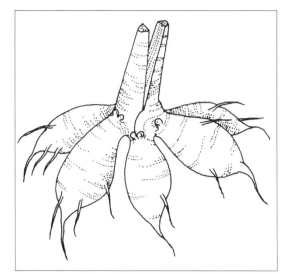

Root Cuttings

Root cuttings are useful for propagating many perennials but are not really applicable to annuals. Dahlias develop a tuberous root system which can be stored over winter and divided as a means of propagating new plants. The handling of Dahlias and other tender perennials that develop a food storage organ and are used as bedding plants is covered in Chapter 6, page 36.

HARDINESS

Hardiness, especially winter hardiness, as it applies to both woody plants and herbaceous perennials, is a familiar term to northerners. One of the great advantages of growing true annuals and the tender perennials that we handle as annuals is that we do not have to worry about bringing them through the winter season. However, among these so-called annuals and bedding-out ornamental plants there are differences in their ability to withstand cold and windy weather. For this reason the classifying of annuals as hardy, half-hardy, and tender is often done. It is a somewhat arbitrary system that does not have widespread application since plants considered hardy in one region may be tender in another. In general, hardy annuals are those you can seed outdoors in the fall or very early in the spring whereas half-hardy kinds should not be seeded until late spring when the soil has warmed up. Tender annuals are those best started indoors or in a greenhouse. For our northern climatic conditions only those classified as hardy would be expected to be capable of being seeded directly outdoors, but this is not always true. Many of those classed as half-hardy and even a few of the tender types can be direct-seeded outdoors with excellent results.

Cultivating Annuals

In order for annuals to grow and thrive, the soil must contain the **essential elements** and be at an optimum **pH.** Temperature, moisture, and light conditions must also be favorable.

SOIL FOR ANNUALS

Preparation of the soil is not as critical as it is for perennials since the plants only last one growing season. Therefore, deep cultivation to allow deep rooting is not necessary since annuals, for the most part, are shallow-rooted; their limited life span does not allow time for development of an extensive root system. It is the upper 6 in. (15 cm) or so of the soil that needs to be well-tilled and of good organic matter content with nutrient reserves. The lower levels need not be disturbed provided the ground is not compacted and natural drainage is good. It is for this reason that annuals perform much better than perennials when planted near a shrub or hedge or underneath trees. The disturbance of the surface soil in preparation for the planting of the bedding-out plants destroys any surface roots of the woody

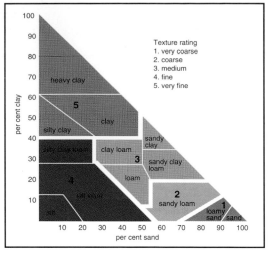

Figure 22

Textural triangle
for soil

plants. This allows the annuals to compete favorably with the woody plants for moisture and nutrients. By the time competition is re-established, the season is nearly over and the life span of the annuals is running out. With perennial flowers, on the other hand, competition would become keen and the woody plants would have the advantage over the herbaceous ones which must begin top growth at ground level every spring.

Any good garden soil will grow annuals. A medium garden loam of good tilth is ideal, but almost any soil can be modified to approach this ideal. For example, a very sandy soil can be made into loamy soil by the incorporation of peat, compost, or well rotted manure. This **organic matter** increases the water-holding capacity of the soil, helps bind the sand together, and yet maintains excellent drainage. Oddly enough, a soil high in clay can have its tilth greatly improved with the same treatment. In this instance the organic matter dilutes the clay, preventing it from compacting and becoming sticky, thus improving both the drainage and the aeration.

Figure 23

Components of soil

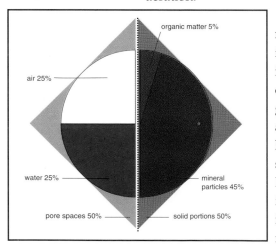

Clay soils may also benefit from the incorporation of coarse or large-grained sand as well as organic matter to help stabilize a good soil structure. However, clay plus fine sand can result in "concrete" so care must be taken in amending heavy, clay soils so that a good proportion of organic matter is incorporated along with the sand. It is this tilth or soil structure that is of utmost importance since there must be both air and water surrounding the roots in the soil if the roots are to remain alive and continue to grow and function.

ESSENTIAL ELEMENTS

Most of the nutrients required by plants are absorbed through their root systems. Therefore it is essential that these materials be present in the soil in adequate amounts. All 16 **essential elements** for plant growth are usually present in soil but not always in optimum quantities. Of the 16, 6 are required in relatively large amounts. These **macronutrients** are nitrogen, phosphorus, potassium, calcium, magnesium, and sulphur. Of this group nitrogen, phosphorus, and potassium are the three most likely to become short in supply and need to be added regularly as fertilizer.

It is the balance of nitrogen, phosphorus, and potassium (N, P and K) available to plants that regulates the growth and development of a plant, provided all other factors essential to plant growth are in place. Nitrogen encourages vegetative development and is particularly important in the early part of the growing season. However, if nitrogen is available in large quantities in relation to phosphorus and potassium, it can delay flowering and restrict root growth. Phosphorus is particularly important for healthy root growth and both phosphorus and potassium are important in flowering and fruiting. This is why a complete fertilizer (10-30-10, 20-20-20, or 5-10-5) is recommended for gardens rather than a lawn fertilizer which is high in nitrogen (the first number) and low in phosphorous and/or potassium. Some prairie soils are naturally high in potassium and may require N-P fertilizer only (16-20-0 or 11-48-0).

SOIL pH

For plants to be healthy and productive, not only must all the essential elements be present in the soil, but they must also be available to the roots. To be available they must be in a soluble ionic form. This explains why the pH or degree of **acidity** or **alkalinity** of a soil is so closely tied to soil fertility. Each nutrient is soluble over a range of pH but will be most soluble at a specific pH reading. The best average pH reading for ensuring that all the essential elements will be soluble is about 6.2. Therefore for most annuals the ideal pH range for the soil is 6.0 to 6.5 which is slightly acidic (7.0 is neutral).

Although incorporation of compost or well rotted manure to the soil each fall or spring will maintain an adequate balance of nutrients for annuals, many annuals will perform better if given supplementary applications of chemical fertilizers. To determine the amount and frequency of fertilizer to add, have your soil tested regularly. Soil testing is provided by both commercial and government laboratories for a fee. You will receive recommendations for bringing the soil fertility into balance for the crop you intend to grow.

Be careful when you purchase top soil or manures for use in the home garden. Some topsoils have been treated with a non- or slowly-degradable herbicide to eliminate weeds before the top soil is removed for sale. This treated topsoil is toxic to most plants grown in it afterward. Also be aware that animal wastes can concentrate certain pesticide residues present on the feed consumed by the animals. This in turn can cause toxicity symptoms on plants whose roots come in contact with these toxins. Ask questions about the quality of the products. Get some sort of insurance in writing if you have any suspicions about the integrity of the product.

TEMPERATURE AND MOISTURE

Soil temperature and moisture also influence plant growth. A properly prepared soil with good structure should have good drainage, but if the top soil is shallow and the subsoil is compacted or rather impervious to water, drainage tiles may have to be installed to ensure proper drainage. To do this, lay tiles made of fired clay, concrete or plastic, or possibly perforated pipe, underground at about 18 to 24 in. (45 to 60 cm) in depth in lines spaced about 24 to 40 in. (60 to 100 cm) apart. These lines should slope very slightly toward the outlet at a pitch of about 3 in. per 45 ft (8 cm per 15 m). Good drainage ensures that the soil warms up quickly in the spring. Soil may be mounded into raised beds of up to 12 to 24 in. (30 to 60 cm) depth as an alternative method to the installation of drainage tile.

WIND PROTECTION

Protection from wind is also important in preventing moisture loss from soil which, in turn, affects soil temperature. The plants themselves will provide wind protection during the growing season, but plants that do not tolerate wind well may need protection themselves. To ensure year-round protection, provide wind breaks in the form of shrubs, trees, or man-made structures. This is particularly important on farms or acreages where winds can sweep across large open areas of land. If trees or shrubs are used, species which have tap roots or limited root systems should be chosen to minimize the competition for moisture and nutrients between these woody plants and the annuals.

Figure 24

Solubility of nutrients at various pH levels

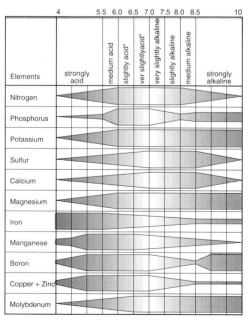

*ideal range for most plants (6.0 - 6.5)

MULCHING

Covering the soil surface with either plastic or organic mulches is another way of conserving soil moisture and controlling soil temperature. Plastic will trap solar energy and warm the soil, which is ideal for warm season crops such as gourds and Morning Glories. However, some annuals, such as Sweet Peas, prefer a cool but moist soil. That is what makes organic mulches ideal since they insulate the soil surface from the hot sun yet reduce evaporation of water. Mulching also reduces mud splash, cushions the soil against compaction, and prevents crusting of the soil surface, a condition that hinders the percolation of rain and irrigation water down into the soil. An organic mulch also gradually decays adding to the organic content of the soil. The organisms that bring about this decay release nutrients in the organic matter making them available to the plant roots. Leaf litter, straw, ground corn cobs, wood chips, and many other materials can be used as a mulch, but coarse peat moss is most commonly used. Care must be taken when using wood chips since some kinds such as fir are toxic to many plants. A depth of 2 to 4 in. (5 to 10 cm) is adequate.

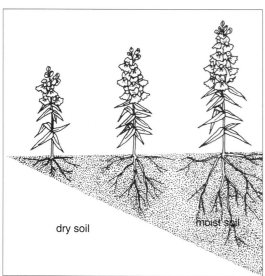

Figure 25

Roots will grow downward only to the depth of moist soil

dry soil

moist soil

IRRIGATION

Seldom is the natural precipitation adequate to maintain a flower bed at its peak of perfection throughout the growing season. It is important to monitor the soil moisture level regularly and add irrigation when required. To determine soil moisture, dig down into the soil to a depth of about 6 to 12 in. (15 to 30 cm), take a handful of soil and squeeze it into a ball. If upon releasing the hand pressure the ball falls apart, the moisture content is too low; if it stays closely packed together it is too wet; and if it partially breaks apart the moisture content is ideal. Soils of different texture (varying proportions of sand, silt and clay) react somewhat differently in this test, but experience will improve your ability to interpret this test for different soils. If irrigation is necessary, add sufficient water to ensure that it penetrates into the root zone. The amount of water required depends upon the soil texture and the organic matter content. Clay particles and humus can absorb copious amounts of water in comparison to sand and silt. Avoid frequent but sparse watering which encourages very shallow rooting that makes the plants susceptible to the stresses of heat, cold, wind, and drought.

If you use rain water for irrigation, discard the initial runoff when rain occurs after an extended dry spell. After many weeks without rain, there may be significant air pollutant fallout on the roofs of buildings that could be concentrated enough in the initial runoff to be toxic to plants.

Water can be applied using a watering can or garden hose. Allow water to gently flood the soil surface around the plants. Water can also be applied by soaker hoses or sprinklers in the same fashion used for watering lawns. However, with overhead watering it is important to time the application so that the plants are not exposed to hot sunshine but will dry off quickly after irrigation is stopped. This means applying sprinkler irrigation early in the morning before the heat of the day or during the daytime when the weather is cloudy. Such irrigation is not recommended later in the day or at night since relative humidity tends to increase as the sun sets and temperatures drop, thus slowing down evaporation. Moisture-laden plants provide ideal conditions for mildew and leaf-spotting diseases to develop.

LIGHT

Among the many annual flowers that can be successfully grown in northern climes the requirement for sunlight varies all the way from full sun for at least 6 hours per day to constant shade. Most plants require a fair amount of sunlight to flower at their best, but many of these can be very attractive or even more attractive in partial shade. Plant size, leaf size, leaf color, and the overall textural appearance of plants are modified by the amount of light the plant receives. So when we talk about shade-loving and sun-loving plants we are referring to the level of light at which a plant will achieve its aesthetic excellence.

PURCHASING BEDDING PLANTS

Supermarkets, department stores, farmers markets, and various other retail outlets including backyard entrepreneurs all have bedding plants of various kinds available for sale in the spring. However, the garden centers and larger greenhouse grower operations are the best sources of good quality materials. These specialty outlets also have a large selection of species and cultivars. They also provide service in the form of instruction for planting and care, and may have a replacement policy. Many retail outlets such as supermarkets obtain their bedding plants from reputable growers, but because the material is being cared for in most cases by untrained personnel, it can deteriorate rapidly from improper watering, exposure to excessive heat (hot sun), and other factors. Damage may not be evident when the plants are purchased but can show up later after the plants have been transplanted to the garden. However, if you are a knowledgeable gardener and a good shopper, there are bargains to be had at the non-specialty outlets.

It is important that bedding plants be **"hardened off"** or acclimatized to the outside environment before they are transplanted to beds, borders, or fixed planters. The low temperature tolerant plants can be conditioned to withstand frost or near freezing temperatures, if properly prepared by gradual exposure to cooler and cooler conditions. On the other hand, tender tropical or sub-tropical kinds are more safely hardened off by withholding water and nitrogen fertilizer. This procedure prevents the production of lush, tender growth that is particularly vulnerable to low temperature and desiccation from wind. When you purchase plants, it is often difficult to determine whether or not the plants have been acclimatized and are ready to plant out. Therefore, leave purchased plants in their containers and set them out where they are to be transplanted for at least a few days to allow them to adjust to their new location. Then transplant them.

Plants that have been mishandled can become severely hardened to the extent that they virtually go into a state of dormancy. When this happens, the plants fail to respond to tender loving care and simply stand still for days, or sometimes weeks, before they take off. Excessive hardening off by the bedding plant grower to extend the shelf-life of the product or to have it withstand the rigors of the blacktop parking lot sales area may explain why the consumer sometimes runs into this problem of "sulky" plants.

Figure 26

Bedding plants in "cell pak", tray, and pots

One of the greatest advantages of buying bedding-out plants is the "jump on the season" that you can achieve. Many bedding plants are sold already in bloom so that planting them into the beds and borders results in instant color. Buying plants in flower also lets you know exactly what the flowers are like, both in size and form as well as color. However, when the choice of selecting plants in bloom or not in bloom is available, you may wish to choose those that have not yet come into blossom. These less-advanced or slower developing specimens will often take off faster in the garden than those already well into flower in the cell paks or trays.

TRANSPLANTING TO THE GARDEN

Since many annuals are either purchased as started plants or started indoors or in a cold frame, the plants are transplanted at least once if not two or more times. Each transplanting results in a "pruning" or "pinching back" of the root systems, which in many plants is beneficial and encourages the development of a well-branched, compact root system. Each time the roots are disturbed, there is an increased demand for phosphorus which plays an important part in encouraging rapid recovery of plants from "transplant shock". For this reason, it is recommended that bedded-out plants be watered in with a solution of fertilizer such as 10-52-10 or 10-52-17 (at the dilution recommended on the label).

These highly soluble, high phosphate fertilizers are often called starter solutions because of their benefit to new transplants. Repeat applications of starter solution once every week for the first 2 or 3 weeks, followed by applications of a more balanced fertilizer (such as 20-20-20 at the dilution recommended on the package) every 2 weeks or so thereafter, should ensure continued growth and flowering of most annual flowers. Because these plants have developed compact root systems, they tend not to "forage" very far beyond their original root zone after being placed in the garden. Therefore, they respond better to regular applications of soluble fertilizer than they do to nutrients naturally occurring or incorporated as granules into the garden soil prior to planting.

When you transfer container-grown plants or seedlings to the garden, plant them to the same depth that they were growing previously. If the soil bed has been properly prepared to a good tilth there should be no compaction around the root system and the new transplants should adapt to their new location quickly.

SPACING

Spacing will vary with each kind of plant and how dense you want the planting to appear. However, the mature height, spread, and vigor of growth are the main factors to consider. Large plants such as Castor Bean *(Ricinus communis)* can occupy up to a cubic meter of space and so should be planted 36 to 40 in. (90 to 100 cm) apart from one another. The vast majority of annuals have less than half the spread of Castor Beans and are planted about 15 to 18 in. (38 to 45 cm) on center. Mat-forming plants or ground covers such as Portulaca or Mesembryanthemum can be planted at various spacings depending on how dense or solid a mat you want to develop. Most recommended plant spacings should be considered as guidelines only.

4

Designing with Annuals

BEDS AND BORDERS

Unlike perennials, annual flowers must be replanted each year. Furthermore, they provide a shorter season of color than a well-planned planting of mixed perennials. Their advantage, however, is that they can provide vivid splashes of color that remain throughout the frost-free summer period. In addition, you can choose a different color scheme each year. This is not to say that annuals cannot be used in a mixed planting of several kinds in the same manner as a well-planned perennial border, but the season of interest will be shorter, extending from sometime in May to early June until the first killing frost which may be as early as late August to early September. Some of the plants included in this book are indigenous or well adapted to our northern continental climate and will self-propagate from seed. These are ones that are ideal for a mixed planting or wild flower garden that is every bit as long-lasting as a perennial border.

Ed Toop

Figure 27

Annual flower display
in Enkhuizen, Holland

Ed Toop

Figure 28

Carpet or mass
planting of annual
flowers

Figure 29

Annual planting
utilizing different
height zones

Ed Toop

The popular annuals or bedding plants such as Petunias, Marigolds, Pansies, or Geraniums, to name a few, are available in a wide range of brilliant colors that can be used in mass plantings to give large splashes of solid color in natural asymmetrical **"drifts"** or in formal geometric patterns. The scope of their use is as broad as your imagination. You can combine colors that complement each other or colors that match or complement the color of the house itself.

But even annuals are not chosen entirely for the color of their blooms. Many are chosen for growth habit, mature height, or the color and texture of the leaves. However, more care must be taken in planning color combinations among annuals than among perennials. There is more purity of **hue** among annuals, especially those cultivars that have been developed by the plant breeders, than is generally found among perennial flowers. Therefore, take care to choose color combinations that are compatible and do not clash with one another.

Annual flower beds and borders can be very striking using only color combinations and patterns as the focus of interest. In other words, there is little, if any, difference in plant height across the entire planting. Often the entire bed may be planted to one kind or even one cultivar of a specific color. In fact, many of the popular kinds, of which there are a myriad of cultivars, have been bred for compactness and low stature to fit this very purpose of carpet or mass planting.

When you combine annuals of different heights, place the shortest kinds at the front and the tallest at the back or the center of a bed if it is to be viewed from all sides. In a large bed or border of this type, the same principles as those involved in a herbaceous perennial border apply. There could be up to 6 height zones with the rear zones being twice the width or depth of the front 2 or 3 zones to give the most pleasing perspective to the planting.

ANNUALS FOR THE PLAINS AND PRAIRIES

CHOOSING A SHAPE

A bed or border may be rather formal with a geometric shape such as a rectangle or informal with a natural-looking, curved edge and variable width or depth. Avoid a patterned or scalloped edging, however, because it detracts from the beauty of the flowers. A natural edge that interfaces with the lawn, a turf walkway or possibly a paved walkway is preferable to a raised edging of stones or brick. An edging of bricks or similar material laid flat and flush with the lawn is a compromise that is unobtrusive yet reduces the maintenance normally required with a direct lawn-garden interface. A simple and effective way to develop a natural looking curvature to a bed or border edge is to lay down a piece of rope or flexible garden hose to outline the desired shape. Be sure that any curvature on the lawn-garden interface can be accommodated by the lawnmower. You can then spade the bed out to this traced marking.

PREPARING A PLAN

Annual flower beds and borders are generally much less complicated than perennial flower beds and borders, but nonetheless a plan, outlined to scale on paper, is well worth the effort. Color zones and height zones can be designed and sketched onto the plan. Kinds and cultivars can then be chosen to meet the required specifications and the number of plants required calculated. For each plant listed in the reference section of this book, a spacing between plants is suggested. Therefore, if the area of the bed or section of the bed in question is determined from the scaled outline, the number of plants required can be easily determined.

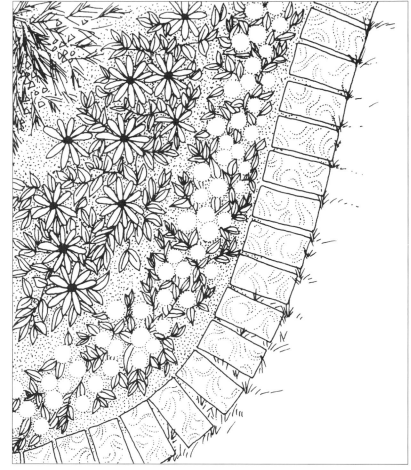

Figure 30

A decorative brick edging reduces maintenance

COLOR

As indicated earlier, many of the more popular annuals have brilliant striking colors that do not always blend well with one another. This can increase the challenge in designing flower beds with different combinations of flowers in plantings that are **monochromatic, complementary,** or **analogous** in their color scheme.

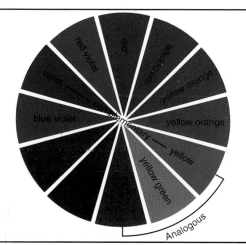

Figure 31

Color wheel

Figure 32

Complementary color
scheme

The **Birren** system for outdoor
color uses six basic colors which are listed
here in descending order of the amount of
light reflected from each (a value scale):

White 80%	Yellow 55%	Green 35%
Red 25%	Blue 20%	Black 0%

Masses of high value color are not
too effective in full sunlight; they tend to
produce glare. For those borders located in
strong sunlight, lower values should
predominate. In shady borders, use colors
of high value more freely. In deep shade,

colors which possess a high degree of
luminosity (orange and scarlet) are more
satisfactory than yellow or white in spite of
the fact that both yellow and white have
higher color values.

Flower colors are seldom pure.
Usually they are tints, shades, or tones of
the pure color or hue.

Tints are derived from yellow,
green, red, or blue by the addition of white.
Shades of these colors are obtained by the
addition of black. Tones result from the
addition of gray. In each case (tint, shade,
or tone), when a quantity of white, black or
gray is added to a pure color, that color
decreases in strength or purity. This
decrease is said to be a decrease in **chroma**.

In spite of the fact that light,
climate, and humidity play an important
part in the way colors can be arranged in
the landscape, it is still possible to use
either complementary or analogous colors
(those which adjoin one another in the
color circle) for harmonious results.

Suggested Combinations
Blue
- With scarlet and buff.
- With white and yellow.
- With orange and scarlet.
- With yellow or orange of the same
  chroma (use sparingly).

Figure 33

Planning a flower bed
based on height and
color zones

72 plus in. 180 plus cm
48 –72 in. 120 – 180 cm
36 – 72 in. 90–120 cm
20 – 36 in. 50 – 90 cm
10 – 20 in. 24–50 cm
6 – 10 in. 15–24 cm
below 6 in. below 15 cm.

Violet, Purple and Magenta (These colors lie between red and blue.)

- Those hues nearer blue: group together or use with tints and shades of blue.
- Those hues nearer red: group together or use with tints or shades of red.
- Violet or purple should be used with plenty of yellow or yellow-green foliage.
- Violet and purple can be contrasted with whites and yellows of equal chroma.

Red and Scarlet

- With dense green backgrounds.
- For sharp contrast, with white or clear blue.
- With analogous hues, red-violet and red-orange.

Pink (Tint of Red)

- Will gain more strength if interspersed with white.
- Goes well with other colors of the same chroma.

Orange

- With darker colors: red, browns, and bronzes.
- With turquoise blue (complementary).
- With purple flowers and bright green foliage (split complementary).
- With creamy white or yellow.

Yellow

- With blue of equal chroma.
- With white (use sparingly).
- Small amounts will liven up dark, heavy compositions.

White

- Frequently turns out to be a tint of one color or another. If so, use with other chromas of the same color or as a contrast with that color's complement.
- If interspersed among low value colors, it softens them.
- If interspersed among high value colors, it strengthens them.

Figure 34

Yellow and orange flowers enhanced with darker shades

Greens

- There are a great many foliage greens varying from deep, dull green through to the darkest of the evergreens. Foliage color must be secondary to flower colors and be carefully chosen to intensify the effect of anything placed in front of it. Thus, yellow-green or blue-green foliage can spoil the effect of a carefully arranged harmony that does not go well with yellow or blue.

Gray and Silvery Foliage

- This foliage can be used to lighten heavy or monotonous masses of dark green and, at the same time, heighten the effect of distance. They can also bring conflicting colors into pleasing

Figure 35

Use of white within an analogous color grouping

relationships. They are ineffective when dotted among bright color but effective in similar surrounding if used in mass. Gray or silvery foliage is most effective with light-tinted flowers.

Figure 36

Silvery foliage used to lighten large masses of green and red

Flower colors are usually tints, shades, or tones of pure hues. Light tints are often referred to as pastels. One of the ways to intensify the hue of pastel flowers is to plant white flowers next to them. Similarly plants with grey or silvery foliage are most effective when planted next to light-tinted flowers. An excellent way to use white-flowered and/or silvery-gray foliaged plants is in a "white" or "night" garden. Such a garden makes extensive use of white, pink, and light yellow flowering plants as well as those which are fragrant.

IMPLEMENTING THE PLAN

There are two aspects to carrying out or implementing the plan. The first is preparing the site, and the second is the actual planting.

Site Preparation

Begin by measuring and staking out the site. Then remove or transplant sod and other plant materials from the site. The bed is now ready for soil preparation prior to planting. It is important that the soil be in good tilth to a reasonable depth (6 to 12 in. (15 to 30 cm)) to ensure good drainage and adequate root development. Incorporate fertilizer and peat or compost into the top soil of the entire bed, either by spade or rototiller, shortly before planting. Fertilizer application based on soil test results is best, but in lieu of a soil analysis,

a fertilizer such as 10-30-10 applied at a rate of 25 to 35 oz. per 10 yd^2 (700 g to 1 kg per 10 m^2) is recommended.

Planting

Young plants, either seedlings or rooted cuttings, may be planted out when the soil is settled and conditions are favorable. A good planting plan will aid greatly in ensuring proper placement and spacing. Transplants should be well firmed and then watered in to ensure good soil contact with the roots. Watering-in with a starter solution (e.g., 10-52-10 or 10-52-17 at dilution recommended on label) is recommended for transplants since it encourages rapid establishment of the roots.

PLANTER TUBS, BOXES, AND HANGING BASKETS

Annuals are well adapted to growing in containers of various types because many of them have a relatively small and condensed root system. Perennials, on the other hand, require more volume for root expansion and special insulation in or around the containers to allow them to survive the winters. Annuals that trail or have a cascading habit of growth are ideal for window boxes or hanging baskets, providing a sense of calm and tranquillity to their surroundings. Containers that are portable allow you to extend the season by moving them indoors whenever the weather is unsettled or frost is predicted, particularly in the early spring and again in the late summer and fall. For gardeners with limited yard space, container growing allows them to make full use of both the vertical and horizontal dimensions available. Planters of varying sizes allow you to bring the flower garden onto the balcony, deck, or patio, as the case may be.

Ed Toop

Ed Toop

Figures 37, 38 and 39

Decorative planter boxes and window boxes

Plants can be spaced closer together when planted in containers than when put into the open ground. This gives a fuller appearance to the planting which is usually viewed from closer at hand than a bed or border. However, this does mean extra care in the form of more frequent watering and fertilizing because of the limited soil or potting mix around the roots. A potting mixture containing a high percentage of peat will provide a sponge-like reservoir for holding water to help reduce the frequency of watering. Similarly, plants that tolerate drought conditions are often good choices for growing in containers.

ANNUALS AS VINES

Vines are useful for providing out-door screens or dividers that define outdoor "rooms", giving a feeling of privacy and protection. They are also useful for adding interest to a blank wall, covering unsightly structures, or serving as a ground cover for rough ground areas or compost heaps. Hardy perennial vines, are functional year-round, but annual vines are fast-growing and serve their purpose well during the period of the year when they are needed most.

Ed Toop

John Beedle

Figure 40

Tropeolum peregrinum as a decorative cover

Figure 41

Ipomea purpurea
used to visually soften
an archway

Figure 42

Helianthus annuus
as a hedge

Brian Porter

Ed Toop

HEDGES AND OTHER USES

Some annuals have the size and stature to serve as temporary hedges or "shrubs". Examples include Castor Bean *(Ricinus communis),* Sunflower *(Helianthus* spp.), Cosmos *(Cosmos bipinnatus),* and Summer Cypress *(Kochia scoparia trichophila).* The latter, as the common name implies, looks like a conifer and makes an attractive light green or silvery-green, upright shrub. As a surprise bonus, it turns a magenta red color at the end of the season. If planted close together in a row and sheared as necessary to even out differences in plant size, Summer Cypress can provide a very attractive low hedge, albeit temporary.

Some annuals are also useful for filling in bare spots in a perennial border where plants have died or where early spring bulbs have finished flowering and faded away. Certain annuals also adapt well and look attractive in rock gardens and can be useful to fill in spots where perennial species have died over winter.

Annuals are also a good choice as accent plants either in a shrub border or for foundation planting against the house. Because they are temporary and their root systems are not extensive, they compete well with the woody plants. They can add a bit of color and interest to an evergreen shrub planting and help fill in between the plants when the planting is young and the shrubs are still small.

Routine
Care

Routine care consists of vigilant weeding and cultivating, timely watering, regular fertilizing, constant insect and disease control, and fall cleanup.

WEEDING AND CULTIVATING

Regular shallow cultivation is the best weed control approach for annual flower beds and borders. It destroys young weeds and weed seedlings before they can become fully established. Cultivation also prevents surface crusting of the soil thereby maintaining good aeration and rapid percolation of rain or irrigation water into the soil. Annuals are frequently used in mass plantings to produce a solid carpet of color. When the plants are given this close spacing, there is little room left for weeds to become established; hence, little cultivation is required for weed control once the planting is established.

Figure 43

Shallow cultivation with a hoe for weed control

Spading the soil and turning it over during fall cleanup destroys any weeds that may have established a foot hold. If the spaded surface is left rough, it allows frost to act on the clumps of soil, thus improving soil structure and preventing soil compaction.

WATERING

Proper watering is the key to successful gardening. Although you have little control over natural precipitation, you can ensure a well structured soil with good drainage properties to reduce the potentially devastating effects of too much water. In addition, you have control of irrigation water to supplement natural precipitation to allow healthy plants to achieve their full potential.

WATER-HOLDING CAPACITY OF SOIL

The water-holding capacity of a soil can be adjusted or modified through the addition of peat, compost, sand, or even clay. The higher the clay content of a soil the higher its water-holding capacity. Organic matter such as peat or compost also has a high water-holding capability. It is interesting that a clay soil high in organic matter will not only hold more water than a clay soil lacking organic matter, but it will have better drainage properties. Organic matter causes the fine clay particles to aggregate into a crumb-like structure creating pore spaces. However, when mixed with sand, organic matter has a binding effect. In short, the addition of organic matter to any type of soil is beneficial.

Much of the water requirements of plants can be met through soil modification. For example, plants with a high water requirement or requiring a constantly moist situation will do best in soils high in organic matter, particularly a clay loam, whereas plants that thrive under hot dry conditions will do best in sandy soils with low to moderate organic content. The chart below shows the water-holding capacity of the different soil textures.

Figure 44

Spading to leave clumps of soil in preparation for winter

Soil Texture	Water-Holding Capacity, %*
Sandy Loam	12 – 18
Silt Loam	24 – 32
Clay Loam	32 – 48
Peat	100+

* As a percentage of the dry weight of soil or peat.

HOW MUCH WATER?

Add sufficient water to permit percolation to a depth of 12 in. (30 cm) or more. Deep watering encourages strong deep rooting, but the actual depth needed depends upon the potential for rooting depth of the plants being watered. Some annual flowers are capable of sending roots down to a depth of over 12 in. (30 cm) whereas many will form a mat of roots only 6 in. (15 cm) or less in depth, regardless of the depth of moist soil. However, if moisture is not available beyond a certain depth roots will not grow beyond that depth (see Chapter 3, Figure 25). Even plants with the potential for deep rooting will only produce roots in the moist surface layer of soil if a dry zone separates this surface layer from moist subsoil. How and when you water depends upon weather conditions and the rate of water use by the plants.

FERTILIZING AND MULCHING

Annual incorporation of compost or well-rotted manure in the fall or before planting in the spring will usually maintain an adequate balance of nutrients for annuals. An annual application of 10-30-10 or an equivalent analysis ratio at 1 to 1.25 oz per yd^2 (40 to 50 g per m^2) is often suggested prior to setting out bedding plants. If peat is used in place of compost or manure, supplementary fertilization is more strongly suggested. The use of water soluble fertilizer, such as 20-20-20, at the dilution rate recommended on the package and applied with a watering can is also an option. If particular plants in the border are showing "hunger" signs, use this method of applying supplemental fertilizer. Watering-in bedding plants with starter solution (10-52-10 or 10-52-17) is highly recommended, (see Chapter 3, page 20).

Organic mulch in the form of peat, grass clippings uncontaminated by weed-killing chemicals, chopped straw, or other available material is very beneficial. It keeps the soil cool for plants that require a cool root zone. It helps to conserve soil moisture by preventing evaporation from the soil surface. It also replaces the need for cultivation to prevent crusting of the soil surface as well as encourage micro-organism activity which in turn improves soil structure and the availability of nutrients to the plant roots. These mulches can be incorporated into the soil when the beds are dug over in the fall.

PINCHING, DISBUDDING, AND PLANT HYGIENE

Many plants, if left to develop naturally from seedling to flowering maturity, will produce only one central stem that terminates in a single flower or inflorescence. Once this flower or flower head matures, it usually triggers the growth of lateral stems which eventually produce flowers as well. For plants of this nature, it is possible to speed up the process by "pinching out" (removing) the growing point of the seedling when it is about 5 to 8 cm tall. This triggers the branching response immediately, resulting in attractive compact plants for bedding-out or development in the garden if direct seeded. This procedure does not work for every kind of plant and is not necessary for many of the cultivars on the market that have been bred for dwarfness or a natural compact growth habit.

Disbudding involves the removal of flower buds, which seems to be a paradox since most annuals are grown for their flowers. However, there are instances in which disbudding can be desirable. For example, if you are growing Sweet Peas and wish to produce the largest spikes with the largest number of large florets that is genetically possible, this can be achieved by allowing each plant to produce only one stem that terminates in only one flower stalk. The ultimate in achievement depends on ensuring that the plants also receive abundant water, nutrients, and excellent weather conditions. It is usually only the keen competitor at flower shows that is willing to spend this amount of effort in "grooming" flowers. A more practical reason for disbudding is to prevent flowering in order to enhance foliage development. Plants such as Coleus retain a brighter coloration in the foliage if all flower stalks are prevented from developing by removing them in the small bud stage.

Plant hygiene is concerned with the removal of all dead and dying leaves, as

Figure 45

Pinching a young plant to encourage branching

COMPOSTING

Composting is a method used to decay plant and animal refuse by microbial action to form humus, a vital soil ingredient.

CONSTRUCTION OF A COMPOST PILE

Construction depends on your preference and situation. No structure at all offers complete flexibility in the movement of the pile. Unprotected compost piles must be kept moist at all times by frequent waterings. A structure can be provided by using grass sods as walls, building a bottomless wooden box of convenient dimensions with a lid, or digging a pit for which a cover or lid is provided.

The conventional system for composting is to place the organic wastes in layers approximately 6 in. (15 cm) thick, alternating with layers of old grass sods or soil. The material is watered down and kept moist at all times. It should be forked occasionally to avoid overheating but is generally kept covered and relatively undisturbed for 1 to 2 years until it is thoroughly decayed.

A newer method developed at the University of California in Berkeley provides for high temperature and rapid composting through improved aeration. While it requires considerable labor, its advantages lie in the absence of foul odors and a rapid recycling of wastes. It is this method that is well adapted to the urban scene and will be described here.

THE FRAME

A wooden frame with either slatted or wire mesh side walls and a capacity of about 1 cu. yd. (1 m^3) is adequate for the average urban lot. It should have no top or bottom and will, therefore, require sturdy construction to retain its shape. It should be lightweight with the sides slightly tapered toward the top for easy removal when the pile requires turning. To turn the pile, lift off the frame, set it beside the pile, and fork the compost back into the empty frame. A single-bin or two-bin frame can also be used with posts set into the ground. With this type of construction, a removable front panel is required.

PROCEDURE

Autumn is a good time to start a compost since there is an abundance of materials available at that time. Store all garden cleanup materials in the compost box until spring. Larger material should be cut up into 8 to 10 in. (20 to 25 cm) lengths for better consolidation and easier future handling. Little, if any, decomposition will occur over the cold winter months. In the spring, add rakings and the first grass clippings, turning the pile to mix the old and new material. Add water if the material is dry. The pile will usually heat up in 3 days. Continue to add grass clippings and other materials as they become available and turn the pile at least once a week. Frequent turning and thorough mixing is essential to supply air to the interior of the pile. Add water as the pile is turned to provide uniform moisture throughout the pile. Enough moisture is present when the particles of compost glisten. Foul odors indicate too much moisture; the remedy is more frequent turning to speed up evaporation and improve aeration. Once the odors disappear, resume the regular routine of turning every 5 to 7 days.

At the end of August, stop adding additional material but continue to turn the pile and keep it moist. Fall cleanup material can be used to start a new pile for composting the following season. It is finished when the pile will not heat up even though moisture and air are adequate. Finished compost is a uniformly dark color with an earthy odor. Shredding it with a mechanical shredder makes it easier to incorporate into the garden soil.

THE COMPOSTING PROCESS

Composting is brought about by the activity of bacteria, fungi, and actinomycetes. All these organisms are present in garden residues. No additives, such as compost starter, fertilizer, lime, or soil are necessary to make the pile work. The first organisms involved in this process are active at ambient temperatures. These are succeeded by organisms active at successively higher temperatures. The internal temperature of a small compost pile of the type described here will reach 130 to 150°F (55 to 65°C) or more. This range of temperature is high enough to kill flies (in all stages of development), weed seeds, and plant pathogenic organisms.

Composting organisms require a suitable carbon:nitrogen ratio for peak activity. Mixing dry garden wastes (high carbon:nitrogen ratio) with grass clippings (low carbon:nitrogen ratio) usually produces a suitable ratio. If the ratio is too high, sprinkle in nitrogen fertilizer (such as 21-0-0 or 33-0-0) on each successive layer of the pile to improve the balance.

Figure 46

Composting frame

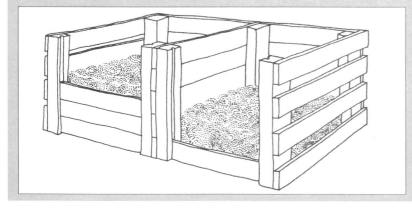

well as faded flowers. The removal of faded flowers is not always practical but can help to keep plants looking attractive and in some cases keep the plants producing more and more flowers. Many of the popular bedding plants have been bred to be **sterile** and therefore do not set seed. This triggers a response in the plant to keep producing flowers in a vain attempt to produce progeny. Removal of fading flowers creates the same response and will invoke continuous flowering in those kinds of annuals that tend to be short-lived and prolific self-seeders.

The removal of dead leaves and any plants that die during the summer season also aids in controlling the spread of possible diseases that cause the death of leaves or whole plants. It also keeps the plantings looking tidy and attractive.

INSECT AND DISEASE CONTROL

You can do much to control disease and plant pests without resorting to chemical pesticides. The first line of attack is to start with healthy plant material and provide the proper care to keep it healthy and vigorous. The second line of attack is to take action quickly when you discover pests or disease. The third line of attack is sanitation.

Sanitation involves the removal of dead flowers and leaves as soon as possible during the growing season and removal of all plants before the onset of winter or alternatively in early spring, well before new plants are bedded-out. If this clean-up is delayed until spring, you run the risk of infection from overwintered pathogens or an outbreak of other pests that have survived in the debris.

To prevent the spread of diseases, such as Botrytis, avoid wetting the foliage when you water the plants. Some diseases, such as Mildew and Yellows, are often controlled by planting resistant varieties (e.g., wilt-resistant China Asters).

Despite good management and proper care, pest problems and disease will arise on occasion. When they do, take immediate action to have the pest or disease identified and apply the appropriate controls.

FALL CLEAN-UP AND PREPARATION FOR WINTER

Remove all plants after they have been killed by frost and before the onset of winter to prevent the overwintering of possible pathogens or insects in the debris. Although this debris can act as a snowtrap over winter, it is safer to provide a snow fence or other wind-breaking device if you wish to trap snow onto any windswept beds. Some plants, even though dead, may provide interesting textural forms throughout the winter months and could be left until spring before removal.

TOOLS FOR THE JOB

If you wish to start your own plants indoors, then depending on the extent of your project, you will require a sunny window ledge, an artificial light set-up, or a small greenhouse. A small greenhouse or a "lighted" table or bench where temperature can be controlled to provide cool conditions during the night or the dark period when lights are turned off is ideal for the purpose. Keeping seedlings sturdy and young developing plants compact and vigorous-looking requires high light levels during the day and cool temperatures during the night. Tools and materials required will include a "dibber", containers, and potting mixtures (see Chapter 2 *Starting Seedlings Indoors).*

For transplanting bedding plants to the garden, whether they have been purchased or are home grown, you will need a trowel to dig holes of appropriate size to accommodate the roots of each plant. Watering-in the plants and applying fertilizer solutions such as 10-52-10 or 20-20-20 is best accomplished with a large watering can. For regular watering, you need a garden hose as well as a soaker hose and possibly a sprinkler.

Cultivation and weeding can be done with various tools such as hand-held cultivators, long-handled cultivators or hoes. A stirrup-shaped weeding hoe consisting of a thin and narrow blade mounted on an arched frame can be efficient for destroying young weed seedlings by simply pushing the blade back and forth just below the surface of the soil. The conventional hoe can accomplish the same task but with a little more effort required. However, the regular hoe is also useful for disturbing the soil to a greater depth to aid in soil aeration and the percolation of rain or irrigation water down into the soil. It is also a useful tool for removing more mature and deeply rooted

weeds. Cultivators break the soil surface and alleviate compaction to whatever depth the cultivator tines penetrate. This depth depends mainly on the effort exerted by the person handling the cultivator.

Spade all flower beds once a year, preferably in the fall rather than the spring. A good garden spade that will penetrate 8 to 12 in. (20 to 30 cm) is generally sufficient for preparation of annual flower beds. A longer-bladed spade for a deep turning of the soil every 3 or so years is beneficial in preventing a hardpan or layer of compacted soil just below the usual depth of soil preparation. It also brings nutrients that have leached down below the major root zone depth to the surface where they are available to new bedding plants.

Rototillers are useful for preparing flower beds, particularly for mixing peat, sand, compost, or other additives with the top soil. However, if rototillers are used exclusively for preparing garden beds for planting year after year, the soil structure can be destroyed and a serious hardpan formed just beneath the maximum depth of penetration of the rotary blades.

One final useful tool for the preparation of flower beds is the metal-tined garden rake. It is an aid in leveling off the soil and filling in depressions prior to planting. It is also useful in raking out small lumps and stones to provide a fine textured surface layer of soil particles for direct seeding, either broadcast or in closely spaced rows.

Figure 47

Tools for the job

6

Annuals That Require Winter Care

Some of the plants that we grow as annuals or bedding plants are herbaceous perennials that require special handling. These include tropicals and subtropicals that are slow to develop from seed to flowering or must be maintained as greenhouse plants during the fall, winter, and early spring. Others are tender plants that produce an underground storage organ that can be dug and stored over the winter months.

TROPICALS AND SUBTROPICALS

Some of the tender perennials that will flower outside during the summer can be started from seed during the late winter and will reach maturity by summer. Plants of this type have been included in the plant description section; examples are Wax Begonia, Patience Plant, and Bedding Geranium. There are some exotic plants in this category which require special handling and have not been included in this book; examples are *Acidanthera* spp. (Peacock Orchid), *Hymenocallis* x *festalis* (Ismene or Spider Lily), *Tigridia pavonia* (Tiger Flower), and *Freesia* x *hybrida* (Freesia). Plants of this type are available from garden centers in the spring for bedding-out purposes, particularly for use in planters and hanging baskets where they can be afforded added protection from the vagaries of our summer climate.

Figure 48

Tuberous root of Begonia

Figure 49

Begonia x *tuberhybrida*

Brendan Casement

PLANTS WITH UNDERGROUND STORAGE ORGANS

There is another group of tender perennials that are well known and regularly grown as outdoor annuals in northern regions. They produce an underground storage organ which can be harvested in the fall and stored in a dormant state through the winter months for replanting in the spring. This group includes *Begonia* x *tuberhybrida, Canna, Dahlia,* and *Gladiolus,* all of which are described below.

Begonia x *tuberhybrida*
Hybrid Tuberous Begonia

Tuberous Begonias are usually purchased as started plants or as tuberous roots but can also be started from seed. For information about the propagation, culture, and use of Tuberous Begonias in the garden, see page 57 of the plant descriptions section.

Since Tuberous Begonias form a corm-like tuberous root, this structure can be harvested after the plants are blackened by the first killing frost at the end of the summer. Rub off all the fine fibrous roots attached to the underside of the central tuberous root, taking care not to unduly bruise the skin of this storage structure. It is best to cut the stems off close to their point of origin rather than snapping them off since they may break so close to the tuberous root surface that a portion of the storage root tissue will break away with the stem, destroying **adventitious** buds. Wash the tuberous roots gently to remove all remnants of soil and allow them to dry in a warm ventilated place for several hours. This "curing" process will allow the small wounds left by removing the fibrous roots to form protective scabs.

The clean, dry tuberous roots can be stored in vermiculite, peat moss, or sand in a container of convenient size at a temperature of 40 to 50°F (5 to 10°C). They should be checked regularly to ensure that the roots remain healthy. Remove any roots showing evidence of decay. If the storage medium is slightly damp, it should prevent the roots from losing moisture and becoming soft or shrivelled, yet not be damp enough to encourage mold or rot.

When the buds on the upper surface of the corm-like roots begin to swell, plant the roots in flats or trays of peat or a peat-lite mix (peat-perlite or peat-vermiculite), water them and keep them in strong light but cool temperatures. Hopefully, this breaking of dormancy will not occur until late March or early April. A cool but sunny window ledge or a greenhouse will ensure that the growth remains strong and sturdy until it is safe to put the plants into the garden.

Store the roots with the top portion containing the buds kept uppermost in the storage medium. When the buds begin growth, they will elongate rather rapidly in the dark medium and grow upward against the pull of gravity. If the roots are upside down, the growth will extend along the surface of the root and around its edge. When the root is turned over for planting, these new shoots will be growing downward into the potting medium rather than upward from the center of the storage root. Although the shoots will reverse their direction, this original twisted growth will remain, leaving the stems with a weak, non-supportive basal attachment.

Canna x generalis and Canna x orchiodes
Common Garden Canna and Orchid-flowered Canna

Common Garden Canna varies in height (24 to 48 in. (60 to 120 cm)) and color of foliage (shades of green to red and bronze). Flowers are up to 4 in. (10 cm) in diameter, gladiola-like in appearance, and ranging in color from red, orange, yellow to salmon, pink, rose, and yellowish-brown.

Orchid-flowered Canna has very large flowers up to 6 in. (15 cm) across, tubular at the base with reflexed petals. Colors range from yellow to red in striped and splashed patterns. Leaves are green.

All Cannas produce fleshy **rhizomes** that can be dug when the leaves die down (but before the first major freeze) and stored over winter in a warm, dry place in sand, peat, or vermiculite. In the spring, these rhizomes can be cut into sections (each section with a bud) and started indoors 10 to 12 weeks before the last spring frost is expected. Plants can be planted outdoors after all danger of frost is past. Space them 12 to 15 in. (30 to 38 cm) apart in ground that has been dug deeply and enriched with compost or peat and fertilizer. Cannas do best in full sun in a warm or sheltered location with plenty of moisture.

Cannas can be raised from seeds, but this is rarely done except in the production of new varieties.

Cannas are very stately, regal plants that are often used in formal circular flower beds in public gardens. For the smaller home garden, they make excellent specimen plants in pots or focal points in flower beds.

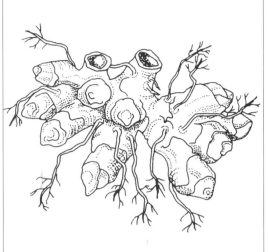

Figure 50

Canna rhizome

Figure 51

Canna blossom

John Beedle

Figure 52

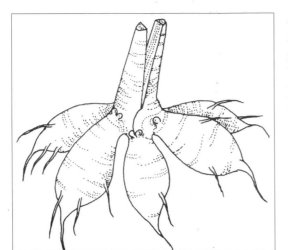

Figure 52

Dahlia tuberous roots

Olds College Collection

Figure 53

Collarette Dahlia

Hybrids of *Dahlia coccinea* and *Dahlia pinnata*

Dahlia

The large-flowered and taller growing Dahlias are usually propagated from their tuberous roots rather than from seed, which is the preferred method for Bedding Dahlias (see p. 88). These tuberous roots can be dug and stored over winter for replanting in the spring.

Dahlias, other than the dwarf bedding types, come in a variety of heights, flower forms, and flower sizes. They have been classified into a number of divisions based on flower head diameter from over 8 in. (20 cm) to under 4 in. (10 cm). A further extension to these size groups are the Pompons, which must be under 2 in. (5 cm),

and Miniature Ball Dahlias, which are 2 to 4 in. (5 to 10 cm) in diameter. Other flower form classifications besides Pompons and Ball include Anemone-flowered, Collarette, Peony-flowered, Cactus, Semi-cactus, and Decorative (Formal and Informal). There is a wide range of color in Dahlia flowers embracing every conceivable shade and combination of shades with the exception of blue.

Dahlia tubers are planted directly into the garden when the soil is warm about a week before the last spring frost is expected. Young plants, on the other hand, are not put into the garden until the danger of frost has passed. Dahlia plants will not tolerate any frost. Each tuberous root is planted with its top end about 4 in. (10 cm) deep. When you divide clumps of Dahlia roots for planting, it is essential to include a portion of the old stem with each piece of root. The fleshy root tissue itself does not have the capacity to initiate shoot growth. Shoots will only develop from adventitious buds located in this basal stem tissue.

Many of these taller-growing, large-flowered Dahlias require staking to prevent them from breaking off due to the wind or from large flowers made heavy with rain. Plant a short stake with the tuberous root that can later be replaced with a sufficiently tall stake or pole to which the plant can be tied. This procedure prevents a support stake being driven through a fleshy root.

After the first killing frost at the end of summer, cut back the blackened tops to leave about 4 in. (10 cm) of basal stem (stump) above the soil. Delay digging up the roots for storage until there is danger of a hard freeze, one that could damage the roots in the soil. After lifting, turn the clumps upside down to allow water to drain from the hollow stems. Gently remove soil from around the plump roots, taking care not to damage them. They are very brittle at this stage and will break apart quite easily. Roots that have broken away from the basal stem area (crown) cannot be saved for replanting in the spring.

The ideal place for storing Dahlia roots is on an earthen floor in a cool, frost-free cellar. Since not many people have such cellars, a comparable substitute must be found, such as a heated garage or the coolest storage available in a basement. The usual recommendation is to dust the cleaned roots with a fungicide and store them in containers of moist peat or vermiculite. Storage temperature should be maintained in the range of 35 to 45°F (2 to 7°C) if possible to prevent sprouting. Success will depend on maintaining a moisture level that will prevent drying and shrivelling of the roots but will not be sufficient to encourage molding and rotting.

An alternative method that appears to work quite well, especially when humidity and temperature are difficult to control, is to store the roots with the garden soil still intact around them in a cool spot. When the soil begins to dry and crack, sprinkle it with water periodically to keep it from separating from the roots. This procedure works well with clay loam soils which have a high water-holding capacity and do not crumble readily upon drying. The roots tend to remain turgid throughout the winter storage period using this approach.

In large gardens, a spectacular effect can be achieved by planting entire beds or borders to Dahlias alone. With the wide range of height, flower size, and flower color available, Dahlias can provide a very interesting flower bed unto themselves. They are also valuable for filling in gaps in a herbaceous perennial border and as a contributor to annual beds and borders. They are also a popular cut flower.

Gladiolus x hortulanus
Gladiolus, Gladiola, Sword Lily

The garden Gladiolus, or Gladiola as it is often called, does not represent a single species but is the product of hybridization of a few of the more than 250 species in the world. This genus is native to the Mediterranean region of Europe, the Near East, and Africa, but most species are found in tropical and South Africa. The species found in Europe are known as Corn Flags usually, whereas the common name Sword Lily can be applied to all species. The name is derived from the Latin *gladius,* a "sword", and alludes to the sword-shaped leaves.

There are many excellent cultivars of Gladiolus covering a wide range of flower size, color, and texture. The erect spike inflorescences, reaching heights up to 56 in. (140 cm), contain tightly-arranged florets that open progressively from the base to the tip of the flower stalk. The florets may be arranged in pairs (formal type) or in a staggered, alternate arrangement (informal type). Cultivars are classified by flower size into five categories from the giants (500 series with the bottom floret 6 in. (15 cm) or more across) to the miniatures (100 series with the bottom floret less than 2.5 in. (6.5 cm) across). The large spectrum of flower colors includes white, cream, yellow, buff, orange, salmon, scarlet, pink, red, rose, lavender, purple, violet, and smoky.

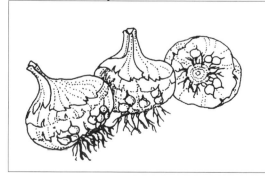

Figure 54

Gladiolus corms with cormels

Figure 55

John Beedle

Gladiolus

Gladiolus corms are planted in the garden as soon as the soil can be prepared in the spring. Corms with a high crown (convex shape) are better quality than those that are flat or concave. Corms are planted 3 to 4 in. (8 to 10 cm) deep and as close as 3 in. (8 cm) apart. When grown as a commercial cut flower crop, they are grown 3 to 6 in. (8 to 15 cm) apart in rows 24 to 36 in. (60 to 90 cm) apart to facilitate cultivation and harvesting.

Gladiolus plants tend to lean at various angles from the effects of wind and rain as their flower spikes mature. For this reason, they do not lend themselves to massed plantings or even additions to showy beds and borders unless individually supported with stakes. Their formal attractiveness is best displayed when they are cut and used in basket bouquets and arrangements.

Although Gladiolus flowers are destroyed by the first killing frost at the end of the summer season, the plants will survive and should be left to develop and mature good-sized corms before being cut down and lifted for storage. When you do dig them, cut off the tops first at about 1 in. (2 cm) above the corms and leave the corms to dry in the sun for a few hours. Then store the corms for two weeks in a warm, dry place to cure (80 to 95°F (27 to 35°C) is recommended). When the old corms will separate easily from the new ones, clean them off and remove any soil or loose outer skin in addition to the old corms. Gladiolus store best over winter if placed in shallow layers in trays or paper bags with good ventilation and a temperature between 40 and 50°F (5 and 10°C). Before storing, dust the corms with a "bulb" dust containing Captan and Carbaryl or Captan and Malathion.

Gladiolus, or Glads for short, are propagated vegetatively since cultivars do not come true from seed. They produce a corm as a storage organ which can be cut into segments as a means of increasing plants, provided each section has at least one eye (bud). When these corm segments are planted, the eye or bud develops into a plant with a flowering shoot and by the end of the growing season will have produced a replacement corm at the base of the stem underground. When whole corms are planted, the same sequence of events occurs, but there is no increase in the number of corms produced over what was planted. Occasionally a large, vigorous corm will produce 2 shoots and subsequently 2 replacement corms, but this "2-for-1" event is not predictable. All planted corms or corm segments shrivel and die as the new corms form immediately above them.

Gladiolus also form small "baby corms" or cormels around the periphery of the "mother" corm. These can be saved and replanted as a means of propagation. New corms that develop from these cormels will vary in size, but many will be large enough to flower the second year (1 to 1.5 in. (2.5 to 3.5 cm) diameter is the minimal size for flowering usually).

Plant
Descriptions

How to use this section

Low, mat-forming, edging material up to 10 in. (24 cm) tall

Medium height, foreground to middle ground material (10 to 35 in. (24 to 90 cm) tall)

Medium to tall background material (35 to 70 in. (90 to 180 cm) tall)

Tall background or climbing material (70 in.+ (180 cm+))

The descriptions of the specific plants dealt with in this section are accompanied by the icons illustrated here to allow the reader to see at a glance the general height of each species or group of hybrids. The sunlight requirements and soil moisture requirements of each individual kind of perennial cannot be accurately depicted by these icons, but they do help in categorizing the plants according to average height and the environmental conditions under which they should thrive. An unhighlighted icon indicates no special requirements in that category. More detailed and accurate information is given in the text and in the master reference chart. If you are searching for a plant by common name, there is an English-Latin index on page 207.

Full sun

Partial shade

Shade

Requires dry soil or is drought resistant

Requires moist or evenly moist soil combinations

Plant Descriptions

Ageratum houstonianum
Ageratum, Flossflower

History: This plant hails from Mexico and is sometimes listed as *Ageratum mexicanum*. The word *Ageratum* is derived from a, "not", and geras, "old", indicating the long lasting character of the flowers.

Description: Most cultivars grow in compact mounds 3 to 6 in. (7 to 15 cm) tall and 8 to 10 in. (20 to 25 cm) across but a few cultivars can reach 24 in. (60 cm) in height. They all have abundant fluffy or fuzzy clusters of individual blossoms that are 1.5 to 3 in. (0.6 to 1.2 cm) in diameter in lavender blue or, less commonly, pink or white.

Propagation and Culture: Ageratum are usually grown from seeds that germinate in 5 to 10 days at 54 to 60°F (12 to 15°C). Young plants develop slowly requiring 6 to 8 weeks development in a greenhouse before being set outdoors after the last frost is due. Plants are spaced 6 to 9 in. (15 to 22 cm) apart in the garden and require a warm sunny location in average soil.

Use: Low growing cultivars are well suited for borders, edging material, or groundcovers, as well as for window boxes and planters. Tall growing types can be used for background plantings and as cut flowers.

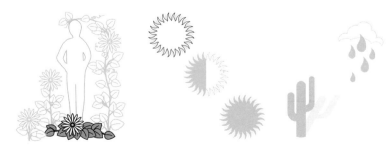

Brian Porter

Ageratum houstonianum 'Blue Danube'

Ed Toop

Ageratum houstonianum

Agrostis nebulosa

Ed Toop

Agrostis nebulosa
Cloud Grass

Description: As a member of the bent grasses, Cloud Grass is useful for garden ornament. It produces long clusters of small, white flower spikes (panicles) on stems 12 to 15 in. (30 to 38 cm) high.

Propagation and Culture: Seeds may be sown as early in the spring as the soil can be worked and later thinned to a spacing of about 6 in. (15 cm). Seedlings can be transplanted easily. Cloud Grass flourishes in any well drained garden soil in full sun.

Use: Plants produce a soft hazy effect when grouped. They are useful for concealing spindly stems of background plants in a border as well as making interesting additions to cut flower arrangements. If picked just before the blossoms open and hung upside down to dry in a cool place out of the sunlight, they can be saved for year-round use in dried arrangements.

Alcea rosea

John Beedle

Alcea rosea (Althaea rosea)
Annual Hollyhock

History: Hollyhocks are traditionally biennial but there are annual, biennial, and short-lived perennial forms or strains available today. Hollyhocks are native to the Orient but are grown around the world.

Description: There are annual strains of Hollyhock that produce robust plants from 48 to 70 in. (120 to 180 cm) in height. Their stalks bear great numbers of single, semi-double, or double flowers, 4 in. (10 cm) or more in diameter, some frilled at the edges in red, rose, pink, yellow, cream, and white.

Propagation and Culture: Seeds may be sown indoors 6 to 8 weeks before the last frost is due. Seedlings can be transplanted into individual 3-in. (7.5-cm) peat pots when the first true leaves appear. They can be grown-on in a cold frame until night temperatures do not fall below 50°F (10°C) before bedding them out in the garden. Plants should be spaced about 12 to 24 in. (30 to 60 cm) apart in the garden. They thrive in full sun and average soil.

Use: Hollyhocks are attractive as background plants in a flower border, or planted in rows against a fence or wall. They are useful as attention-getting accent plants.

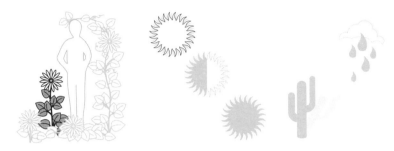

Alcea rosea

Amaranthus caudatus
Amaranth, Love-lies-bleeding, Tassle Flower

History: Species of *Amaranthus* (commonly called Amaranths) originated in the tropics of India, the Philippines, and other far eastern countries. The botanical name conveys the meaning of "not withering" and refers to the extremely long lasting qualities of the blooms.

Description: Love-lies-bleeding grows to 36 in. (90 cm) or more in height and produces long, drooping, cord-like flower stalks bearing blood-red to dark, reddish-purple blooms.

Propagation and Culture: Seeds may be sown indoors about 6 weeks before the last frost is due or in the garden when the soil is warm and night temperatures do not fall below 40 to 50°F (5 to 10°C). Light may increase germination. Amaranths should be spaced 18 to 24 in. (45 to 60 cm) apart. They are easy to grow in any average to dry soil as long as they are in full sun.

Use: Amaranths are tall enough to serve as a temporary substitute for shrubbery or even a hedge, but their brilliant coloration can overwhelm if they are not used with discretion.

Amaranthus caudatus

Amaranthus caudatus

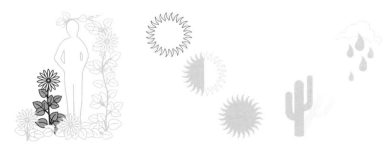

Amaranthus 'Green Thumb'

Amaranthus 'Pygmy Torch'

Amaranthus hybridus var. *erythrostachys* (*A. hypochondriacus*)
Amaranth, Prince's Feather

Description: Prince's Feather has purple, red or green leaves and stem tips that are crowned with large erect spikes of tiny, bright red flowers. It grows to 40 to 50 in. (100 to 130 cm) in height. It is the cultivated form of the Common Pigweed, the wild beet *(Amaranthus hybridus)*.

Propagation and Culture: Seeds may be sown indoors about 6 weeks before the last frost is due or in the garden when the soil is warm and night temperatures do not fall below 40 to 50 °F (5 to 10°C). Light may increase germination. Amaranths should be spaced 18 to 24 in. (45 to 60 cm) apart. They are easy to grow in any average to dry soil as long as they are in full sun. They do not perform well in a rich soil.

Use: Amaranths are tall enough to serve as a temporary substitute for shrubbery or even a hedge, but their brilliant coloration can overwhelm if they are not used with discretion.

Amaranthus tricolor

Amaranthus tricolor (*A. melancholicus*)
Amaranth, Joseph's Coat, Molten Fire, Summer Poinsettia

Description: These amaranths are grown for their highly colored leaves and are relatively short (12 to 24 in. (30 to 60 cm)). Typically Joseph's Coat has red, yellow, and green leaves, but some selections range from brilliant red to scarlet to carmine-colored leaves.

Propagation and Culture: Seeds may be sown indoors about 6 weeks before the last frost is due or in the garden when the soil is warm and night temperatures do not fall below 40 to 50°F (5 to 10°C). Light may increase germination. Amaranths should be spaced 18 to 24 in. (45 to 60 cm) apart. They are easy to grow in any average to dry soil as long as they are in full sun.

Use: Because of their shorter stature, these amaranths are more adaptable to mixed flower beds or small mass plantings than other amaranths.

Amaranthus tricolor

Ammi majus
Bishop's Flower, False Queen Anne's Lace

History: Bishop's Flower is indigenous to northeast Africa and Eurasia, but has become naturalized in North America as well. It is one of about 8 species in the genus *Ammi*.

Description: Bishop's Flower is similar in appearance to the wild carrot or Queen Anne's Lace *(Daucus carota carota)*. Plants produce white lacy heads (6 in. (15 cm) across) on stems up to 30 in. (75 cm) tall. Flower heads are broader and fuller than those of *Daucus carota carota*.

Propagation and Culture: Seeds may be sown in the garden as soon as the soil is warm and all frost danger is past. They may be sown indoors also about 4 to 6 weeks before the last spring frost is due. Plants should be spaced about 12 to 18 in. (30 to 45 cm) apart, but can be planted closer than this when grown for cutting and drying. They grow well in ordinary soils in full sun.

Use: Bishop's Flower is an easily-grown annual that can contribute to the middle-ground height zone of a flower border. It also makes an excellent filler for fresh flower arrangements and is useful in dried, cut flower arrangements.

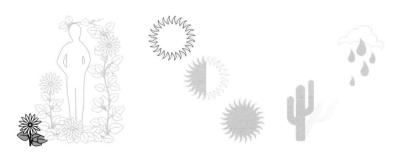

Ammi majus

Ammi majus

Ammobium alatum

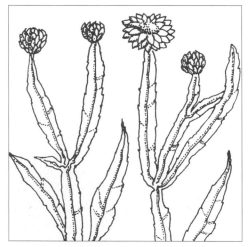

Ammobium alatum

Ammobium alatum
Winged Everlasting

History: A native of Australia, Winged Everlasting gets its name from the raised ridges or "wings" on its stiff stems. The genus name *Ammobium* is Latin for "living in sand".

Description: This composite produces flower heads 1 to 2 in. (2.5 to 5 cm) in diameter made up of a yellow center (florets) surrounded by an involucre of pearly-white, dry petal-like bracts. Leaves at the base of the plant are javelin-shaped, and the stem leaves are small and sparse. Winged Everlasting grows 18 to 36 in. (45 to 90 cm) in height, is erect and branchy, and produces many stems from the crown.

Propagation and Culture: This plant is really a perennial but usually responds as an annual. Seeds should be sown indoors about 6 weeks before the last frost is due and seedlings planted outdoors after all danger of frost is past. Seeds may also be sown outdoors as soon as the soil has warmed up in the spring. They are easy to transplant at any stage of development and thrive in full sun in sandy soils. Plants should be spaced 12 in. (30 cm) apart.

Use: This is a popular Everlasting or Immortelle for use in winter bouquets. For this purpose they should be cut just before the flowers are fully open and hung upside down to cure in a dry, shady place.

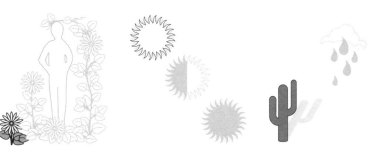

Anagallis arvensis
Scarlet or Common Pimpernel, Shepherd's Clock, Poor Man's Weather Glass

History: The name *Anagallis* is from the Greek meaning "delighting". The common names refer to the fact that the flowers open and close in response to sunlight.   Description: This species from the Primrose family is truly annual and produces bright red to orange blossoms 1.5 in (0.6 cm) in diameter on trailing stems. Blue and white flowered cultivars are also available. Height ranges from 6 to 9 in. (15 to 23 cm).

Propagation and Culture: Seed may be sown indoors about 10 to 12 weeks before the last frost is due, or directly outdoors when the soil is warm and danger of frost is past.

Anagallis arvensis

However, direct seeding outdoors may be too late to have plants come into flower before a late-summer killing frost. Plants should be spaced 6 in. (15 cm) apart in full sunlight. They thrive in light sandy loam soil.

Use: They are very suitable for planting near the edge of a flower border or in dry pockets of the rock garden. They are also useful in hanging baskets and planter boxes.

Anagallis arvensis

Calgary Zoo

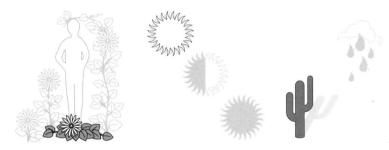

Anagallis monelli subsp. *linifolia (A. linifolia, A. grandiflora)*
Flaxleaf Pimpernel

Description: A native of north Africa, this species and its varieties are compact plants 6 to 18 in. (15 to 45 cm) tall and bear flowers that are 6.5 in. (2.6 cm) in diameter produced in clusters. The flowers are generally blue on top and reddish beneath.

Propagation and Culture: Seed may be sown indoors about 10 to 12 weeks before the last frost is due. Plants should be spaced 6 in. (15 cm) apart in full sunlight. They thrive in light, sandy loam soil.

Use: This species is very suitable for planting near the edge of a flower border or in dry pockets of the rock garden. They are also useful in hanging baskets and planter boxes.

Anagallis monelli subsp. linifolia

Anchusa capensis

Anchusa capensis 'Blue Angel'

Anchusa capensis
Summer Forget-me-not, Cape Forget-me-not, Alkanet, Bugloss

History: This member of the Borage family, *Anchusa capensis*, is native to South Africa. The genus name means "paint for the skin" and refers to the use made of some of the species of *Anchusa*.

Description: Many blue-flowered annuals tend to be more lavender or purple than blue, but this plant is the exception. The cultivar 'Bluebird' in particular has flowers that are true sky blue. The flowers have white centers resembling Forget-me-nots but are larger (1.5 to 3 in. (0.6 to 1.2 cm)) and in clusters on hairy 15 to 18 in. (38 to 45 cm) stems. There is also a pink cultivar, 'Pink Bird', and a white-flowered variety (*Anchusa capensis alba*).

Propagation and Culture: Seeds should be started indoors 6 to 8 weeks before the last frost is due or seeded directly outdoors after all danger of frost is past. Plants should be spaced 10 to 12 in. (25 to 30 cm) apart. If trimmed back after the first flush of blooms to within 6 in. (15 cm) of the ground, they will rejuvenate quickly and develop more compact and floriferous plants. They thrive in moist fertile soil in partial shade.

Use: Summer Forget-me-nots are most effective in massed plantings that dramatize their unusual color (beds and borders).

Antirrhinum majus
Snapdragon

History: Snapdragons are native to the Mediterranean region. The name *Antirrhinum* is derived from *anti* meaning "like" and *rhin* meaning "snout" or "nose", a reference to the form of the flower. In mild climates this species is perennial. Snapdragons tend to shatter (drop blossoms prematurely shortly after being fertilized by bees), but plant breeders have developed shatterproof strains.

Antirrhinum majus

Description: This species produces vertical flower spikes which bloom from the base toward the top, may be faintly fragrant ,and occur in a wide variety of bright colors. Cultivars range in height from short (6 to 9 in. (15 to 23 cm)) and intermediate (18 to 24 in. (45 to 60 cm)) to tall (40 in. (100 cm) and taller). A single plant may produce 7 or 8 blossom spikes in one summer. A strain with open-faced, cup-shaped blossoms comes in both single and double flowers (butterfly type).

Propagation and Culture: Seeds may be sown indoors 6 to 8 weeks before the last frost is due and the seedlings moved outside as soon as the planting beds can be worked in preparation for planting. Seeds germinate in one to two weeks at 55°F (13°C) and may respond to light. Some hybrids are best started at 60 to 64°F (16 to 18°C). Seeds may also be sown outside directly, but because the seed is very fine and the spring seedlings quite delicate, controlled growing conditions give better germination and young seedling development. Plants should be spaced 6 to 12 in. (15 to 30 cm) apart, depending on the ultimate size of the cultivar selected. Pinching off the stem tips of young plants will increase the numbers of flower spikes produced. Cutting mature spikes for bouquets and removal of fading flower spikes will also keep new spikes coming until the plants are ultimately killed by severe frost. Snapdragons flourish in fertile soil in full sun.

Use: The tall growing cultivars are popular as cut flowers and are grown commercially for this purpose in greenhouses and outdoors. The more popular for garden use are the intermediates which require no staking but are stately additions to the flower border and can be used as cut flowers as well. The dwarf bedding Snapdragons are particularly useful for splashes of color in mass plantings, as edging plants, and as additions to the rock garden.

Antirrhinum majus 'Rembrandt'

Antirrhinum majus 'Sweetheart White'

Antirrhinum majus 'Bright Butterflies'

Arctotis stoechadifolia

Arctotis stoechadifolia (A. grandis)
Blue-eyed African Daisy, Arctotis

History: The name *Arctotis* is Greek for "Bear's Ear" and alludes to the shape of the seed (achenes). This plant is native to South Africa.

Description: Arctotis has woolly gray leaves and single stemmed daisy-like flower heads that are 3 in. (7 cm) across. The gold-rimmed, steel-blue centers are surrounded by pearly-white ray florets that have lavender backs. There are also hybrid strains in shades of yellow, pink, brown, terra cotta, wine, and mauve. Most cultivars are less than 12 in. (30 cm) tall, but some may exceed 24 in. (60 cm).

Propagation and Culture: Seeds should be sown indoors about 6 to 8 weeks before the last frost is due or outdoors when the soil is warm. Seeds germinate in 2 to 3 weeks at 68°F (20°C). Plants should be spaced about 12 in. (30 cm) apart. Plants will withstand drought and do best in light, sandy loam in full sun. They thrive in areas where nights are cool.

Use: The long stems make this a flower that is desirable for flower arrangements, although the flowers close at night. It is ideal for beds and borders in a warm, sunny spot.

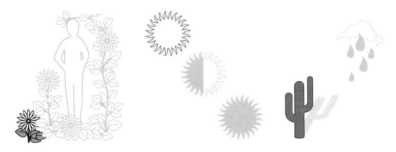

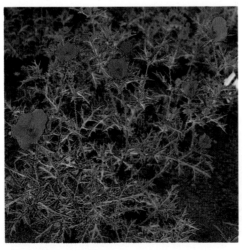

Argemone mexicana

Gail Rankin

Argemone grandiflora and *Argemone mexicana*
Argemony, Prickly Poppy

History: These plants are members of the Poppy family and are of Mexican origin. The name *Argemone* is from the Greek meaning "cataract "or "eye disease" for which this plant was reputed to be a remedy.

Description: The flowers of *Argemone grandiflora* are satiny white and about 4 in. (10 cm) in diameter, whereas those of *Argemone mexicana* , often called Mexican Poppy, are yellow and 2 to 3 in. (5 to 7 cm) across. Both species grow to about 24 in. (60 cm) in height with leaves that have scalloped edges tipped with tiny spines.

Propagation and Culture: Seeds may be sown indoors about 6 weeks before the last frost is due. They should be started in individual 3- to 3.5-in. (7- to 8-cm) peat pots since they do not transplant well. Seed may also be sown directly in the garden where they are to grow after all frost has left the soil. Plants should be thinned or planted to stand about 9.5 in. (22 cm) apart. They thrive in light, sandy loam soil in full hot sun.

Use: Prickly Poppies make dramatic border plants.

Argemone grandiflora

Asarina spp. (*Maurandya* spp.)
Chickabiddy

History: There are several species of this genus in North America and Europe. They are all tender, herbaceous perennials and mostly climbers by means of coiling petioles. They are often referred to as Climbing Snapdragons or Creeping Gloxinia. The three main species grown as garden annuals are *Asarina antirrhinifolia, Asarina barclaiana,* and *Asarina erubescens.*

Description: Depending on the species and cultivar grown, these plants will grow from 40 to 120 in. (100 to 300 cm) or more in height. The "two-lipped" flowers vary from white through rose to purple and blue. Flower size varies also with species and cultivar from about 1 to 2.5 in. (2.5 to 6 cm).

Propagation and Culture: Seeds may be sown indoors at least 6 to 8 weeks before the last spring frost is due. Plants should be spaced about 12 to 24 in. (30 to 60 cm) apart depending on the vigor and spread of the species or cultivar in question. A trellis or string support of sufficient height will need to be provided unless the plants are used as a ground cover rather than as a climber. They grow well in average, well-drained, slightly alkaline soil in full sun to light shade. Seeds are not readily available commercially.

Use: These attractive vines or trailing plants can be used to cover lattices, pergolas and gazebos as well as to screen walls or fences. They are also useful in hanging baskets, window boxes, or raised planters.

Asarina spp.

Carmen's Nursery

Asclepias curassavica

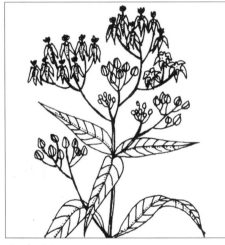

Asclepias curassavica

Asclepias curassavica
Bloodflower, Bloodflower Milkweed

History: The name *Asclepias* is derived from the Greek *asklepios,* the god of healing. Bloodflower is native to tropical America but can be handled as an annual flower in northern climates if it is started indoors from seed or cuttings.

Description: The flowers are about 1 in. (2 cm) in diameter, deep purplish-red and orange in color and appear in clusters from the base of leaves and at the top of 24- to 48-in. (60- to 120-cm) stalks. The plants bloom in late summer.

Propagation and Culture: Seeds may be sown indoors at least 10 to 12 weeks before the last frost is due and seedlings set in the garden when danger of frost is past. Branching will be enhanced if plants are pinched when the shoots are 4 to 6 in. (10 to 15 cm) tall. Plants should be spaced15 to 17 in. (38 to 45 cm) apart in moist, fertile soil in a sunny location. Heavy, dry soils should be avoided.

Use: Bloodflowers are eye-catching in summer gardens, especially as a background planting. The seed pods, if they mature before the first killing frost at the end of the season, make interesting material for dried arrangements. Mature plants left in place over winter can add interest to the winter landscape.

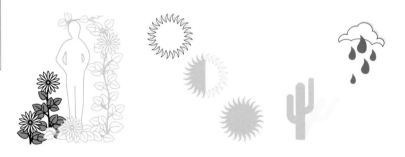

Asperula orientalis

Asperula orientalis (A. azurea setosa)
Annual Woodruff

History: The name *Asperula* comes from the word asper meaning "rough" and refers to the texture of the leaves. This genus contains both perennial and annual species found wild in many countries around the world. It is a member of the *Rubiaceae* family. Annual Woodruff is native to the Caucasus.

Description: This little annual bears clusters of tiny, very fragrant, pale blue flowers on 9- to 12-in. (23- to 30-cm) tall plants. The flower stems trail on the ground clothed in whorls of slender bristly leaves.

Propagation and Culture: Seeds can be scattered on the ground where they are to grow as soon as it can be cultivated in the spring. For best results seedlings should be thinned so that plants stand 4 to 6 in. (10 to 15 cm) apart. Plants should bloom 10 to 12 weeks after seeding. Annual Woodruff may scatter its own seeds in favorable locations so that the plants renew themselves each spring. Seeds are not readily available commercially. This is one of the few annual flowers that is at its best in a moist, shady place.

Use: It makes a fine edging plant, especially near a stream or water course. It may also be used as a short-stemmed cut flower.

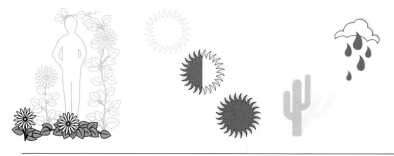

Atriplex hortensis (A. hortensis astrosanguinea)
Garden Atriplex, Orach, Sea Purslane

History: This fast growing annual from Asia is a member of the *Chenopodiaceae* or Goosefoot family. It is sometimes referred to as Asiatic Mountain Spinach and is occasionally cultivated as a vegetable. It makes a good cooked edible green (potherb).

Description: Strains of this plant with dark red foliage make attractive ornamentals. The leaves are arrowhead-shaped and covered with a crystalline substance when the plants are young. Plants reach a height of 48 to 70 in. (120 to 180 cm) and produce tiny purplish flowers in spike-like clusters.

Propagation and Culture: Seeds may be sown outdoors when danger of frost is past and the seedlings thinned so that plants stand 12 in. (30 cm) apart. Seed may also be started indoors 4 to 6 weeks earlier. Plants thrive is almost any soil in open sunny areas and will withstand wind. Garden Atriplex will self-seed readily.

Use: Garden Atriplex is often used as a temporary summer hedge or screen because of its rapid growth and tall stature. It is also useful as a cut flower, mainly because of its attractive foliage.

Brian Porter

Atriplex hortensis rubra

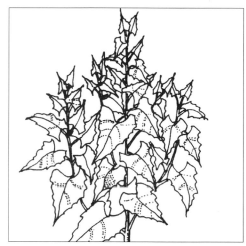

Atriplex hortensis

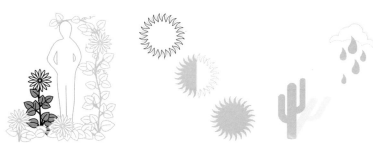

Begonia x *semperflorens*

Begonia x *semperflorens*

Begonia x *semperflorens*

Begonia x *semperflorens – cultorum* and other hybrid cultivars
Fibrous Begonia, Bedding Begonia, Wax Begonia

History: Wax Begonias are natives of Brazil and are actually tender herbaceous perennials. However, they are popular bedding plants because they will flower prolifically the first year from seed. They are also popular as year-round house plants.

Description: Wax Begonias usually grow only 6 to 9 in. (15 to 23 cm) tall and bear 1 to 2 in. (2.5 to 5 cm) clusters of delicate pink, white, or red flowers. Some cultivars produce single flowers whereas others have double flowers, some so dense and broadly petalled that the clusters resemble miniature Christmas-tree balls. The blooms grow close together hiding much of the glossy red or green foliage.

Propagation and Culture: Begonias take a long time to develop from seed (4 to 6 months), so most people prefer to buy plants or to root cuttings taken from house plants in the spring. Plants may be set out in the garden after all danger of frost is past and night temperatures do not drop below 46 to 50°F (8 to 10°C). Plants should be spaced 6 to 8 in. (15 to 20 cm) apart. They flourish in shade as well as full sun, provided they have rich moist soil. However, some cultivars may scald if planted in full sun.

Use: Wax Begonias are among the most versatile and popular of bedding plants. They are superb for window boxes, beds, and borders, and can be wintered over as house plants.

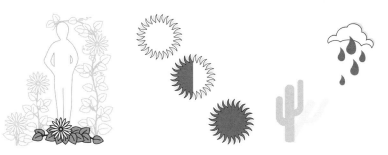

Begonia x *tuberhybrida*
Hybrid Tuberous Begonia

History: Tuberous Begonias have been developed as the result of extensive crossing and back-crossing of several species of begonias that grow wild in South America. The resultant hybrid species, *Begonia* x *tuberhybrida,* is therefore a very variable species including cultivars with single, semi-double, and double flowers in almost every color except blue.

Description: The plants have stout fleshy stems about 17 in. (38 cm) in height and large, deep green, glossy leaves. Cultivars that have a drooping habit of growth are suitable for use in hanging baskets. In some cultivars the edges of the flower petals are frilled; in others they are crested. They produce an underground corm-like tuber or tuberous root that can be stored over winter in a dormant state.

Propagation and Culture: Many people prefer to buy the tuberous roots or started plants, but Tuberous Begonias, like Wax Begonias, may be started from seed. It does, however, take 4 to 6 months to develop flowering plants when starting from seed. The tubers on the other hand can be started in peat moss or a highly organic soil mixture indoors 6 to 8 weeks before the last frost is due. Plants should not be planted outdoors until all danger of frost is past and night temperatures are well above freezing. Plants should be spaced 12 in. (30 cm) apart in partial shade in moist, organic soil. They will flower well in partial to full shade and should not receive direct sunlight except in the cool hours of early to mid-morning. They also require protection from wind and wind-driven rain. For information on how to harvest and store the tuberous roots over winter, see Chapter 6.

Use: Tuberous Begonias add an exotic and colorful dimension to the flower garden. They are useful as edging plants or in mass carpet plantings. The trailing types are excellent in hanging baskets or raised planters in shady areas.

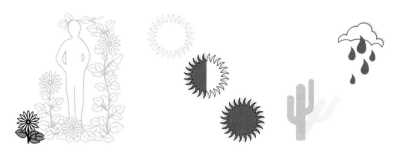

Begonia x *tuberhybrida* 'Non-stop White'

Begonia x *tuberhybrida*

Begonia x *tuberhybrida*

Brachycome iberidifolia
Swan River Daisy

History: This is a delightful annual from Australia that is a member of the *Asteraceae* or Sunflower family. The genus name comes from the Greek meaning "short hair" and refers to the pappus or bristles that are attached to the seed (achene).

Description: Swan River Daisy produces a multitude of fragrant, daisy-like blossoms of pastel blue, rose, violet, or white coloration, and are about 1.5 in. (4 cm) in diameter. Plants rarely exceed 12 in. (30 cm) in height.

Propagation and Culture: Seeds may be sown indoors 4 to 6 weeks before the last frost is due or sown outdoors in late spring after danger of frost is past and the soil is warm. Plants should be spaced 6 in. (15 cm) apart. Bushy twigs or short wire supports should be placed around the plants to support their slender stems. They require rich soil and full sun.

Use: Masses of Swan River Daisies are very effective when used in borders, window boxes, and patio planters. They can also be used as short-stemmed cut flowers.

Brendan Casement

Brachycome iberidifolia

Brachycome iberidifolia

Brassica oleracea acephala and Brassica oleracea capitata
Ornamental Kale and Ornamental Cabbage

History: These plants are merely colorful strains of their vegetable "siblings" and are tender biennials grown for their rosette pattern of foliage. They are also susceptible to the same insects as their edible relatives.

Description: It is their foliage rather than flowers that make these low growing plants notable. The two species look very much alike and are usually sold interchangeably or as a mixture. The leaves develop and open out from a central growing point and become either off-white or deeply tinged with pink, rose, red, or purple, especially toward the centers. The coloration becomes more prominent towards the end of the growing season as the plants mature and night temperatures become cooler. They will withstand the early frosts that kill the more tender annual flowers.

Brian Porter

Brassica oleracea acephala

Propagation and Culture: Seeds may be sown indoors 4 to 6 weeks before the last frost. The plants are then set outside when night temperatures are not expected to drop below freezing. Seeds may be sown directly in the garden as soon as the soil can be worked in the spring. Plants should be spaced 12 to 18 in. (30 to 45 cm) apart. Later seedlings will produce plants with smaller leaves useful in fall arrangements. They grow in average soil conditions but require full sun. They are most colorful in cool weather.

Use: Ornamental Cabbage and Kale make unusual bedding plants and can extend the attractiveness of flower beds well into the autumn. They are also prized by flower arrangers because their colorful leaves complement the shades of gold and russet that predominate in the fall colors of our native trees and shrubs.

Brian Porter

Brassica oleracea capitata

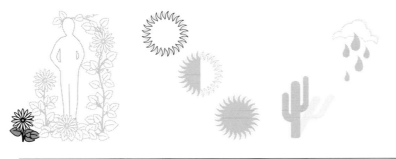

Briza maxima (B. major) and *Briza minor (B. gracilis, B. minima)*
Large or Big Quaking Grass and Lesser or Little Quaking Grass

Description: The ornamental feature of Quaking Grass is its colorful seeds that are grouped into arrowhead-like shapes that droop from slender stems and tremble in the slightest breeze. The seed heads of Large Quaking Grass are about 1 in. (2.5 cm) long hanging on stems 18 to 24 in. (45 to 60 cm) tall. The seed heads of Lesser Quaking Grass are only about 0.1 in. (0.3 cm) in size on stems 9 to 12 in. (23 to 30 cm) tall. The colors of the seeds include silvery-red, reddish-brown, and purplish-green.

Propagation and Culture: Seeds may be sown outdoors in early spring as soon as the ground can be cultivated. Germination should be evident in 10 to 14 days after seeding. Seedlings may be thinned if necessary to a spacing of 6 to 8 in. (15 to 20 cm) between plants. Quaking Grass thrives in average or dry soil and full sun.

Brian Porter

Briza maxima

Use: In general, ornamental grasses, including Quaking Grass, add a special textural interest to flower beds or serve as specimen plants of special interest. They can also serve as ground cover in place of turf, especially in rough areas or areas that are difficult to access. Perhaps the greatest use of ornamental grasses is in decorative dried arrangements. For this purpose stems should be cut right after flowering to prevent the seeds from maturing and falling off. The cut stems should then be hung upside down in small bundles to cure in a dry, shady location.

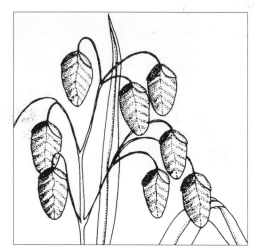

Briza maxima

Browallia speciosa

Brian Porter

Browallia speciosa and *Browallia viscosa*
Browallia, Bush Violet

History: The genus *Browallia* is named after John Browall, Bishop of Abo, Sweden. It is a member of the *Solanaceae* , the Potato or Nightshade family, and contains about 6 species, all indigenous to South America.

Description: Bowallias are close relatives of the petunia and have a similar trumpet-like shape and velvety texture to their blossoms. Cultivars of *Browallia speciosa* have blue or white flowers 1 to 2 in. (2.5 to 5 cm) across. *Browallia viscosa* has dark blue, white-throated blossoms about 1 in. (2.5 cm) in diameter. All grow to a height and spread of 12 to 15 in. (30 to 38 cm).

Propagation and Culture: Plants can be started from seeds sown indoors 6 to 8 weeks before the last frost is due, but most gardeners buy young plants. Seeds take 2 to 3 weeks to germinate at 68°F (20°C). Like Wax Begonias and some of the other popular tender bedding plants, Browallias can be brought indoors as potted house plants that will flower freely all winter. Cuttings can be taken in September or March and rooted in a warm greenhouse. Plants should be spaced 8 to 10 in. (20 to 25 cm) apart in flower beds. They grow and flower well in average to moderately rich soil, in warm temperatures, in either full sun or partial shade.

Use: With their slender, graceful trailing stems, Browallias make excellent plants for window boxes and hanging baskets.

Browallia speciosa

Calendula officinalis
Pot Marigold, Calendula

History: The name *Calendula* comes from the Latin *calendae* or *calends* meaning "throughout the months" and alludes to the almost continuous flowering character of this plant. They are native to the Mediterranean region and the dried flowers have been used to flavor soups and stews as well as to color butter. It has also been used in medicine in the past to heal wounds, settle upset stomachs, and remove warts.

Description: These colorful floriferous plants produce either daisy-like or chrysanthemum-like flowers in white through cream and lemon, to bright yellow, apricot, and orange. Flower size ranges from 2 to 3 in. (5 to 8 cm) in diameter and plant height ranges from 12 to 18 in. (30 to 45 cm).

Propagation and Culture: Seeds can be planted outdoors as soon as the ground can be cultivated in the spring. Plants should be thinned and transplanted to stand 12 to 15 in. (30 to 38 cm) apart. Calendulas transplant very easily and thrive in full sun, fertile soil, and cool temperatures. They will flower satisfactorily in partial shade as well. Removal of faded flower heads to prevent seed formation will prolong the flowering season. Calendulas can be susceptible to Aster-Yellows. See culture of Annual Aster (*Callistephus chinensis*) for control measures.

Use: Calendulas are excellent for cut flowers and make bright flower bed plantings. They are also good for planters and window boxes.

Calendula officinalis 'Bon Bon Yellow'

Calendula officinalis 'Family Circle'

Callistephus chinensis
Annual Aster, China Aster

Callistephus chinensis 'Early Charm'

Brian Porter

History: This plant is native to the Orient and closely related to the asters of the genus *Aster*. The name *Callistephus* comes from the Greek word *kallistos* meaning "most beautiful" and *stephos*, a "crown", and refers to the appendages on the fruit (seed).

Description: The flowers of China Asters vary from 1.5 to 5 in. (4 to 12 cm) in diameter and take on a wide variety of forms; some are like daisies, some like chrysanthemums, some like tight little pompons, and others quite shaggy. Colors range from white through creamy yellow and pink to red, blue, lavender, and purple, often with yellow centers. Cultivars range in height from 8 to 36 in. (20 to 90 cm).

Callistephus chinensis 'Mini-Lady Blue'

Brian Porter

Propagation and Culture: Seeds can be sown indoors 5 to 6 weeks before the last frost is expected. Seed should be barely covered. They germinate in 2 to 3 weeks at 68°F (20°C). Young plants, preferably in small peat pots, should be hardened off in a cold frame and set out in the garden after all danger of frost is past. Plants should be spaced 9 to 12 in. (23 to 30 cm) apart and the ground covered with 1 to 1.5 in. (2 to 3 cm) of peat or grass clippings to keep the soil cool and help maintain moisture. China Asters have very shallow root systems. Seed may also be sown directly outdoors when all danger of frost is past, but because of our short growing season, late-started plants may not bloom before the first killing frost. It is best to choose the earlier blooming cultivars for the same reason. China Asters are also subject to diseases, especially Aster-Yellows, which causes stunting and wilting. The pathogen causing "yellows" is transmitted by leaf hopper insects. To reduce the incidence of this disease, only wilt-resistant cultivars should be planted and the plants kept free of leaf hoppers. It is not advisable to plant China Asters in the same location for two successive years because they are susceptible to pathogens that can build up in the soil from year to year if a "crop rotation" is not practiced. They are best grown in full sun and a rich porous soil. They succeed best when nights are relatively cool and days are warm and dry but not hot.

Use: Annual Asters are grand flowers for late summer and early autumn. They are useful additions to flower beds and are particularly popular as cut flowers.

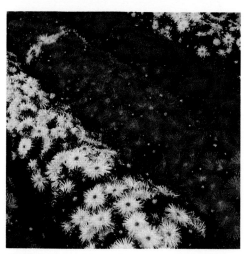

Callistephus chinensis

Ed Toop

Campanula macrostyla
Anatolian Bellflower

History: The genus *Campanula,* known as Bellflower, Harebell, and Bluebell, is a large group of attractively flowering herbs, containing some of the most hardy and popular garden perennials. This bellflower is native to central Turkey; hence the common name, Anatolian Bellflower.

Description: Anatolian Bellflower is a branching, hardy annual with broad, solitary purple, pink, or white flowers. The leaves are small and the whole plant is covered with bristles. Flowers are broad, 2 to 3 in. (5 to 7.5 cm) in diameter, with long and prominent styles and stigmas. Plants grow about 18 in. (45 cm) tall.

Propagation and Culture: Seeds can be sown directly in the garden as soon as the soil can be cultivated. Seedlings do not transplant easily. The space between plants should be about 12 in. (30 cm). They should thrive in average garden soil in full sun.

Use: Anatolian Bellflower is an interesting addition to the annual flower beds or borders.

Campanula macrostyla

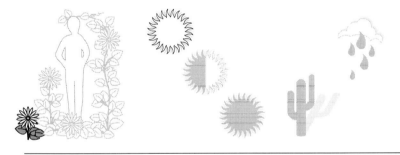

Campanula medium (C. grandiflora)
Canterbury Bells

History: Biennial forms of Canterbury Bells, which are native to southern Europe, have been garden favorites for generations.

Description: Canterbury Bells will not survive our winter climate and therefore cannot be grown as a biennial. However, if young plants are produced in a greenhouse for bedding-out in the spring, they will flower as an annual and reach a height of 24 in (60 cm) or more. Some forms will flower the first year from seed planted in the spring (early) and perform like a regular annual. Annual Canterbury Bells develop into 18 in. (45 cm) tall pyramids that become covered in late summer with spikes of large bell-shaped blossoms of white, pink, rose, lavender, and blue hues. Each flower is 2 in. (5 cm) or more in length. The "cup and saucer" variety (*Campanula medium* 'Calycanthema') bears flowers with double bells, one inside the other. This cultivar is biennial but will bloom the first year if started indoors early enough.

Campanula medium

Propagation and Culture: Annual forms can be started indoors 8 to 10 weeks before the last frost is due. However, it can take 6 months from seeding until flowering even for these annual forms. Biennial forms are best purchased as plants that have been grown through their first-year developmental stage and are ready to produce flower stalks. Plants should be set in the garden at a spacing of about 12 in. (30 cm) when all danger of frost has passed. They require full sun and a rich, moist soil.

Use: Canterbury Bells are attractive additions to the flower border and make unusual, long-lasting cut flowers.

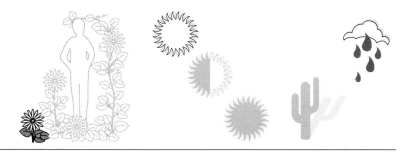

Cardiospermum halicacabum
Balloon Vine, Heartseed, Love-in-a-puff

Cardiospermum halicacabum

History: The names for this plant are all very descriptive of its appearance. The genus name *Cardiospermum* is from the Greek meaning "heart-seed" and refers to the heart-shaped white spot that occurs on the round black seeds. These seeds form in balloon-shaped seed pods about 1 in. (2.5 cm) in diameter. This plant is a native to tropical America, India, and Africa.

Description: The four-petalled flowers of the Balloon Vine are small and white, but the inflated seed pods are the decorative and interesting feature of this plant. It will grow and climb by tendrils to a height of 10 ft (3 m) or more in a summer.

Propagation and Culture: Seeds may be sown in individual small pots 6 weeks before the last frost is due and the seedlings transplanted to the garden after all danger of frost is past. Plants should be spaced 12 in. (30 cm) apart and provided with a 2.5- to 3-yd (2.5- to 3-m) tall trellis or other support on which the vines can climb. Balloon Vine thrives in average, moist garden soil in full sun.

Use: Balloon Vine provides a quick-growing decorative screen when planted beside a fence, trellis, or wall.

Cardiospermum halicacabum

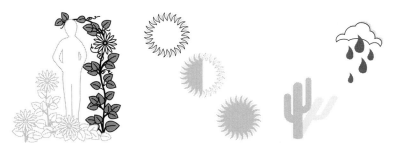

Carthamus tinctorius
Safflower, Saffron Thistle

History: Safflower comes from Asia and its generic name is derived from an Arabic word *quartom* meaning to "paint". The yellow florets of the flower head can be used to produce a rose-colored dye used in cosmetics and for dying cloth, especially silks. The seeds also contain an oil used for culinary purposes, for leather dressings, and for illumination.

Description: The thistle-like flower heads, about 1 in. (3 cm) across, terminate in a globular crown of orange florets. Safflower has egg-shaped, spiny-toothed leaves, almost as broad as long, and grows to a height of 36 in. (90 cm). There are newer cultivars such as 'Lasting White,' 'Lasting Orange,' and 'Tangerine' that have expanded the color range to white, yellow, and red.

Propagation and Culture: Seed may be sown indoors 6 to 8 weeks before the last frost is due or sown outdoors in spring when the soil is warm and the main danger of frost is past. Direct-seeded plants will not reach flowering stage until late summer. They grow well in ordinary to dry garden soil in full sun. Plants should be thinned or transplanted to a spacing of 8 to 12 in. (20 to 30 cm).

Use: Safflower is very suitable for a wild garden or as an interesting addition to a flower bed.

Carthamus tinctorius

Brian Porter

Catananche caerulea
Cupid's Dart, Blue Cupidone, Blue Succory

History: The name *Catananche* is derived from the Greek *katanangke* meaning a "strong incentive", a reference to its ancient use as a love potion. It is native to southern Europe where it survives as a herbaceous perennial.

Description: Cupid's Dart grows about 24 in. (60 cm) tall with long, narrow, grayish-green leaves and slender stalks. The stalks are topped with blue flower heads up to 2 in. (5 cm) in diameter with stiff chaff-like fringed "petals" (florets), not unlike Zinnias. There is also a blue and white flowering cultivar (*Catananche caerulea* 'Bi-color') and a white flowering cultivar (*Catananche caerulea* 'Alba').

Catananche caerulea

Carmen's Nursery

Catananche caerulea

Propagation and Culture: Seeds may be sown indoors 6 to 8 weeks before the last frost is due or outdoors as soon as the soil can be cultivated. Seeds germinate in 2 to 4 weeks at 68 to 86°F (20 to 30°C). Plants should be spaced about 9 in. (23 cm) apart. They grow well in a dry, well-drained, ordinary garden soil in a sunny location.

Use: These flowers make a colorful addition to the garden border or a wild flower garden, but their greatest asset is the fact that they can be dried for winter flower arrangements without losing their shape or color. To dry them, cut the flower stalks when the blooms are at their peak and hang them upside down in a cool, shaded place to cure.

Catharanthus roseus 'Pretty in Rose'

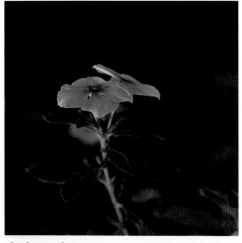

Catharanthus roseus

Catharanthus roseus (Vinca rosea)
Madagascar Periwinkle

History: Madagascar Periwinkle is native to tropical areas of the world and is often known in the trade as *Vinca rosea*.

Description: Madagascar Periwinkle is quite bushy, growing from 10 to 18 in. (25 to 45 cm) tall with glossy leaves and 1 to 2 in. (2.5 to 5 cm) diameter flowers. Blossoms come in rose, pink, and white as well as white with pink centers.

Propagation and Culture: Seeds of this periwinkle may be started indoors 3 to 4 months before the last frost is due. Unless you have a greenhouse, it is better to buy the plants for bedding out. Plants should be put out in the garden at a spacing of 8 to 10 in. (20 to 25 cm) after all danger of frost has passed. They flower most freely in hot weather but prefer some shade. They thrive in ordinary soil and will tolerate full sun if kept well watered.

Use: Madagascar Periwinkles are valued for the splashes of color they provide in beds, borders, and planters.

Celosia cristata
Cockscomb, Woolflower

History: Cockscomb is native to the Asian tropics and a member of the Amaranth family. The name *Celosia* comes from the Greek *kelos* meaning "burned" and refers to the burned look of the flower of some species.

Description: Cockscomb is notable for its striking flower heads that range from 2 to 10 in. (5 to 25 cm) in width in variously crested, plumed, or feathered spikes. One group, often listed as *Celosia argentea cristata,* has inflorescences that look like the combs of roosters whereas those of another group, often incorrectly listed as *Celosia argentea plumosa,* are dense sprays not unlike ostrich plumes. This latter plumosa group is often called Feathered Amaranth. Both types and their cultivars come in brilliant shades of yellow, orange, red, and even purple. They also vary from 8 to 30 in. (20 to 90 cm) in height. The flower heads, like those of *Amaranthus,* are extremely long-lasting (up to 8 weeks) before fading.

Propagation and Culture: Seeds may be started indoors 4 weeks before the last frost is due or sown directly in the garden in the spring when the soil can be cultivated and has warmed up. Plants should be spaced 9 to 12 in. (23 to 30 cm) apart. Care should be taken in transplanting since Celosias do not tolerate root disturbance well. They will grow in average garden soil and will tolerate dry conditions. They require full sun.

Use: Because of their intense colors, Cockscombs must be used discreetly in most gardens in much the same way as the Amaranths. They make colorful and interesting cut flowers and are suited for drying to use in winter bouquets. For this purpose, flowers should be cut when they are at their peak and hung upside down in an airy, shaded place.

Ed Toop

Celosia cristata

Ed Toop

Celosia cristata

Ed Toop

Celosia cristata

Centaurea americana

Centaurea americana
Basket Flower

History: This member of the genus *Centaurea* gets its common name from the fact that the flower head buds appear to be enclosed in little baskets.

Description: The blooms of Basket Flower look like its cousin, Cornflower, but much larger, 4 to 5 in. (10 to 13 cm) in diameter on plants that can reach 60 to 70 in. (150 to 180 cm) in height. The color range includes pink, lavender, and white.

Propagation and Culture: Seed should be sown outdoors as soon as the soil can be cultivated in the spring and plants thinned to a spacing of 6 to 10 in. (15 to 25 cm). Plants will thrive in any well-drained soil in the sunshine. Seed is difficult to obtain commercially.

Use: Basket Flowers are effective when massed in flower beds or borders as background materials. They are also useful as cut flowers.

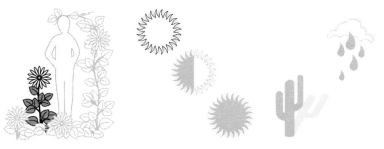

Centaurea cyanus 'Blue Diadem'

Brian Porter

Centaurea cyanus
Cornflower, Bachelor's Button

History: This species of *Centaurea* grows wild in the grainfields of southern Europe and hence its common name of Cornflower. It is one of the world's most widely grown annuals and is known by various common names including Bluebottle, Ragged Sailor, and French Pink.

Description: Cornflower blossoms are about 2 in. (5 cm) in diameter and borne on plants 12 to 36 in. (30 to 90 cm) tall with gray-green foliage. In addition to the old favorite blue Cornflower, there are newer cultivars in pink, red, maroon, lavender, and white.

Propagation and Culture: Seeds may be sown indoors 4 weeks before the last frost is expected and the seedlings transplanted to the garden as soon as the danger of frost is past. Seeds germinate in 3 to 4 weeks at 68 to 86°F (20 to

30°C). They may also be sown directly in the garden in the fall (late October to early November) or in the spring as soon as the soil can be cultivated. It appears that germination is enhanced with the chilling of the seed, either naturally outdoors or by stratification for one week. Plants should be spaced about 12 in. (30 cm) apart. Cornflowers bloom prolifically with little care provided they are in a sunny, well-drained location. They commonly self-seed.

Use: Cornflowers are effective when massed in flower beds or borders. They are also useful as cut flowers.

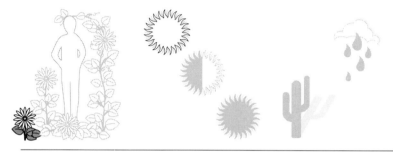

Centaurea cyanus

Centaurea gymnocarpa and *Centaurea cineraria* (*C. candidissima*)
Dusty Miller

Description: These two species of *Centaurea* are similar and are grown for their silvery-white, fern-like leaves. *Centaurea gymnocarpa* grows about 24 in. (60 cm) tall whereas *Centaurea cineraria* grows only 10 to 12 in. (25 to 30 cm) tall. In mild climates, they are flowering perennials that grow to 36 in. (90 cm) in height once established.

Propagation and Culture: Dusty Millers are slow growing so should be started indoors 6 to 8 weeks before the last frost is expected, at which time they can be moved outdoors. Seeds germinate in 2 to 4 weeks at 68 to 86°F (20 to 30°C). They should be spaced about 8 to 10 in. (20 to 25 cm) apart. They thrive in ordinary to dry soil in sunny locations.

Use: The shorter Dusty Millers are useful as edging plants, acting as a "frame" to the flower bed. Tall Dusty Millers, as specimen plants within a border, can act as focal points or so-called "dot" plants (tall plants set in flower beds filled with shorter plants, often in the center of groupings as a design feature).

Centaurea cineraria

Centaurea moschata

Centaurea moschata 'The Bride'

Brian Porter

Centaurea moschata (C. suaveolens, C. odorata, C. amberboii)
Sweet Sultan

History: This species of *Centaurea* comes from the near east.

Description: Sweet Sultans bear fuzzy flower heads up to 4 in. (10 cm), but more commonly 2 in. (5 cm), in diameter, delicately scented and in shades of yellow, pink, and lavender as well as white. They grow about 24 in. (60 cm) tall.

Propagation and Culture: Seed should be sown outdoors as soon as the soil can be cultivated in the spring and plants thinned to a spacing of 6 to 10 in. (15 to 25 cm). Plants will thrive in any well-drained soil in the sunshine.

Use: Sweet Sultans are effective when massed in flower beds or borders, especially near patios or decks where their perfume can be appreciated. They are also useful as cut flowers.

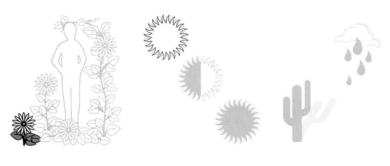

Cerinthe aspera
Honeywort

History: The name is derived from the Greek *keros* meaning "wax" and *anthos* meaning "flower" since the ancients thought that bees visited the flower to gather wax. Honeywort is a member of the Borage family and native to southern Europe.

Description: At the ends of the 12- to 24-in. (30- to 60-cm) long stems of this plant are pendant clusters of yellow tubular flowers (bell-shaped) with whorls of chocolate-colored bracts around the base of each flower. Each flower is about 1 in. (3 cm) long. The stems are clothed in smooth, gray-green clasping leaves.

ANNUALS FOR THE PLAINS AND PRAIRIES

Propagation and Culture: Seeds may be sown indoors about 8 weeks before the last spring frost is expected, or sown directly outside in spring as soon as the soil has warmed up and can be cultivated. Plants should be spaced about 6 in. (15 cm) apart. These plants should thrive in average garden soil and will withstand wind and wind-driven rain. They flower best in full sun but will tolerate partial shade. Seed may be difficult to obtain commercially.

Use: This plant is rather unusual in form and color so can add interest to a flower bed or planter.

Charieis heterophylla
Charieis

History: The name of this plant is Greek for "elegant". This attractive, hardy garden annual of the Daisy family is native to South Africa and was previously catalogued under the old name of *Kaulfussia amelloides*.

Description: Charieis is a compact, much-branched plant 6 to 12 in. (15 to 30 cm) tall with bright blue, yellow-centered blooms about 1 in. (2.5 cm) across and borne singly on slender, hairy stems. They are also delicately fragrant and long-lasting.

Propagation and Culture: Seeds may be sown indoors 4 to 6 weeks before the last frost is due or sown directly outdoors in the spring as soon as the soil has warmed and dried enough to be cultivated. Plants should be spaced 6 in. (15 cm) apart. They prefer a sunny location and a light, sandy loam soil. Seed may be difficult to obtain.

Use: Charieis is well suited for edging purposes or as an addition to the rock garden. Because of their short, sturdy stature, they hold up well in wind and rain. Because of their delicate fragrance and long-lasting qualities, they make good cut flowers, but remain open only during daylight hours.

Charieis heterophylla

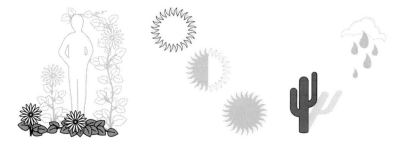

Cheiranthus cheiri

Cheiranthus cheiri

Cheiranthus cheiri

Carmen's Nursery

Donna Balzer

Cheiranthus cheiri
English Wallflower

History: This is an old garden favorite from southern Europe and a common plant on the stone walls in England. It is a somewhat woody perennial, but is best renewed frequently by young plants from seed. It normally takes two years from germination to maturity and the production of flowers.

Description: Plants bear spikes of four-petalled flowers, each about 1 in. (2.5 cm) across in shades of yellow, orange, red, purple, or maroon-brown. Cultivars vary in height from 6 to 9 in. (15 to 23 cm) (dwarf) to others that grow as tall as 18 in. (45 cm). Wallflowers are usually biennial in habit, but early strains will flower in about 5 months from seed. If starting your own plants from seed, look for packets marked "early flowering" or "annual variety". Most cultivars should be scented.

Propagation and Culture: To grow Wallflowers as annuals, you really need a greenhouse to develop good plants that are mature enough to flower as bedding plants when placed in the garden in spring after the danger of frost is past. So-called "annual selections" may perform successfully if started indoors 8 weeks before the last frost is due in spring. Seeds germinate in 2 to 3 weeks at 55°F (13°C) and may respond to light. Plants should be spaced about 6 to 12 in. (15 to 30 cm) apart. Wallflowers will grow in full sun or partial shade and prefer cool, damp nights. They thrive in ordinary soil provided it is not acidic (neutral to slightly alkaline), which is not usually a problem on the prairies where the soils are predominantly alkaline.

Use: Dwarf cultivars are useful in rock gardens and particularly in "dry walls" (unmortared rock retaining walls). Taller annual cultivars may be massed for late-summer color in flower beds. Longer-stemmed cultivars make good cut flowers.

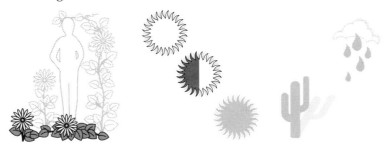

Chrysanthemum carinatum, Chrysanthemum coronarium, and Chrysanthemum segetum Hybrids
Annual Chrysanthemum

Chrysanthemum carinatum 'Merry Mixture'

History: The hardy Annual Chrysanthemums have been developed through cross-breeding and selection from the three species listed above. They are often commonly called either "mums" or "chrysanths".

Description: Annual Chrysanthemums vary tremendously in flower size and form but flower heads are usually single (daisy-like) to semi-double, about 2 to 3 in. (5 to 7 cm) across in colors ranging from yellow through orange, salmon, and scarlet to purple and white, usually with a ring of contrasting color near the center of each flower head. Most cultivars grow about 24 in. (60 cm) tall.

Propagation and Culture: Most Annual Chrysanthemums grow rapidly from seed which can be sown shallowly in the garden as soon as the earth can be worked in the spring. Seedlings should be thinned and transplanted to stand about 18 in. (45 cm) apart. Chrysanthemums transplant easily at any time. Annual Chrysanthemums grow well in ordinary soil in full sun or light shade.

Use: Annual Chrysanthemums provide masses of color in flower beds if they are planted in rich soil in full sun. They provide fine cut flowers as well.

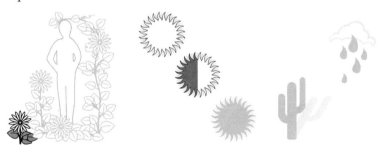

Chrysanthemum Hybrids

Chrysanthemum multicaule and Chrysanthemum paludosum
Annual Yellow or Butter Daisy, Yellow Buttons and Annual White Daisy, White Buttons

Chrysanthemum multicaule

History: These two annual daisies or marguerites are quite similar except for color.

Description: Ray florets are short and rounded, giving the flower heads the appearance of buttons up to 1.5 in. (4 cm) in diameter. Yellow Buttons (*Chrysanthemum multicaule*) produce compact plants that are 6 to 12 in. (15 to 30 cm) tall, whereas White Buttons (*Chrysanthemum paludosum*) is more vigorous, producing plants that are more open and up to 4 in. (10 cm) taller. The Yellow Buttons' flowers tend to close at night.

Propagation and Culture: These daisies can be grown from seed sown shallowly in the garden as soon as the earth can be worked in the spring. Seedlings should be thinned and transplanted to stand about 10 to 12 in. (25 to 30 cm) apart. These annual chrysanthemums grow well in ordinary soil in sun or partial shade.

Use: These annuals can provide masses of color in the front of flower beds or in planters. They make good edging plants for beds and borders. The Yellow Buttons are particularly good as ground covers, but do not make good cut flowers because they close in low light.

Chrysanthemum paludosum

Chrysanthemum parthenium (Matricaria capensis, Pyrethrum parthenium)
Feverfew, Matricaria

History: Feverfew is one of the "old-fashioned" plants common about yards and waste places. There are many rather distinct horticultural forms varying in height, form, flower size, leaf form, and color. Feverfews give off a strong scent something similar to Chamomile *(Anthemis nobilis),* and the dried flowers have been used in the treatment of fevers.

Description: There are two main types of Feverfew, one that grows about 24 in. (60 cm) tall bearing double white blooms and another that grows only 6 to 9 in. (15 to 23 cm) tall with double white or yellow flowers. Feverfews are actually half hardy perennials that flower the first year from seeds. There is a dwarf horticultural variety called 'Golden Feather,' which has yellow foliage that later changes to green if flowers are allowed to form. It is useful for carpet-bedding.

Propagation and Culture: Seed may be sown indoors 6 to 8 weeks before the last frost is due in spring for early flowering or sown directly in the garden as soon as the soil can be cultivated in the spring. Seeds germinate in 2 to 4 weeks at 68°F (20°C). Plants should be spaced about 20 to 30 cm apart for the shorter types and about 18 in. (45 cm) apart for the taller types. They grow in full sun or light shade in ordinary to dry soil.

Chrysanthemum parthenium 'White Stars'

Chrysanthemum parthenium 'White Wonder'

ANNUALS FOR THE PLAINS AND PRAIRIES

Use: The shorter Feverfews are useful as edging plants as well as mass plantings for splashes of white or yellow color. They can be used as a substitute for Sweet Alyssum because of their resistance to flea beetles in areas where Canola is widely grown. The taller Feverfews are excellent cut flowers for bouquets, as well as contributors to flower beds and borders.

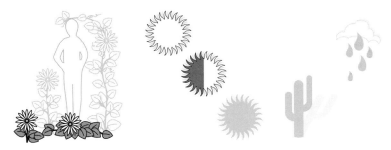

Chrysanthemum parthenium

John Beedle

Chrysanthemum ptarmiciflorum (Cineraria candicans)
Silver Lace Dusty Miller

Description: Silver Lace Dusty Miller is the showiest of all the plants called Dusty Miller. It is relatively tall (up to 16 in. (40 cm)) with fine-textured lacy foliage.

Propagation and Culture: Like other Dusty Millers, Silver Lace is slow growing and should be started indoors about 6 to 8 weeks before the last frost is due. Plants should be spaced about 10 in. (25 cm) apart. They thrive in an ordinary to dry soil in a sunny location.

Use: This plant, when mixed with brightly colored flowering annuals, tends to tone down their intensity. When mixed with pastel-colored flowers, they enhance or brighten their hues.

Chrysanthemum ptarmiciflorum

Brian Porter

Chrysanthemum ptarmiciflorum

Ed Toop

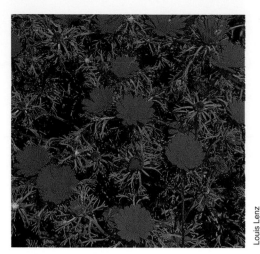

Cladanthus arabicus

Cladanthus arabicus

Cladanthus arabicus (C. proliferus, Anthemis arabica)
Palm Springs Daisy, Cladanthus

History: The name of this plant comes from the Greek *klados*, "branch", and *anthos*, "flower", alluding to its branching habit which distinguishes this genus from *Anthemis*. A member of the Daisy family, *Cladanthus arabicus* (the only species) is indigenous to southern Spain and Morocco.

Description: Cladanthus, because of its recurrent branching pattern, becomes a compact mound clad in a dense covering of golden-yellow, daisy-like flowers. The lacy, cosmos-like foliage has a strong but not unpleasant odor. Plants may become 24 to 36 in. (60 to 90 cm) tall and equally broad.

Propagation and Culture: The seeds of this plant often take a month to germinate after sowing and the subsequent seedlings take an additional 3 to 3 1/2 months to reach the flowering stage. Therefore, this is a plant that requires a lot of attention under greenhouse conditions before it is planted in the garden. Plants should be spaced about 12 in. (30 cm) apart in the garden. Cladanthus grows well in most soils in a sunny well-drained location.

Use: This cheery plant provides an abundance of bright yellow flowers in an annual border.

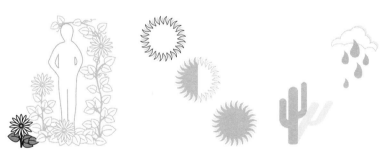

Clarkia amoena 'Sybil Sherwood'

Clarkia amoena (Godetia amoena)
Godetia, Farewell-to-spring, Satin Flower

History: Until recently the common garden Godetia or Farewell-to-spring was classified as the species *Godetia amoena,* but now it is considered to be more correctly a part of the closely-related genus *Clarkia.* Godetias are named for the Swiss botanist, C. H. Godet. Farewell-to-spring is native to the west coast of North America but is a popular garden flower in many parts of the world.

Description: Farewell-to-spring grows 12 to 24 in. (30 to 60 cm) tall with satin-petalled, cup-like blossoms, 3 to 5 in. (7.5 to 12.5 cm) in diameter, clustered along its stems. Flower color ranges from white to pink, red, or lilac. Foliage is gray-green.

Propagation and Culture: Godetias do best in cool weather so seeds may be sown outside in spring as soon as the soil can be worked to form a good seed bed. They should be seeded where they are to be grown since they are not easy to transplant. Seedlings should be thinned to a spacing of 6 to 12 in. (15 to 30 cm). They grow well in light, sandy soil that is not too fertile since a rich soil tends to produce plants with much foliage and few flowers. They do well in either sun or partial shade.

Use: Godetias are showy plants and make an attractive addition to annual flower beds or planters. Tall varieties make lovely cut flowers.

Clarkia amoena 'Azalea Flowered'

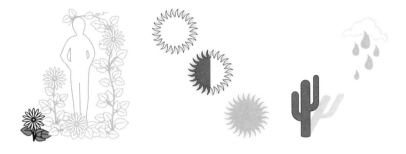

Clarkia unguiculata (C. elegans) and *Clarkia pulchella*
Clarkia and Rocky Mountain Garland

History: These beautiful hardy annuals of western North America are named after Captain William Clark of the Lewis and Clark expedition. They are members of the Evening Primrose family *(Onagraceae)*.

Description: Clarkias produce spike-like stems bearing delicate blossoms, each about 1 in. (2.5 cm) across, all along their wiry length. Seeds of double-flowered cultivars are available in shades of salmon, pink, mauve, rose, carmine, purple, red, or white, but usually a few single-flowered types, like the wild native types, appear among the seedlings. They usually grow to 18 to 24 in. (45 to 60 cm) in height.

Propagation and Culture: Seeds may be sown outdoors early in the spring as soon as the ground can be cultivated. If plants are started indoors to achieve earlier flowering, they must be kept in cool temperatures (i.e., a cool greenhouse). Seeds will germinate in 1 to 2 weeks over a wide temperature range (55 to 90°F (13 to 32°C)). Seeds of some strains require light to germinate. Plants should be spaced about 10 in. (25 cm) apart in the garden. Clarkias thrive in cool summers and dry sandy loam soils low in nitrogen fertilizer. They grow and flower well in either full sun or partial shade.

Clarkia unguiculata
'Royal Bouquet Double Mixed'

Use: Clarkias can be a good choice for a partially shaded, cool spot in the prairie garden. They make long-lasting, decorative, cut flowers.

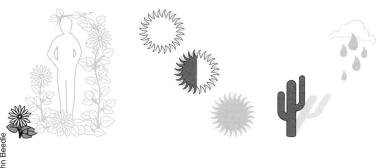

Clarkia unguiculata

John Beedle

Cleome hasslerana

Brian Porter

Cleome hasslerana 'Violet Queen'

Brian Porter

Cleome hasslerana (C. spinosa, C. pungens) and *Cleome lutea*
Cleome, Spider Flower and Yellow Spider Flower

History: *Cleome hasslerana* is a native of tropical America, whereas *Cleome lutea* is a wild flower of western parts of the United States.

Description: Cleome hasslerana grows quickly to a dramatic height of about 4 ft (120 cm) producing large, airy terminal flower clusters 6 to 8 in. (15 to 20 cm) in diameter in pink, lavender, or white. *Cleome lutea*, as the name implies, has golden-yellow flowers but otherwise is similar to its cousin. Each flower is graced with a tracery of long stamens, and as the blossoms fade, decorative seed pods develop beneath the advancing flower clusters like spider legs. Cleomes are better appreciated at a little distance, especially since the pungent scent of their blossoms and leaves can be overpowering.

Propagation and Culture: Seeds may be sown indoors 4 to 6 weeks before the last spring frost is expected. Seeds germinate in 1 to 2 weeks at 55 to 90°F (13 to 32°C). Seeds may respond to light. Cleomes grow in almost any soil but prefer rather hot, dry locations. They will, however, tolerate some shade. Plants should be spaced 12 to 24 in. (30 to 60 cm) apart, depending on how dense a planting you wish to have.

Use: Cleomes are effective as a background planting, especially beside a wall or along a fence. With relatively close spacing (12 in. (30 cm)), they will form an effective temporary hedge. They also make interesting specimen plants in patio or terrace pots.

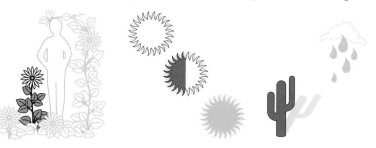

Cobaea scandens
Cup-and-saucer Vine, Cathedral Bells, Mexican Ivy

Cobaea scandens

Description: The showy cup-like blossoms of the Cup-and-saucer Vine are about 2 in. (5 cm) long and 1.5 in. (4 cm) wide and look as though they are sitting in large green saucers of foliage. Colors range from greenish-purple to violet as well as white (cv. 'Alba'). This vigorous climber can grow to a height of 15 to 25 ft (450 to 750 cm).

Propagation and Culture: The large seeds should be planted on their edge, with soil just covering the top edge. Plant two seeds to a 3-in. (8-cm) pot, indoors, 6 to 8 weeks before the last frost. Germination is slow and may take 3 weeks. If both seeds germinate, the weaker one should be removed. The plants should be acclimatized outdoors after all danger of frost is past and planted into the garden at a spacing of 18 to 24 in. (45 to 60 cm). A trellis, wall, or strings should be provided for the plants to climb on. They require a rich, light soil and full sun.

Use: Cup-and-saucer Vine makes an ideal, although temporary, cover for a wall, fence, or gazebo.

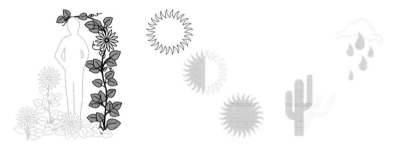

Coix lacryma-jobi
Job's Tears

Coix lacryma-jobi

History: Job's Tears is an ornamental grass native to India. The name is of ancient Greek origin and was used by Theophrastus to designate a reed plant. It is a member of the Grass family, *Poaceae (Gramineae)*.

Description: This annual grass forms a dense tuft about 3 ft. (90 cm) tall bearing clusters of pretty white, pearl gray, black, or brown seeds about the size of cherry pits in the summer.

Propagation and Culture: Before planting, seeds should be soaked in water for a day to soften the seed coats and hasten germination. They may be started indoors 4 to 5 weeks before the last frost is due or planted in the garden in average to dry soil in a sunny spot after all danger of frost is past. Plants should be spaced about 12 in. (30 cm) apart. This plant is likely to be a challenge to the northern gardener since experience seems to be lacking in the successful growing of this annual grass in the prairie climate.

Use: Stems with seeds intact make interesting additions to winter dried flower arrangements. Stems should be cut before the seeds are mature enough to fall off. After cutting, the stems should be set to dry in a cool, airy place. Stems may be set upright in a container or hung upside down, depending on whether straight or curved stems are desired. Individual seeds can be used to make necklaces or bead curtains.

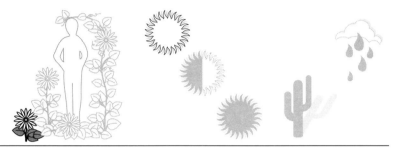

Coleus x *hybridus* 'Wizard Mix'

Coleus x *hybridus* 'Saber Mix'

Coleus x *hybridus* (Hybrids of *C. blumei* and *C. pumilus*)
Coleus, Flame Nettle, Painted Leaves

History: Coleus are tender perennial herbs from the islands of the South Pacific grown for their colorful foliage rather than their flowers.

Description: Coleus hybrid selections range in height from 6 to 24 in. (15 to 60 cm) and are admired for their bizarre foliage which may be chartreuse, yellow, pink, red, or green, usually in multi-hued patterns. A selection known as the "Wizard" strain is considered to be an improvement over the older "Rainbow" and "Prize" strains because it produces dwarf, self-branching plants without the need to "pinch back".

Propagation and Culture: Seeds may be sown indoors 10 weeks before the last frost is expected. Seeds germinate in 2 to 3 weeks at 68 to 86°F (20 to 30°C). Although the seeds are small, the seedlings grow rapidly. It is important to pinch out the growing point of young plants to create compact plants that are a mound of foliage. Plants should not be set out in the garden until the weather is settled and warm since they will not tolerate cold, wet weather. They should be spaced 8 to 10 in. (20 to 25 cm) apart. They have no special soil requirements and will thrive in sun or partial shade provided the air is warm.

Use: Coleus make spectacular plants for beds, borders, planters, or window boxes.

ANNUALS FOR THE PLAINS AND PRAIRIES

Collinsia heterophylla (C. bicolor)
Collinsia, Chinese Houses, Pagoda Collinsia, Innocence

History: These pretty, hardy annuals are members of the Snapdragon family and native to California and other parts of western North America. Collinsia is named after Zaccheus Collins, an American promoter of the sciences.

Description: Collinsias grow 12 to 24 in. (30 to 60 cm) tall and bear stems with whorls of blossoms, each composed of two deeply cleft lips, with the upper one white and the lower one pink or lavender. Individual blooms are about 1 in. (2.5 cm) in diameter. There are also cultivars with all white flowers.

Propagation and Culture: Seeds may be sown indoors a few weeks before the last frost is due or seeded directly outdoors as early in the spring as the soil can be worked. The ultimate spacing of the plants should be about 12 in. (30 cm) apart. They will thrive in partial shade in ordinary soil. They tolerate dryness but not heat.

Use: Collinsias make beautiful, free-flowering border plants and because of their tolerance to dry soil are often used in rock gardens. As cut flowers, they are long-lasting.

Collinsia heterophylla

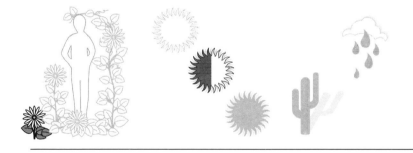

Hybrids of Consolida ambigua (Delphinium ajacis) , Consolida regalis (Delphinium consolida) and Consolida orientalis
Larkspur, Annual Delphinium

History: Larkspurs or Annual Delphiniums used to be classified as species of the genus *Delphinium* and still appear under that name in many seed catalogues. Larkspurs are native to southern Europe. They are grown commercially as a cut flower.

Description: Larkspurs produce tall, beautiful spikes of feathery petalled flowers in shades of blue, salmon, rose, lilac, purple, or white set amid and above lacy green foliage. There are two strains, a branching type that produces several flower stalks on each plant, and a hyacinth-flowered type

Consolida

Brendan Casement

Consolida ambigua

Ed Toop

that has only one massive flower stalk per plant. Each type will grow 36 to 60 in. (90 to 150 cm) tall. Among the hyacinth-flowered cultivars, there is a dwarf strain that grows only 12 in. (30 cm) tall but bears large, lovely flowers.

Propagation and Culture: Seeds may be sown outdoors where the plants are to bloom either in the fall or as early in the spring as the soil can be prepared. They do not transplant well; therefore, if started indoors, they should be seeded in individual small pots. The earliness of seeding will affect the height the plants will reach. The earlier they are started, the taller they will be when flowering occurs. Plants should be spaced 8 to 16 in. (20 to 40 cm), depending on type and anticipated height. Tall cultivars may require staking to keep them upright. Larkspurs require fertile, well-drained soil in full sun or light shade (especially if summers are hot).

Use: The tall, stately, heavily-flowered spikes of the taller strains provide a mass of color as a background planting against a fence, along a wall, or at the back of a flower bed or border. The long-lasting spikes and graceful appearance make them ideal cut flowers for bouquets and arrangements. Spikes in full bloom can also be cut and dried by hanging them upside down in a dark, airy place.

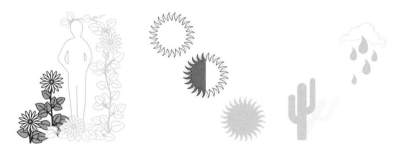

Convolvulus tricolor

Brendan Casement

Convolvulus tricolor
Dwarf Morning Glory

History: The name *Convolvulus* comes from *convolvo*, to "entwine", and refers to the climbing and entwining growth habit of many of the members of this genus. A common name for the group is "bindweed" and many of the perennial species can be very troublesome weeds. *Convolvulus tricolor*, however, is a non-climbing, safe and easy to grow annual flower.
Description: These lovely plants make solid mounds of blue, lilac, red, pink, or white flowers, usually about 12 in. (30 cm) tall and of even greater spread. The name *tricolor* refers to the fact that each flower has a band of white between its yellow throat and the flaring trumpet portion which may be of any of the colors listed. Blossoms are 2 in. (5 cm) across.

Propagation and Culture: Plants can be given a head start by planting the seeds indoors in individual 3-in. (8-cm) pots 5 to 6 weeks before the last spring frost is due. To speed germination, the hard seeds should be nicked with a file before planting two seeds per pot. After germination, the weaker of the two seedlings in each pot should be discarded. Seeds may be sown directly outdoors, but not until the soil is warm and night temperatures do not drop below 40 to 50°F (5 to 10°C). Plants should be set 12 in. (30 cm) apart in the garden. Dwarf Morning Glories thrive in dry, sunny locations in almost any kind of soil.

Use: These annuals are among the best flowers for use in planters, window boxes, or hanging baskets, or for edging flower beds.

Convolvulus tricolor

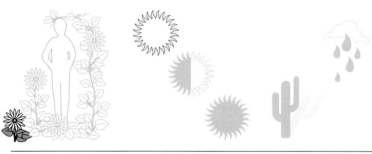

Coreopsis basalis (C. drummondii) and *Coreopsis tinctoria (C. bicolor)*
Calliopsis, Coreopsis, Tickseed

History: The annual species of Coreopsis are usually known as Calliopsis, whereas the perennial ones are commonly called Coreopsis. The name *Coreopsis* comes from *koris*, a "bug", and *opsis*, "like". This is an allusion to the appearance of the seed, and hence the common name "Tickseed".

Description: Calliopsis, of which the two species listed are the most common, bear long-stemmed flowers that are yellow, yellow marked with crimson, dark crimson, maroon, orange, and mahogany. They are daisy-like with toothed petals, often in double layers with brownish-yellow centers and are 1.5 to 2 in. (3 to 5 cm) in diameter. They appear to dance in the slightest breeze on their wire-thin stems. Cultivars vary in height from less than 12 to 36 in. (30 to 90 cm).

Propagation and Culture: Calliopsis are among the easiest of flowering plants to grow. Seeds should be sown very early in the spring, as soon as the soil can be worked. Seedlings are difficult to transplant successfully so they should be seeded where they are to flower and thinned to a spacing of about 6 to 9 in. (15 to 20 cm). Some sort of staking or support is recommended since the thin stems have difficulty holding the heavy flower heads erect. They grow well in most soils but need a sunny location.

Coreopsis tinctoria 'Semi Dwarf Single'

Use: Calliopsis bloom well over the summer season and make a brilliant showing in borders and beds. They are also excellent for cut flower use.

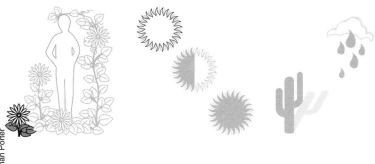

Coreopsis tinctoria 'Dwarf'

Brian Porter

Cosmos bipinnatus 'Sunny Red'

All-America Selections

Cosmos bipinnatus

Ed Toop

Cosmos bipinnatus and *Cosmos sulphureus*
Cosmos and Yellow Cosmos

History: These plants are native to Mexico and sometimes are called Mexican Asters. The name is from the Greek *kosmos*, meaning "beautiful".

Description: The attractive single or double flowers range from white through yellow, pink, and crimson. The plants are large, openly branched plants with delicate feathery foliage. They usually grow 3 to 5 ft. (90 to 150 cm) tall, but newer cultivars of *Cosmos sulphureus*, the traditional Yellow Cosmos, such as 'Ladybird', 'Sunny Gold', and 'Sunny Red' are 12 to 18 in. (30 to 45 cm) tall.

Propagation and Culture: Seeds may be sown indoors 5 to 6 weeks before the last spring frost or outdoors after all danger of frost is past. Plants should be spaced 12 in. (30 cm) apart in the garden. Seedlings transplant easily. Plants may require staking if the site is windy. They grow well in any soil in full sun but will tolerate partial shade.

Use: Cosmos is valuable as a background plant in beds or borders or to fill in empty spaces. They can be used to form a temporary hedge. They also make graceful, long-lasting cut flowers.

Craspedia spp. Hybrids
Drumstick Flower

History: *Craspedias* are native to Australia, New Zealand, and Tasmania. The genus includes about seven species. They are members of the Daisy family but form compound globe-shaped flower heads. Individual florets are all tubular in shape and bisexual.

Description: These plants have silvery foliage and bright yellow, drumstick-like flower heads on strong wiry stems. They grow up to 18 in. (45 cm) tall, usually with flower heads up to 1.5 in. (3 cm) in diameter. Plants should be spaced 8 to 10 in. (20 to 25 cm) apart.

Propagation and Culture: Seeds may be sown indoors 5 to 6 weeks before the last frost is due or outside after all danger of frost is past in the spring. They require well-drained soil and full sun.

Use: As well as being an interesting addition to the garden flower beds, Drumstick Flowers make excellent cut flowers, both fresh and dried.

Craspedia spp.

Crepis rubra (Barkhausia rubra)
Hawk's Beard

History: This plant is native to Italy and Greece.

Description: The blooms of Hawk's Beard resemble pink dandelions in size and shape, and are about 1 in. (2.5 cm) in diameter. The slender flower stalks are about 12 in. (30 cm) tall arising from clumps of slender leaves at the base of the plant. There are varieties or cultivars of different shades of pink as well as white.

Propagation and Culture: Seeds may be sown outdoors in spring as soon as the soil can be cultivated. Plants should be thinned and transplanted to a spacing of 4 in. (10 cm). They thrive in poor soil if given full sun.

Crepis rubra

Use: Hawk's Beard is effective as an edging border plant and in rock gardens. It does not make a good cut flower since the blossoms tend to close when used for this purpose.

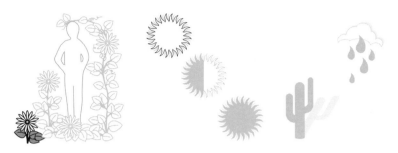

Cucurbita pepo ovifera and related species
Ornamental Gourds

Cucurbita pepo ovifera

History: *Cucurbita pepo ovifera* produce small gourds, whereas *Lagenaria vulgaris* produces large gourds. Several species of other genera produce gourd fruits as well, including *Benincasa, Cucumis,* and *Trichosanthes.* All are members of the *Cucurbitaceae,* the Gourd or Pumpkin family.

Description: Ornamental Gourds are tropical vines that produce brightly colored, hard-shelled, often grotesquely shaped inedible fruit. The plants can grow to over 10 ft. (300 cm) tall with fruit ranging from 2 to 60 in. (5 to 150 cm) in length.

Propagation and Culture: When all danger of frost is past, seeds are sown outdoors in the place where the plants are to develop since they do not transplant well. They may be started indoors in individual peat pots and later transferred to the garden with a minimum of root disturbance in order to gain a few weeks on the season. Seeds germinate in 2 to 3 weeks at 68 to 86°F (20 to 30°C). They grow well in almost any soil provided there is good sunlight.

Cucurbita pepo ovifera

Use: Gourd plants quickly cover fences, porch railings, trellises, arbors, or even compost heaps with heavy foliage. Matured fruit may be gathered before the first frost for use as a table decoration. A thin coat of floor wax will give them a shine and enhance their color. Unless they have hardened and the stems begun to shrivel before harvest, they will bruise easily from handling and are likely to decay.

Cymbalaria muralis
Kenilworth Ivy, Mother-of-thousands, Pennywort, Wall Toadflax

History: *Cymbalarias* are low, creeping herbaceous plants of the Old World that are classified as species of *Linaria* by some authorities. They are members of the Snapdragon family.

Description: Kenilworth Ivy is a trailing plant whose stems root wherever they touch the soil. It self-seeds and can become weedy because of this. It produces small, pale, lilac-blue flowers with a yellow throat about .4 in (1 cm) long. There is a white-flowered variety as well as a form with variegated leaves.

Propagation and Culture: Kenilworth Ivy should be seeded outdoors where plants are to grow as soon as the soil can be worked in the spring. Seeds germinate in 1 to 4 weeks at 54°F (12°C). The plant grows well in any soil in rather dry locations such as spaces between stones or bricks or even in old soft mortar. It thrives in sun or partial shade.

Use: Kenilworth Ivy is a most charming plant to use in a dry wall type of rock garden as well as in pots, window boxes, or hanging baskets. Its stems trail down and flower in a dainty and attractive manner.

Cymbalaria muralis

Cymbalaria muralis

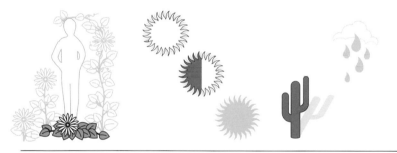

Cynoglossum amabile
Chinese Forget-me-not, Hound's Tongue

History: The name *Cynoglossum* comes from the Greek *kyos* meaning "dog" and *glosse*, a "tongue", and refers to the shape and soft surface of the leaves. The genus *Cynoglossum* belongs to the Borage family. The species Chinese Forget-me-not is native to Eastern Asia.

Description: This plant produces small, blue blossoms 0.25 in (0.6 cm) in diameter resembling those of true Forget-me-nots (*Myosotis* spp.). They are borne along graceful branching stalks 18 to 24 in. (45 to 60 cm) tall. There are also cultivars in white and pink that are less common. The seeds produced are "stick-tights" that adhere to clothing or animal fur.

Cynoglossum amabile 'Firmament'

Cynoglossum amabile

Propagation and Culture: Seeds should be sown outdoors as soon as the soil can be cultivated in the spring and seedlings thinned and transplanted to a spacing of 12 in. (30 cm). Because they start flowering rather quickly from seed, there is little advantage to starting seeds indoors. Chinese Forget-me-not thrives in almost any soil, in full sun or partial shade, and tolerates both wet and dry locations. It tends to scatter its seeds and can become a weedy nuisance.

Use: Chinese Forget-me-not is a pleasant addition to the middle ground of an annual flower bed or border. It is attractive but not long-lasting as a fresh cut flower.

Dwarf *Dahlia* hybrids

Ed Toop

Dwarf *Dahlia* hybrids

Brendan Casement

Hybrids of *Dahlia coccinea* and *Dahlia pinnata*
Dwarf Bedding Dahlia

History: Dahlias are members of the Daisy family named to commemorate Dr. Dahl, a Swedish botanist. They are tender tuberous-rooted summer and autumn flowering plants, native to Mexico, varying greatly in height, flower form and flower size. All can be started from seed but can also be propagated from stem cuttings and/or division of roots. The tuberous roots can be harvested and stored over winter in cold climates (see Chapter 6).

Description: The dahlias described here are the shorter bedding types that come into flower relatively quickly from seed and therefore can be handled like regular annuals. They bloom prodigiously producing 2 to 3 in. (5 to 8 cm) diameter flower heads in every color except blue. Height can range from less than 12 to 18 in. (30 cm to 45 cm).

Propagation and Culture: Seeds should be sown indoors 6 to 8 weeks before the last spring frost is due and the seedlings set outdoors after all danger of frost is past. Seeds germinate in 2 to 3 weeks at 68 to 86°F (20 to 30°C). Dahlias are extremely sensitive to chilling and freezing. Unless you have a greenhouse, purchase plants rather than start them from seed. Although these Dwarf Bedding Dahlias produce tuberous roots that can be stored over winter, plants grown from these tubers are usually not as uniform in height and flowering pattern as plants from seedlings or stem cuttings. They require fertile, well-drained soil and full sun for best flower production. It is important to keep the plants well watered.

Use: Dwarf Bedding Dahlias massed in mixed colors can make attractive flower beds unto themselves. They are also a striking addition to any annual flower bed. They are long-lasting as cut flowers, but the taller types grown from tuberous roots make even better cut flowers (see Chapter 6, page 38). Dahlia flowers also make good candidates for drying using silica gel.

Dwarf *Dahlia* hybrids

Datura metel and *Datura inoxia*
Trumpet Flower, Angel's Trumpet, Downy Thorn Apple

History: Daturas are members of the *Solanaceae* or Potato family and native to the tropics or warm temperate regions, mainly in the New World. The leaves and seeds yield alkaloid drugs with narcotic properties that have been used since ancient times. The flowers, leaves, or fruits are toxic if eaten.

Description: Trumpet Flowers grow from 3 to 5 ft. (90 to 150 cm) tall and produce large trumpet-like blooms up to 8 in. (20 cm) long and 4 in. (10 cm) across. Flowers are fragrant but individual flowers last only one day. *Datura metel* has white flowers typically, but there are yellow or purple-flowered forms. *Datura inoxia* has pink or lavender-colored flowers. There are both single and double-flowered forms.

Propagation and Culture: Seeds should be started indoors in a greenhouse 8 to 12 weeks before the last frost of the spring is due. Plants should be set out in the garden about 18 in. (45 cm) apart after all danger of frost is past. They require rich fertile soil that is rather dry and well-drained and a hot, sunny location.

Use: Individual plants can be spectacular novelties when grown in large pots or planters. They are also suitable for the mixed annual flower border or as a hedge if space permits. Because of their large leaves and large flowers, they can be visually overpowering in a small yard or garden.

Datura metel 'Cornucopaea'

Datura metel

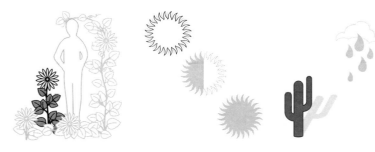

Daucus carota carota

Daucus carota carota

Daucus carota carota
Queen Anne's Lace, White Lace Flower

History: Closely related to the common carrot vegetable *(Daucus carota sativa)*, Queen Anne's Lace is a member of the *Apiaceae (Umbelliferae)*, native to Europe but naturalized in North America. It is naturally biennial in growth habit.

Description: Wild Carrot or Queen Anne's Lace produces flat heads (umbels) of tiny white to yellowish-white flowers giving a lace-like appearance. Plants are 24 to 36 in. (60 to 90 cm) in height with leaves finely cut into very narrow segments that are almost fern-like.

Propagation and Culture: Seeds may be sown in the garden as soon as the soil is warm and all frost danger is past. They may be sown indoors also about 4 to 6 weeks before the last spring frost is due. Plants should be spaced about 12 to 18 in. (30 to 45 cm) apart. They grow well in ordinary soils in full sun.

Use: Queen Anne's Lace is an easily-grown annual that can contribute to the middle ground height zone of a flower border. It can be used as both a fresh and dried cut flower as well. Cut flower stalks can be hung upside down in a dry, airy place and later used as filler in dried arrangements. With the introduction of Bishop's Flower or False Queen Anne's Lace *(Ammi majus)*, Queen Anne's Lace *(Daucus carota carota)* has lost favor. Bishop's Flower is superior in appearance and is a true annual in growth habit.

Dianthus barbatus
Annual Sweet William

History: The species *Dianthus barbatus* comes in annual, biennial, and short-lived perennial selections. Annual forms resemble the more common biennial Sweet Williams. Annual Sweet Williams are native to both southern and eastern Europe.

Description: Annual Sweet Williams have closely packed, flat-topped, non-fragrant flower clusters 2 to 4 in. (5 to 10 cm) in diameter. Flower colors include shades of red, pink, rose-purple, white, or a combination of these colors. The foliage is dark green. Height ranges from 6 to 18 in. (15 to 45 cm).

Dianthus barbatus 'Extra Early Kurokawa'

Propagation and Culture: Annual Sweet Williams will flower by mid-summer if seeds are sown outdoors as soon as the soil can be worked in the spring. For earlier flowering, seeds may be sown indoors 6 to 8 weeks before the last frost is due. They need full sun and well-drained alkaline soil for best growth and flowering.

Use: The shorter cultivars are among the most popular plants for garden edgings. All provide dramatic color effects when massed in beds or borders. They also make long-lasting cut flowers.

Dianthus barbatus

Gail Rankin

Dianthus caryophyllus
Annual Carnation

Description: Annual Carnations are natives of southern Europe and have flowers that rival those of the greenhouse-grown carnations sold by florists. They come in a wide range of colors: yellow, white, red, pink, and mixtures with spicy-scented flowers that are 1 to 3 in. (2.5 to 7.5 cm) in diameter on plants that are 12 to 24 in. (30 to 60 cm) in height. The foliage is blue-gray in color.

Propagation and Culture: Seeds should be sown indoors in a greenhouse. It takes only 10 days for the seeds to germinate but 5 months for the plants to come into flower. It is suggested that young plants be purchased for planting in the garden. Plants should be spaced about 8 to 10 in. (20 to 25 cm) apart. They require well-drained, alkaline soil and full sun to do their best.

Dianthus caryophyllus

Brian Porter

Use: The shorter cultivars are among the most popular plants for garden edgings. All provide dramatic color effects when massed in beds or borders. They also make long-lasting cut flowers.

Dianthus caryophyllus

Ed Toop

ANNUALS FOR THE PLAINS AND PRAIRIES

Dianthus chinensis 'Snowfire'

Dianthus chinensis

Dianthus chinensis
Rainbow Pink, China Pink

History: The name *Dianthus* is derived from *dios*, "divine", and *anthos*, "flower" the name said to have been given by Theophrastus because of the charm and fragrance of the flowers. There are about 300 species in the world with considerable variation in plant form and growth habit among them. Species tend to hybridize easily and even the categories of "annual" or "perennial" fail to apply firmly to species of *Dianthus*. Types that bloom readily from seed the first season may continue to live for several years if hardy enough to survive the winters.

Description: China Pinks, which are native to East Asia, grow 6 to 12 in. (15 to 30 cm) in height and produce many single, semi-double, or frilled flowers on erect stems. Flowers are 1 to 2 in. (2.5 to 5 cm) in diameter in shades of pink, rose, scarlet, crimson, and white; some are even bi-colored. Foliage is gray-green in color.

Propagation and Culture: Seeds may be sown indoors 6 to 8 weeks before the last frost is due, but the temperature should be dropped a month after seeding since seedlings require temperatures around 54 to 60°F (12 to 15°C) for best development (use a coldframe). After danger of frost is past, plants can be put into the garden at a spacing of about 6 to 10 in. (15 to 25 cm). China Pinks do best in a well-drained, alkaline soil in full sun.

Use: The shorter cultivars are among the most popular plants for garden edgings. All provide dramatic color effects when massed in beds or borders, and make long-lasting cut flowers.

Diascia barberae
Twinspur

History: This member of the Snapdragon family is native to South Africa. The name *Diascia* is derived from *diaskeo*, to "adorn".

Description: Twinspur is a lovely annual with slender stalks rising above a mound of gleaming, deep green leaves. These stalks bear clusters of pink flowers with yellow throats about 1 in. (2 cm) in diameter. On the reverse side of each blossom are two curving horn-like spurs which account for the common name. Some strains have deep pink or orange flowers. The height ranges from 10 to 16 in. (25 to 38 cm).

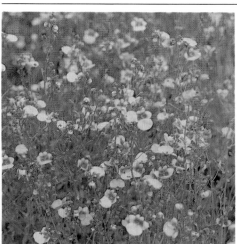

Diascia barberae 'Pink Queen'

Propagation and Culture: Seed may be sown indoors 6 to 8 weeks before the last frost is due in the spring. Successive pinching of the plants, starting when the seedlings are about 2 in. (5 cm) tall, will develop well-branched bushy plants. Plants should be set in the garden at a spacing of 6 in. (15 cm) when all danger of frost is past. Seeds can also be sown directly in the garden as soon as the soil can be cultivated in the spring. Plants flower about 14 weeks after sowing. The removal of faded flowers will encourage repeat flowering throughout the summer. Plants thrive in well-drained average garden soil provided the location is sunny. Seed is not readily available commercially.

Use: Twinspur flowers are delightful in a garden border but are not suitable as cut flowers.

Diascia barberae

Digitalis purpurea 'Foxy Strain'
Annual Foxglove

History: *Digitalis purpurea*, the Common Foxglove, is a typical biennial, self-seeding plant but is not winter hardy in our prairie climate. However, plant breeders have developed an annual strain which is usually referred to as "Foxy". *Digitalis purpurea* is the source of the important cardiac drug digitalis. It is native to southern Europe.

Description: Annual Foxglove grows 24 to 36 in. (60 to 90 cm) tall with sturdy compact flower spikes of 2- to 3 in. (5- to 7.5-cm) long tubular, bell-shaped flowers with mottled throats. Colors include white, cream, yellow, pink, lavender, magenta, and purple.

Propagation and Culture: Since a growing season of about 5 months is needed for these plants to produce flowers after seeding, it is best to purchase plants that are close to the flowering stage. Seeding can be done in a greenhouse, in late fall or early winter. Seeds germinate in 2 to 3 weeks at 68 to 86°F (20 to 30°C) and may respond to light. Plants can be put in the garden in the spring after the danger of hard frosts is past at a spacing of 12 to 18 in. (30 to 45 cm). Foxy often reproduces from its own scattered seeds, but chances of this happening in the prairie garden are rare. Foxgloves provide color in cool, shady spots where few other kinds of plants will flower, but the soil must be well drained. Foxgloves will also do well in full sun.

Digitalis purpurea 'Foxy Strain'

John Beedle

Use: Foxgloves are among the showiest of tall plants to use at the back of a border or as individual accents. The flowers can appear almost fluorescent when blooming under the shade of a woodlot of spruce trees.

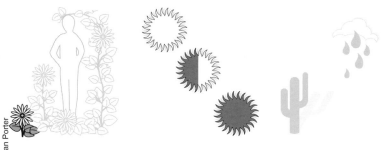

Digitalis purpurea 'Foxy Strain'

Brian Porter

Dimorphotheca sinuata

Brendan Casement

Hybrids of *Dimorphotheca sinuata*
Cape Marigold, Star-of-the-veldt

History: This member of the Daisy family is native to South Africa. The name *Dimorphotheca* is derived from *dimorphos* meaning "two forms" and *theca* meaning a "receptacle". It refers to the two types of florets that make up the individual flower heads.

Description: Cape Marigolds grow about 12 in. (30 cm) tall producing a profusion of 3.5 to 4 in. (9 to 10 cm) daisy-like blossoms whose colors range from white through brilliant shades of yellow to salmon-orange and rose. The reverse side of the "petals" is often colored in shades of blue or lavender.

Propagation and Culture: Seeds may be sown indoors 4 to 5 weeks before the last frost is due, but the young plants should not be put into the garden until the night temperatures are well above freezing. Seeds germinate in 2 to 3 weeks at 68 to 86°F (20 to 30°C). Seed may also be sown in the garden after all danger of frost is past. It takes about 9 to 10 weeks from seeding until flowering occurs. They do particularly well in hot, dry areas of the garden where the soil is well-drained.

Use: Cape Marigolds will provide masses of color in the garden provided they have plenty of sunshine. Since they close at night and on cloudy days, they are rarely used as cut flowers.

Dimorphotheca sinuata

Brendan Casement

Dyssodia tenuiloba (Thymophylla tenuiloba)
Dahlberg Daisy, Golden Fleece

History: Dahlberg Daisy is a member of the Daisy family, *Asteraceae (Compositae)*, and is native to Texas and Mexico. Its old genus name is derived from *thymos*, "thyme", and phylla, a "leaf", and refers to the thyme-like appearance of the foliage.

Description: Dahlberg Daisy seldom grows taller than 8 in. (20 cm) and produces finely divided aromatic foliage. The leaves are almost hidden by great numbers of daisy-like, golden-yellow flowers usually about 0.5 in. (1 to 1.5 cm) across. This plant is quite similar in appearance and growth habit to the Dwarf Signet Marigold.

Propagation and Culture: Seeds must be sown indoors 10 to 12 weeks before the last frost is due since the plants often take 4 months to begin flowering. For this reason, many gardeners will purchase plants ready for bedding-out. Plants should be set in the garden at a spacing of 6 in. (15 cm) after all danger of frost has passed. Dahlberg Daisies do best in full hot sun and well-drained, light, sandy loam.

Use: Dahlberg Daisies are especially good during long periods of very hot weather. They make good edging plants and can brighten up a rock garden. The flowers are also excellent for use in small bouquets or flower arrangements.

Dyssodia tenuiloba

Dyssodia tenuiloba

Echinocystis lobata
Wild Cucumber, Mock Cucumber, Balsam Apple

History: This vine is native to North and South America and grows rapidly in hot weather.

Description: Wild Cucumber can grow to 20 ft (6 m) or more in a long growing season. Its small, fuzzy, greenish-white flowers are followed by spiny, egg-shaped seed pods 2 in. (5 cm) long. The lobed leaves are 3 to 5 in. (7.5 to 12.5 cm) long.

Propagation and Culture: The seeds should be sown indoors 4 to 5 weeks before the last frost is due and the plants put into the garden at a spacing of 12 in. (30 cm) when all danger of frost is past. They may also be sown outdoors as soon as the

Echinocystis lobata

soil can be worked in the spring. They grow in any soil provided they are given a warm, sunny location. They require support for the tendrils to cling to.

Use: This vine provides a quick cover for any unsightly object as well as for a trellis or fence.

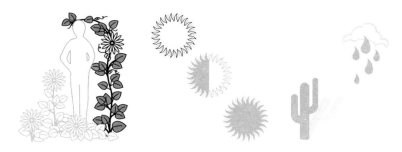

Echium lycopsis (E. plantagineum)
Viper's Bugloss

History: The name *Echium* comes from the Greek word for "viper" and refers to the seeds which look like tiny snakeheads. The name "bugloss" is also derived from the Greeks and means "ox tongue", a reference to the broad, rough, tongue-shaped leaves. Viper's Bugloss is a member of the Borage family and native to the Mediterranean region.

Description: Although the wild species of this plant may grow 24 to 36 in. (60 to 90 cm) tall, the garden forms are usually only 12 to 18 in. (30 to 45 cm) tall. They bear great quantities of bell-shaped flowers in shades of blue, lavender, purple, rose, or white. The flowers, about 0.5 in. (1.3 cm) across, appear along branching stems covered with bristly gray hairs. The cultivar 'Blue Bedder' has masses of violet-blue blossoms that turn pink as they age.

Propagation and Culture: Seeds may be started indoors 6 to 8 weeks before the last frost is due and moved to the garden when the danger of frost is past. They also can be sown in the garden as soon as the soil can be worked in the spring. Plants should be spaced 16 to 18 in. (38 to 45 cm) apart. They will become compact, bushy plants, ready to flower about 3 months after sowing. They thrive in dry, sunny locations with poor soil and self-seed readily.

Use: Viper's Bugloss is a long-flowering annual ideal for a hot, sunny spot. In rich soil, the plants tend to have much foliage and few flowers.

Echium lycopsis

Brendan Casement

Echium lycopsis

Emilia javanica (E. coccinea, E. flammea, and E. sagittata)
Tassel Flower, Flora's Paintbrush

Description: Tassel Flowers are grown for their small but brilliantly colored tassel-like flower heads of red, golden orange, or yellow. The blooms are borne on wiry stems about 18 to 24 in. (45 to 60 cm) tall above a low cluster of gray-green foliage.

Propagation and Culture: Seeds should be started indoors about 4 to 6 weeks before the last spring frost is expected and the young plants moved to the garden at a spacing of 6 to 8 in. (15 to 20 cm) when frost danger has passed. They also may be seeded in the garden when all danger of frost is past. They thrive in dry to average soil in a sunny location. Seed is not widely available commercially.

Use: Tassel Flowers add a dash of brilliant color to a flower bed or border and are also good as long-lasting cut flowers.

Emilia javanica

Eschscholzia californica
California Poppy

History: This plant was discovered on the Pacific coast of North America by a Russian expedition in 1815 and was named after a member of the expedition, Dr. John Friedrich Eschschotz. It is the state flower of California.

Description: California Poppies produce silky cup-like blooms of gold, bronze, scarlet, terra cotta, rose, or white, 2 to 3 in. (5 to 7.5 cm) in diameter. Some cultivars have semi-double or double flowers, often with crinkled petals edged in a darker shade. However, the most common type is the single-flowered gold to bronze. The blossoms appear above mounds of finely cut, silvery-green foliage about 12 in. (30 cm) tall, but the stems tend to cascade outward giving the plants a greater width than height.

Eschscholzia californica

T & T Seeds

Eschscholzia californica

Propagation and Culture: Seeds are sown in the garden where the plants are to grow since California Poppies are not easy to transplant. Seeds can be sown any time in the fall or as early in the spring as the soil can be worked. Plants should be spaced 6 to 8 in. (15 to 20 cm) apart. Since the common types readily self-seed, they will return every year but will require rigorous thinning to prevent overcrowding or even self-annihilation. Needless to say, they will thrive in any soil but prefer well-drained sandy soil sites in full sun.

Use: California Poppies are spectacular in the garden in mass plantings. They also thrive in window boxes, planters, and hanging baskets.

Euphorbia heterophylla

Euphorbia heterophylla
Annual Poinsettia, Mexican Fire Plant, Fire-on-the-mountain

History: There are 600 or more kinds of *Euphorbia* or spurge found wild in various countries. They range in appearance from uninteresting weeds to beautiful flowering shrubs, from tree-like forms to cactus-like species. Euphorbias contain a milky sap that exudes after any injury to stems or leaves. This sap is acrid and can cause a skin rash in some people. The name *Euphorbia* commemorates Euphorbus, physician to Joba, King of Mauritania.

Description: The actual flowers of Annual Poinsettia are small and unattractive, but they are subtended by bracts which are sometimes leaf-like and brightly colored. Annual Poinsettia is closely related to Christmas Poinsettia and somewhat resembles it. It grows 24 to 36 in. (60 to 90 cm) tall and by mid- to late summer the top leaves turn from dark green to red, sometimes with white markings that resemble a gigantic "flower".

Propagation and Culture: Seeds of Annual Poinsettia should be sown indoors about 6 weeks before the last frost is due and the plants moved to the garden after all danger of frost is past. Plants should be spaced 12 in. (30 cm) apart. They will thrive in light sandy to ordinary soil, but should be grown in a protected, warm, sunny location.

ANNUALS FOR THE PLAINS AND PRAIRIES

Use: Annual Poinsettias make showy border plants or specimen displays in patio pots or planters. The branches may be used as "cut flowers" if the stem ends are seared over a flame or dipped into boiling water before arranging in vases of warm water. This procedure prevents wilting caused by bleeding of the sap and its coagulation and blockage of the stems.

Euphorbia heterophylla

Euphorbia marginata
Snow-on-the-mountain

Description: Snow-on-the-mountain is a wild flower of the central United States and a plant that is easy to grow. It grows 18 to 24 in. (45 to 60 cm) tall with upper leaves that have a margin of clear white and an occasional leaf that may be totally white. The true flowers at the tips of the stems are as insignificant as are the true flowers of Annual Poinsettia.

Propagation and Culture: Seeds of *Euphorbia marginata* may be sown directly outdoors in the spring as soon as the soil is workable. Plants should be thinned to a spacing of about 10 to 12 in. (25 to 30 cm). Plants do not transplant well. They thrive in light, sandy loam to ordinary poor soil in full sun.

Use: Snow-on-the-mountain is a showy plant for beds or borders. It can also be used as a cut flower. (See *Euphorbia heterophylla* for special handling of cut flowers.)

Euphorbia marginata

Louis Lenz

Euphorbia marginata

Eustoma grandiflorum

Eustoma grandiflorum (E. russellianum, Lisianthus russellianus)
Prairie Gentian

History: *Eustoma* represents a small group of plants that are natives of America from Nebraska to Colorado and south to Texas and Mexico. They belong to the Gentian family. The name is from *eustomos,* meaning "of beautiful countenance".

Description: The original species is biennial but there are strains and hybrids available that are annual in habit. Cultivars vary in height from 6 in. (15 cm) to over 24 in. (60 cm). Plants have smooth, oval-shaped leaves and large flowers (2 to 3 in. (5 to 8 cm) deep) that are bluish-purple and funnel-shaped. There are also double rose-like selections in a wide range of colors including pink, rose, wine red, cream, and white as well as blue and purple.

Propagation and Culture: Prairie Gentians take a long time from seed to flower (over 5 months) so unless you have a greenhouse it is best to purchase plants for bedding out in the garden in the spring. Plants should be spaced 6 to 12 in. (15 to 30 cm) apart, depending on the ultimate size of the strain being grown. They require a well-drained, sunny location.

Use: A delightful plant for a flower border or in pots or planters. They make excellent long-lasting cut flowers.

Fuchsia x *hybrida*

Fuchsia x *hybrida*
Fuchsia, Lady's-eardrops, Ladies'-eardrops

History: Fuchsias are woody perennial plants that thrive under cool growing conditions. They are grown outdoors as shrubs in mild climates but are popular as house plants in colder regions.

Description: Fuchsias reach a height of 36 in. (90 cm) when grown as shrubs in warm climates but seldom exceed12 in. (30 cm) when used as bedding-out plants. The flowers are composed of a tube with four spreading sepals subtending a corolla in various color combinations of red, white, and purple. The berries that may develop after the flowers fade are also very attractive. The attractiveness and pendulous nature of both the flowers and the fruit accounts for the common names.

Propagation and Culture: Fuchsias are propagated by cuttings of soft green wood. They flower well outdoors in the summer and can be kept over winter as house plants in a cool window. They should be cut back after blooming. They are difficult to maintain as attractive flowering plants in the home unless they can be given plenty of sunlight or artificial light and kept at about 60°F (15°C) or lower at night. However, plants can be dried-off, overwintered in a defoliated state in the dark at 40°F (5°C), then pruned, repotted, and re-started in the early spring at a temperature of 54 to 60°F (12 to 15°C) in good light. They thrive in a well-drained, fertile, loamy soil in full sun to partial shade.

Use: Fuchsias are excellent as bedding-out plants for use in hanging baskets and planter boxes.

Fuchsia x *hybrida*

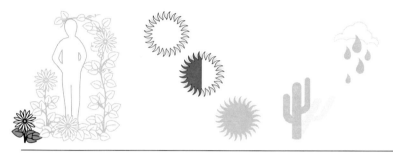

Gaillardia pulchella picta
Annual Gaillardia, Annual Blanket Flower

History: There are both perennial and annual species of Gaillardia that are popular garden flowers. Most annual garden forms are likely to belong to the species *Gaillardia pulchella*, variety *picta*, but hybrids of the species *Gaillardia amblyodon* are also common. Gaillardias are descendants of wild plants of the American west but named for the French patron of botany, M. Gaillard de Martentoneau.

Description: Most Annual Gaillardias grow about 18 in. (45 cm) tall. Some have single and semi-double, daisy-like blooms, while others have shaggy, ball-shaped flower heads as large as 3 in. (7.5 cm) in diameter. Colors range from creamy white to yellow, orange, and red. Many have bi-colored flower heads.

Propagation and Culture: Seeds should be sown indoors 4 to 6 weeks before the last spring frost is expected and moved to the garden when danger of frost is past. Seeds germinate in 2 to 3 weeks at 68°F (20°C) and may respond to light. They can also be seeded directly in the garden as soon as the flower beds can be prepared in the spring. Plants should be spaced 8 in. (20 cm) apart. Gaillardias flourish in ordinary to dry soil and will withstand heat waves and drought better than most flowering plants. They require full sun.

Gaillardia pulchella picta
'Red Plume'

Use: Because of their drought tolerance, Gaillardias are useful for window boxes and planters. They make excellent, long-lasting, long-stemmed cut flowers as well. They are also compatible with many other annual flowers in beds and borders.

Gaillardia pulchella picta 'Double Lorenziana'

Gazania ringens

Gazania ringens (G. splendens)
Gazania, Treasure Flower

History: Gazanias are native to South Africa. The name commemorates the scholar Theodore of Gaza.

Description: Gazanias grow 6 to 12 in. (15 to 30 cm) in height and produce single daisy-like blossoms up to 4 in. (10 cm) in diameter in bright yellow, gold, cream, yellow-orange, pink, or bronze-red, each with a dark center. Their 6- to 9-in. (15- to 23-cm) long leaves are usually dark green and thick with a felty white undersurface and variable shape.

Propagation and Culture: Plants can be started from seed sown indoors 7 to 9 weeks before the last spring frost is due. Plants are set in the garden at a 8- to 12-in. (20- to 30-cm) spacing when all chance of frost is past. They require light, sandy soil and prosper even if it is dry. They need full sun and flower best in hot weather.

Use: Gazanias make attractive mass plantings and thrive well in windy places such as balcony planters. They do not make good cut flowers because they close up in cloudy weather and at night.

Gazania ringens

Gilia capitata
Blue Thimble Flower

History: Blue Thimble Flowers are native to the Pacific Coast. They are members of the phlox family and named to commemorate the Spanish botanist Gil.

Description: Blue Thimble Flowers are dainty annuals with feathery foliage that grow 12 to 24 in. (30 to 60 cm) tall and are covered with sky-blue, globe-shaped flower heads about 1 in. (2.5 cm) across. Another annual species of *Gilia (Gilia tricolor)*, commonly called Bird's Eyes, has a few terminal flowers on each flower stalk. Flowers are lilac colored with a yellow throat marked with purple.

Propagation and Culture: Blue Thimble Flowers are easy to grow and can be seeded outdoors after all danger of frost has passed. However, with our short summer season it is advisable to start the seedlings indoors or in a coldframe 4 to 5 weeks before the last frost is due. Plants should be spaced about 8 to 12 in. (20 to 30 cm) apart. They thrive in full sun in dry to average soil.

Use: Blue Thimble Flowers make a colorful addition to a flower bed or border. They also make long-lasting and graceful cut flowers.

Gilia capitata

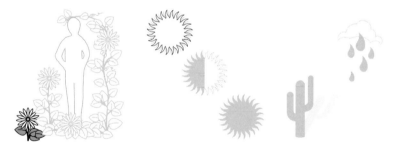

Gomphrena globosa
Globe Amaranth

History: Globe Amaranths are annuals that grow wild in tropical countries and belong to the Amaranth family.

Description: Globe Amaranths grow in neat mounds up to 18 in. (45 cm) tall covered with round flower heads about 1 in. (2 cm) in diameter resembling large-sized clover. Purple and white forms are most common, but orange, red, pink, and yellow types are also available.

Brian Porter

Gomphrena globosa 'Dwarf Buddy'

Gomphrena globosa

Propagation and Culture: Seeds may be sown indoors 6 to 8 weeks before the last frost is due and the young plants moved to the garden after danger of frost is past in the spring. Seeds may take up to 2 weeks to germinate. Plants should be spaced 8 to 12 in. (20 to 30 cm) apart in the garden. Globe Amaranths tolerate hot weather well and should be planted in full sun in well-drained soil.

Use: Globe Amaranths do well in dry windy places such as apartment balconies. They are a good choice for window boxes and planters. Dwarf selections make excellent edging plants and taller cultivars make interesting cut flowers, both fresh and dried. If picked just as the flower heads are fully open and hung upside down to dry in a cool, shady place, they will retain their color and shape for use in dried arrangements.

Gypsophila elegans

Gypsophila elegans
Annual Baby's Breath

History: The name *gypsophila* comes from the Greek *gypsos*, or "gypsum", and *philos*, or "friendship", referring to this plant's requirement for a soil high in lime or gypsum. The vigorous and longer-flowering perennial species, *Gypsophila paniculata*, is more popular than *Gypsophila elegans*, the annual species described here.

Description: Baby's Breath bears dainty 0.2 to 0.4 in. (6 to 10 mm) diameter star-like blossoms in profusion and many-branched stalks forming sprays that give an airy quality to summer gardens and bouquets. The plants grow 8 to 18 in. (20 to 45 cm) tall and come in the familiar white as well as pink, rose, and carmine.

Propagation and Culture: Seeds are sown outdoors in the fall or in the spring when the soil can be cultivated. Seedlings should be thinned to a spacing of about 8 to 12 in. (20 to 30 cm) between plants. Successive seedings every 10 days to 2 weeks at the beginning of the season will ensure flowers throughout the summer. Starting a few seeds in small pots indoors 2 to 3 weeks before the last frost is due will help lengthen the period of flowering even more. Plants should have full sun and a soil low in nutrients.

Use: Annual Baby's Breath flowers for a period of only 6 weeks at most and therefore is better suited to a cutting garden than to a flower border. Its delicate flower heads are valued for fresh flower arrangements, but it is of doubtful value as a dried flower. For extensive continual use as a cut flower, successive seeding is the answer.

Gypsophila elegans 'White Giant'

Helianthus annuus and *Helianthus debilis* subsp. *cucumerifolius*
Common Sunflower and Cucumberleaf Sunflower

History: *Helianthus* is a genus of hardy herbaceous perennial and annual plants that are found chiefly in North America. They belong to the Daisy or Sunflower family, *Asteraceae (Compositae)*. The name is derived from *helios*, "sun", and *anthos*, "flower", and alludes to the sun-like appearance of some of the large-blossomed types. Furthermore, their flower heads track the sun by changing their orientation to remain at right angles to the sun's rays as the sun passes across the sky.

Description: Common Sunflower is a familiar plant bearing huge (8 to 10 in. (20 to 25 cm)) golden, rounded, black-centered flower heads on stems 6 to 10 ft. (200 to 300 cm) tall. There are cultivars of slightly different colors including reddish-yellow, pale yellow, and deep yellow. Cucumberleaf Sunflower, on the other hand, is smaller, bearing flower heads 3 in. (7.5 cm) in diameter on plants that range in height from 18 in. (45 cm) to about 48 in. (120 cm). Flower heads come in both single and double forms and range in color from pure white through shades of yellow, and orange to chestnut, maroon, and even rosy lavender. Some are bi-colored.

Propagation and Culture: Seeds are planted outdoors where the plants are to grow at a depth of 1 to 2 in. (3 to 5 cm) and spaced 24 in. (60 cm) apart when the soil has warmed up and all danger of frost has passed. Sunflowers germinate and grow rapidly. All cultivars thrive best in poor to normal soil with little moisture and, despite their name, will tolerate light shade.

Helianthus annuus

Helianthus annuus

Use: Common Sunflower and taller cultivars of Cucumberleaf Sunflower can be used effectively as temporary hedges and screens. Cucumberleaf Sunflower also provides bright cut flowers. Both kinds produce an abundance of seeds which attract goldfinches and other birds.

Brendan Casement

Helianthus annuus 'Teddy Bear'

Ed Toop

Helichrysum bracteatum

Helichrysum bracteatum
Strawflower, Everlasting Flower, Immortelle

History: Strawflowers are natives of Australia and are the most brilliant of all flowers suitable for drying for year-round display. The name *Helichrysum* comes from the Greek *helios,* "sun", and *chrysos*, "gold".

Description: *Helichrysum bracteatum* grows about 24 in (60 cm) tall and produces daisy-like flower heads 1 to 2 in. (2.5 to 5 cm) in diameter. The parts of the flower heads that look like petals are actually stiff, chaff-like, colorful, modified leaves called bracts. The color range is broad from white through yellow to red, rose, salmon, and purple. There is also a related species, *Helichrysum subulifolium*, that grows only 12 to 15 in (30 to 38 cm) tall. Its cultivar 'Golden Star' produces flowers that are a shining, brilliant yellow.

Propagation and Culture: Seeds can be sown indoors 4 to 6 weeks before the last spring frost is due or sown outside directly in the garden after all danger of frost is past. Plants should be spaced about 9 in. (23 cm) apart. They flourish in almost any soil in full sun.

Use: Strawflowers can be used fresh as cut flowers during the summer or dried for winter bouquets. For drying, flowers should be cut just before the center florets ("petals") open. The leaves should be stripped off and the flowers hung upside down in a dry, shady place. The stems become very fragile once they are dry so are usually reinforced in some way or entirely replaced with wire.

John Beedle

Helichrysum bracteatum

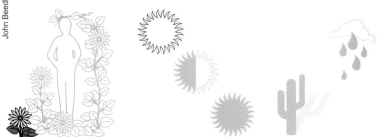

ANNUALS FOR THE PLAINS AND PRAIRIES

Heliotropium arborescens (H. peruvianum)
Common Heliotrope, Cherry Pie

History: Heliotropes are actually tender sub-shrubs in their native Peru but can be grown as annuals in temperate zone gardens. They are sweet-scented members of the Borage family.

Description: Plants grow 12 to 24 in. (30 to 60 cm) tall, depending on the strain, and bear flower clusters as large as 12 in. (30 cm) in diameter in dark violet, white, or heliotrope blue. They give off a sweet vanilla scent.

Propagation and Culture: To propagate these plants from seed, you need a greenhouse in order to start the process in mid-winter. Seeds germinate in 3 to 4 weeks at 68 to 86°F (20 to 30°C) and may respond to light. However, they are generally purchased as bedding plants in the spring. Plants should be spaced 12 in. (30 cm) apart. They require a rich soil and plenty of sun but benefit from a bit of shade during the hottest part of the day.

Use: Heliotropes make colorful as well as very fragrant plants in borders, window boxes, planters, and patio or terrace pots.

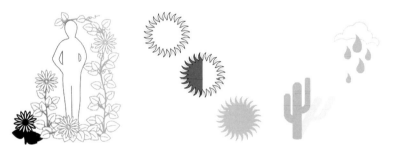

Heliotropium arborescens 'Marine'

Brian Porter

Heliotropium arborescens

University of Alberta Plant Science Collection

Helipterum manglesii (Rhodanthe manglesii); Helipterum roseum (Acrolinium roseum) and *Helipterum humboldtiana (H. sanfordii)*
Rhodanthe, Swan River Everlasting; Acrolinium, Rose Everlasting, Rose Sunray; Humboldt's Sunray, Yellow Everlasting

History: Helipterums are often sold under the name of Acroclinium or Rhodanthe. There are three species that are grown as annual everlasting garden flowers because of their outstanding quality when dried for winter bouquets. They are *Helipterum manglesii, Helipterum roseum,* and *Helipterum humboldtiana.* All are members of the Daisy family and are native to Australia.

Helipterum manglesii

Brendan Casement

Helipterum roseum

Brian Porter

Description: Swan River Everlasting grows 12 to 18 in. (30 to 45 cm) tall with white, pink, and red to purple flower heads with golden centers. Flower heads are about 1 to 1.5 in. (2 to 3 cm) in diameter nodding on long, thin stalks or pedicels. Acrolinium grows 12 to 24 in. (30 to 60 cm) in height with each strong stem terminating in a large flower head about 2 in. (5 cm) in diameter. Blossoms are a bright pink, rose, carmine, or white. Yellow Everlastings grow to 18 in. (45 cm) in height with silvery foliage and fragrant spicy-like clusters of small golden flower heads. Clusters are up to 3 in. (7.5 cm) in diameter.

Propagation and Culture: Helipterums are best seeded outdoors where plants are to flower after the danger of spring frost has passed. However, to obtain earlier flowering, they may be seeded indoors in individual peat pots 6 to 8 weeks before the last spring frost is expected. Early seeding is especially recommended for Humboldt's Sunray. Plants should be spaced 6 to 12 in. (15 to 30 cm) apart. Helipterums flourish in average to dry soil in full sun.

Use: Helipterums can be used as fresh cut flowers but are most outstanding when dried for winter flower arrangements. However, they are fragile when dry. To dry them, flowers should be cut before they are fully open and hung upside down in a dry, shady place. They are an attractive addition to summer flower beds. The shorter and daintier Swan River Everlasting is also useful in the rock garden.

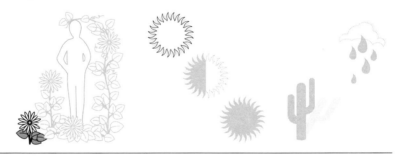

Hesperis matronalis

John Beedle

Hesperis matronalis
Dame's Rocket, Sweet Rocket, Dame's Violet

History: *Hesperis* is a genus of perennial and biennial hardy flowering plants belonging to the Mustard family, *Brassicaceae*. They are native to Japan, Asia Minor, and Europe. The name *Hesperis* is derived from *hesperos,* "the evening" and refers to the flowers of some species which are scented in the evening.

Description: Sweet Rocket is a perennial, sometimes biennial, but self-seeding to the extent of becoming invasive. It grows to 36 in. (90 cm) in height with terminal spike-like branched panicles of four-petalled flowers 0.5 in.

(1.3 cm) or more in diameter in lilac or light purple, varying to white. There are both single- and double-flowered forms. Flowers are fragrant particularly in the evening.

Propagation and Culture: Sweet Rocket is propagated easily from seed planted in the fall or spring and later thinned and transplanted to a final spacing of about 12 to 18 in. (30 to 45 cm). Few if any plants will likely bloom the first summer, but from the second year on they will self-seed and respond as true biennials or short-lived perennials. They thrive in ordinary moist garden soil, in sun or partial shade.

Use: Sweet Rocket is best used in a wild flower garden or in a confined part of the garden where its self-seeding habit can be controlled. Because of its pleasant perfume, it is a good choice for growing on a patio.

Humulus japonicus
Japanese Hop Vine

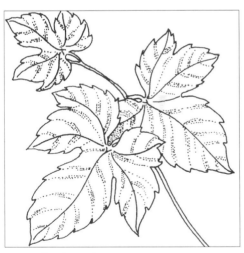

Humulus japonicus

History: This is one of two species of *Humulus* or Hop that is native to Japan and Manchuria. The other is *Humulus lupulus,* the common hop which is grown for use in the brewing industry. The name is derived from *humus,* or "ground", a reference to its trailing nature along the ground if it does not have something to climb on.

Description: Japanese Hop Vine is a coarse, fast-growing annual that climbs to 18 ft. (6 m) or more in a single season by twining around most any kind of support available. It is grown for its foliage. Its leaves are bright green, rough-textured, and hand-shaped with 5 to 7 deeply indented lobes. Leaves are about 6 to 8 in. (15 to 20 cm) across. Its small greenish flowers are rather insignificant from an ornamental perspective.

Propagation and Culture: Seeds are sown in the garden after all danger of frost has passed or started indoors 4 to 6 weeks before the last spring frost is expected. Plants should be spaced about 18 in. (45 cm) apart at the base of the support on which they are to climb – fence, trellis, or strings. Vines grow quickly in ordinary soil in sun or partial shade but are even more vigorous in enriched soil with plenty of moisture and lots of sunshine.

Use: Japanese Hop vines make dense screens and can be used as temporary coverings for unsightly walls, fences, and garage and service areas.

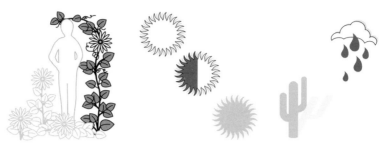

Hunnemannia fumariifolia 'Sunlite'

Hunnemannia fumariifolia
Mexican Tulip Poppy

History: This species is closely allied to California Poppy (*Eschscholzia*). The genus is named for the nineteenth-century English friend of botany, John Hunneman. Mexican Tulip Poppy is native to Mexico and a member of the Poppy family (*Papaveraceae*).

Description: Mexican Tulip Poppy, although perennial, is grown as an annual in temperate zones. It has blue-green, finely cut foliage and 2.5- to 3-in. (6- to 8-cm) satiny yellow flowers. It blooms continuously until frost and reaches a height of 12 to 24 in. (30 to 60 cm).

Propagation and Culture: Although seeds may be sown outdoors after all danger of frost is past and night temperatures are well above freezing, plants will not reach flowering stage in our climate until late in the summer. It is therefore recommended either to buy plants ready for bedding-out or to start seed indoors. Seeds germinate in 2 to 3 weeks at 68°F (20°C). For indoor seedings, 3 to 4 seeds should be placed in individual 3-in. (8-cm) peat pots containing a sandy loam about 4 to 6 weeks before the last frost is due. It is suggested that only the most vigorous seedling in each pot be allowed to develop. Since poppies do not transplant well, plants should be planted in the garden, pot and all, to minimize root disturbance. Because these plants are quite similar to California Poppies, the latter might be a better choice for your prairie garden. Plants do particularly well in dry soil with plenty of sunlight.

Use: Mexican Tulip Poppy can be an excellent choice for flower beds and borders. It also makes a good long-lasting cut flower if picked just before the buds open and the stem ends are singed with a match or dipped briefly into boiling water.

Hunnemannia fumariifolia

Iberis amara (I. coronaria)
Rocket Candytuft, Hyacinth-flowered Candytuft

History: *Iberis* comes from the ancient name for Spain where many species of *Iberis* occur. They are members of the *Brassicaceae (Cruciferae)* or Mustard family.

Description: Rocket Candytuft reaches a height of 12 to 24 in. (30 to 60 cm) and bears fragrant 0.8- to 1-in. (2- to 2.5-cm) white blossoms in dense hyacinth-like clusters.

Propagation and Culture: Candytufts are not easily transplanted so it is best to seed directly in the garden as soon as the soil can be cultivated in the spring. Seeds germinate in 1 to 2 weeks but may need light; therefore, plant seed shallowly. Seedlings should be thinned to a spacing of 6 to 10 in. (15 to 25 cm). It usually takes about 8 weeks for seedlings to reach flowering stage. Candytufts do well in average soil in a sunny location. They do benefit from some shade during the hottest part of day during hot weather.

Use: Rocket Candytuft is a dramatic border plant as well as an excellent long-lasting cut flower.

Iberis amara 'Dwarf Fairy'

Iberis amara 'Dwarf Fairy'

Iberis umbellata

Iberis umbellata

Iberis umbellata
Fairy Candytuft, Globe Candytuft, Common Annual Candytuft

History: *Iberis* comes from the ancient name for Spain where many species of *Iberis* occur. They are members of the *Brassicaceae (Cruciferae)* or Mustard family.

Description: Fairy Candytuft bears tiny flowers in flat-topped clusters in a dazzling array of colors including pink, carmine, lilac, purple, rose, and white. They grow only 7 to 12 in. (18 to 30 cm) tall and have no fragrance.

Propagation and Culture: Candytufts are not easily transplanted so it is best to seed directly in the garden as soon as the soil can be cultivated in the spring. Seeds germinate in 1 to 2 weeks but may need light; therefore, plant seed shallowly. Seedlings should be thinned to a spacing of 6 to 10 in. (15 to 25 cm). It usually takes about 8 weeks for seedlings to reach flowering stage. Candytufts do well in average soil in a sunny location. They do benefit from some shade during the hottest part of day during hot weather.

Use: Candytufts are among the brightest and most easily grown of annuals. Fairy Candytuft is excellent for borders, edgings, and rock gardens. It provides long-lasting cut flowers for indoor bouquets.

Impatiens balsamina 'Color Parade'

Impatiens balsamina
Garden Balsam

History: The Latin genus name *Impatiens* means "impatient" and refers to the fact that the seed pods, when ripe, will burst open on the slightest pressure, scattering the seed. For this reason, they are often called Touch-me-nots. They belong to the *Balsaminaceae* or Jewel Weed family.

Description: Garden Balsam is an old-fashioned flower originally from Asia and among the easiest to grow. The blossoms of most cultivars are double or semi-double, up to 2.4 in. (6 cm) in diameter in white, pink, purple, or deep red, as well as combinations of colors. Some cultivars grow only 8 to 10 in. (20 to 25 cm) tall and are known as "bush balsams". They display their flowers on the tops of the plants. Others become 36 in. (90 cm) tall with camellia-like or rose-like blossoms clinging closely to the main stems.

Propagation and Culture: Garden Balsam seeds may be started indoors 4 to 6 weeks before the last frost is due or sown directly in the garden after all danger of frost has passed. Seeds germinate in 2 to 4 weeks at 68°F (20°C) and may respond to light. Plants should be spaced 18 in. (45 cm) apart for proper development and display of their flowers since the flowers tend to be hidden among the foliage. Balsams transplant easily, even when in bloom, if moved with a good ball of soil around the roots. All types of Garden Balsams do well in rich, moist, light, sandy loam in partial shade or full shade.

Use: The short cultivars of Garden Balsams are excellent for mass bedding purposes as well as edging material. The taller types are excellent additions to a flower border.

Impatiens balsamina

Impatiens 'New Guinea Hybrid'
New Guinea Impatience

History: This magnificent herbaceous plant is the result of much hybridization of several New Guinea species such as *Impatiens hawkeri* and *Impatiens linearifolia* that were collected between 1960 and 1970. Further crosses were made with species from Java and Celebes and selections made from the progeny. These selected hybrids have been commercially segregated into several series of named cultivars.

Description: These 'New Guinea Hybrids' form bushy, spreading plants 10 to 16 in. (25 to 40 cm) tall with each succulent branch topped by a beautiful rosette of frequently corrugated, oval-shaped leaves 3 to 6 in. (8 to 15 cm) long in a riot of color and variegation. These leaves are usually creamy-yellow along the center with green serrate margins and red to milky-white ribs. The showy spurred flowers, 1 to 3 in. (3 to 7 cm) across, come in shades of crimson to scarlet, red, orange, salmon, pink, chartreuse, purple, or blush-white.

Propagation and Culture: The majority and most spectacular cultivars of the New Guinea Impatience are propagated only from cuttings. However, two cultivars, namely 'Spectra Mix' and 'Tango' (orange flowers) can be propagated from seed and handled much the same as

Impatiens 'Tango'

All-America Selections

Impatiens 'Flame Orange'

regular Patience plants. Seed should be sown indoors 6 to 8 weeks before the last frost is due and seedlings transplanted to the garden when all threat of frost is past. All cultivars do well in rich, moist, sandy loam in partial shade or full shade.

Use: These 'New Guinea Hybrids' are ideal for shady spots in flower beds and borders as well as in planters and hanging baskets.

Impatiens wallerana

Impatiens wallerana

Impatiens wallerana (I. sultanii)
Patience Plant, Patient Lucy, Busy Lizzie

Description: Patience Plant is a house plant for the old-fashioned window sill where the cool night temperatures and warm daylight keep it flowering continuously. Old-time cultivars used to become leggy, long-jointed plants, but the cultivars of today are compact, lush plants 6 to 15 in. (15 to 38 cm) tall and 10 to 36 in. (25 to 60 cm) wide bearing an abundance of fiery red, scarlet, pink, orange, purple, and bi-colored flowers as well as more subdued golden yellow and white.

Propagation and Culture: Patience Plant is more delicate and sensitive to cold weather than Garden Balsam. Seeds should be sown indoors 6 to 8 weeks before the last frost is due and seedlings transplanted to the garden when all threat of frost is past. Seeds germinate in 2 to 4 weeks at 68°F (20°C) and may respond to light. New plants can also be propagated from cuttings. All cultivars do well in rich, moist, light, sandy loam in partial shade or full shade.

Use: Patience Plant is especially effective for beds in shady places, as well as for window boxes, planters, and hanging baskets.

ANNUALS FOR THE PLAINS AND PRAIRIES

Ipomea alba (Calonyction aculeatum, I. bona-nox)
Moonflower

History: The old name of *Calonyction* comes from the Greek and means "beautiful night", a reference to the plant's night-blooming habit and large fragrant flowers. They are now considered a part of the Morning Glory genus *(Ipomoea)* and are native to the tropics of both hemispheres.

Description: Moonflowers are twining climbers with large heart-shaped leaves and white trumpet-like blossoms up to 6 in. (15 cm) in diameter that open at sunset and usually close by noon the next day. They are perennial in the tropics but grow well as annuals in the temperate zone.

Propagation and Culture: Moonflowers are difficult to transplant so need to be started in individual small pots 8 weeks before the last frost is due. Seeds germinate in 1 to 3 weeks at 68 to 86°F (20 to 30°C). Seeds should be nicked with a file or soaked in water overnight before planting in order to hasten germination. When night temperatures do not drop below 46 to 50°F (8 to 10°C), the seedlings can be planted outdoors 9 to 12 in. (23 to 30 cm) apart with a 8- to 10-ft. (2.5- to 3-m) high trellis or string support for the plants to climb on. They grow in average garden soil in full sun.

Use: Moonflowers make excellent screens since they grow rapidly to a height of 10 ft. (3 m) or more during the summer season. They also usually produce a heavy fragrance on summer evenings.

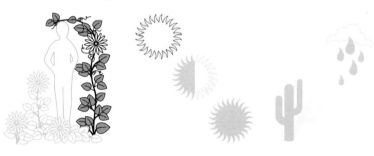

Ipomea alba

Ipomea alba

Carmen's Nursery

Ipomea purpurea and Ipomea tricolor
Morning Glory

History: These two species of *Ipomea* are popular vines grown as annuals in temperate climates. They are members of the *Convolulaceae* or Morning Glory family.

Description: Morning Glories are very fast growing vines that may reach 10 ft. (3 m) or more during the growing season. They produce a daily crop of freshly opened blue, purple, pink, scarlet, white, or multicolored single or double trumpet-shaped flowers. The flowers, which normally are 3 to 5 in. (8 to 12 cm) in diameter, may be as much as 8 in. (20 cm) across. They normally open only from dawn until mid-morning, but newer cultivars tend to hold their flowers open most of the day. The vine's abundant leaves are heart-shaped and 4 to 5 in. (10 to 12.5 cm) long.

Ipomea purpurea 'Heavenly Blue'

Brian Porter

Ipomea purpurea 'Heavenly Blue'

Brian Porter

Propagation and Culture: Seeds may be sown outdoors about 0.5 in. (1.5 cm) deep, 8 to 12 in. (20 to 30 cm) apart after all danger of frost has passed. They may also be started indoors in 3-in. (7.5-cm) peat pots 4 to 6 weeks before the last expected frost is due and set out in the garden when they will not be nipped by a late frost. Each seed should be nicked with a file before planting to help it absorb water and speed up the germination process. Soaking the seeds overnight in tepid water before planting is also recommended. Morning Glories do not tolerate root disturbance so only pot-grown seedlings, transplanted pot and all, are likely to survive any transplanting. Rather infertile, relatively dry soil and a full sun location will encourage the most flowers. Morning Glories will climb on most any support and flower profusely against a background of pale green foliage.

Use: Morning Glories form attractive hedges or screens. They can also serve as a temporary ground cover or be allowed to cascade from a hanging basket or raised planters.

Kochia scoparia trichophylla
Summer Cypress, Burning Bush, Fire Bush

History: Summer Cypress is indigenous to southern France and eastward across Asia to Japan. Plants are grown for their shape and dense feathery foliage, not for their flowers. They are members of the *Chenopodiaceae* or Goosefoot family.

Description: Summer Cypress develop bushy specimen plants about 24 to 36 in. (60 to 90 cm) tall in an attractive, compact globe shape. They grow slowly early in the season, especially if the weather is cool, but develop rapidly with the onset of warm weather. Their feathery foliage is a delicate green during the summer but becomes a bright red to maroon red in the fall. It should be noted that this plant, related to the tumbleweeds, may be a troublesome pest if it is allowed to escape.

Propagation and Culture: Seeds may be started indoors 4 to 6 weeks before the last expected frost or may be sown directly in the garden after danger of frost is past. Seedlings should be spaced about 16 in. (40 cm) apart. They thrive in average to dry soil and require full sun for optimum coloration. They will tolerate very hot weather and windy locations.

Kochia scoparia trichophylla

Gabe Botar

Use: Summer Cypress is often used to make low hedges or screens even though they last but one season. Mature plants can be sheared to achieve a desired height or shape – often a necessary procedure since it is difficult to get a row of plants to grow at a uniform rate and achieve an ultimate uniform size. They can be grown in pots or containers as specimen plants for a balcony, deck, or patio.

Kochia scoparia trichophylla
'Acapulco Silver'

Lagurus ovatus
Hare's-tail Grass, Rabbit-tail Grass

History: Hare's-tail Grass is the only species in the genus *Lagurus*. It is native to the Mediterranean region and cultivated as an ornamental. The name is derived from the Greek *lagos*, a "hare", and *oura*, a "tail".

Description: This ornamental grass produces woolly tufts of seeds, some 2 in. (5 cm) in size, at the end of each slender stem. When mature it reaches 12 to 24 in. (30 to 60 cm) in height.

Propagation and Culture: Seeds are best sown in the garden as soon as the ground can be worked in the spring. However, to ensure that the plants produce flower heads before frost in the fall, seed should be sown indoors 6 to 8 weeks before the last spring frost is expected. Plants should be spaced about 4 in. (10 cm) apart. They thrive in light, well-drained soil in full sun and tolerate heat well.

Use: Hare's-tail Grass makes an unusual edging plant for a garden walk, but in wet weather the flower heads become rain-soaked and will lay flat out on the ground or walkway until they dry out. Hare's-tail Grass is also an interesting addition to either fresh or dried arrangements. For winter bouquets, stems should be cut when the seed heads have developed and hung upside down in a dark, dry place.

Lagurus ovatus

Lagurus ovatus

Lantana camara

Lantana camara

Lantana camara

Lantana camara and *Lantana montevidensis (L. sellowiana, L. delicatissima)*
Common Lantana and Trailing Lantana

History: Lantanas are evergreen flowering plants of tropical America and belong to the Verbena family *(Verbenaceae).*
Description: Common Lantana ordinarily grows 36 in. (90 cm) tall but is available in dwarf cultivars 12 to 18 in. (30 to 45 cm) tall. It is a stiff-branched shrub with 1- to 1.5-in. (2.5- to 3.8-cm) clusters of tiny yellow, pink, white, red, orange, or bi-colored flowers. Both flowers and foliage have a pungent fragrance that is pleasing to some and unpleasant to others. The more graceful Trailing Lantana has smaller clusters of rosy-lilac, yellow-centered flowers, or white flowers borne on cascading stems.

Propagation and Culture: Lantanas take a long time to reach flowering when started from seed, so are usually propagated from cuttings to produce bedding plants. Seeds take 6 to 7 weeks just to germinate. When placed outdoors, the plants should be set about 18 in. (45 cm) apart. A few weeks before the last frost, plants can be pruned back and potted for keeping indoors as winter house plants and as a source of cuttings for next year's garden. Both species do best in a rich, organic soil in full sunshine.

Use: Common Lantana seems to perform best when it is grown in individual pots or planters for use as accent plants on patios, decks, or terraces. The dwarf cultivar can be effective in beds or borders. Trailing Lantana is shown off to advantage in hanging baskets, window boxes, or raised planters.

Lathyrus odoratus
Sweet Pea

History: Sweet Pea is native to Sicily and was introduced into northern Europe about 1700. The natural species produced primarily purple flowers. Other colors came into being when the English florist, Henry Eckford, began a breeding program to improve Sweet Pea in 1870. His success was phenomenal and led to the development of the Spencer strain. Further development can be attributed mainly to plant breeders in California.

Description: Sweet Peas are well known and cherished for their multi-flowered stems of delicate, airy blossoms, 1 to 2 in. (2.5 to 5 cm) in size. They come in a wide variety of colors and are delightfully fragrant. Most have riffled or wavy petals and some are bi-colored, striped, or mottled. Most Sweet Peas climb to heights of 6.5 to 10 ft (2 to 3 m) by attaching themselves to supports by means of tendrils, but there are non-climbing types such as 'Patio' and 'Little Sweethearts' that produce colorful mounds of flowers only 8 to 12 in. (20 to 30 cm) tall. There are also taller bushy types ranging in height from 18 to 30 in. (45 to 75 cm).

Propagation and Culture: Sweet Peas require a deep, cool root run for successful development and should be planted where they are to flower in the garden as early in the spring as possible. It is advisable to soak the seeds in tepid water overnight before planting. This will soften their seed coats and enhance germination. It is advisable to dig a trench 12 in. (30 cm) wide and 24 in. (60 cm) deep and incorporate well-rotted manure or compost with the removed soil before using it to refill the trench to within 4 to 6 in. (10 to 15 cm) of the top. Seed should then be pushed into this mixture to a depth of 0.5 in. (1.5 cm), spacing each seed about 2 in. (5 cm) apart. Seeds take about 2 weeks to germinate. As the seedlings develop, additional soil mixture should be pulled into the trench around the plantlets until the surface is level and the trench no longer exists. When the seedlings are about 4 in. (10 cm) tall, they can be pinched (removal of growing tip) to encourage branching. A support of string or wire should be provided for climbing varieties. A mulch of peat, bark chips, or other insulating material around the base of the plants will help to keep the soil cool. Plants should be watered regularly and old blossoms removed as they die. Sweet Peas require full sun to partial shade and cool night temperatures to flower at their best.

Use: The many different types of Sweet Peas can be used for various purposes. These include screens (for the climbers) to border or bedding plants for the various non-climbing cultivars. All make excellent fragrant cut flowers.

Lathyrus odoratus 'Cuthbertson Salmon'

Lathyrus odoratus 'Bijou'

Lathyrus odoratus 'Burpee's Patio'

Brian Porter

Lavatera trimestris 'Silver Cup'

Lavatera trimestris 'Mont Blanc'

Lavatera trimestris
Annual Rose Mallow, Tree Mallow

History: *Lavatera* commemorates the Swiss Lavater family of Zurich. *Lavatera* belongs to the Mallow family *Malvaceae.* It is native to the Mediterranean region and similar to *Hibiscus* but of shorter stature.

Description: Rose Mallow grows 24 to 36 in. (60 to 90 cm) tall and bears large rose-colored flowers. There is also a white-flowered variety. Flowers are cup-like and up to nearly 3.5 in (8 cm) in diameter. They have hairy stems with maple-like leaves.

Propagation and Culture: Since Rose Mallow does not transplant well, it is best to plant the seed where the plants are to grow as early in the spring as the soil can be worked. Plants should be spaced 24 in. (60 cm) apart. They are easy to grow and flourish in ordinary soil in sunny locations.

Use: Rose Mallows make fine middle-height hedges or screens. They can also be used as short-lived cut flowers.

Layia platyglossa 'Elegans'

Layia platyglossa
Tidy Tips

History: *Layia* is a member of the Daisy family *Asteraceae* or *Compositae* and grows wild in western North America. The name commemorates G. T. Lay, a naturalist.

Description: Tidy Tips forms a solid mound of clean yellow, white-tipped, daisy-like flower head 12 to 18 in. (30 to 45 cm) tall. The small narrow leaves tend to be hidden by the flowers.

Propagation and Culture: Seeds should be sown directly in the garden in the spring as soon as the soil can be cultivated. Seedlings should be thinned and transplanted to a spacing of 4 to 5 in. (10 to 12 cm). Plants thrive in the sun in ordinary to dry soil.

Use: Tidy Tips are well adapted to window boxes and planters, as well as flower beds and borders. Their flowers are also exquisite as cut flowers.

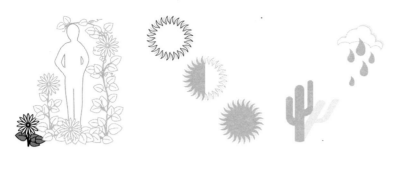

Layia platyglossa

Limnanthes douglasii
Meadow Foam, Fried Eggs

History: Meadow Foam is a beautiful, hardy annual that grows wild in the western United States. Its name is derived from *linne,* a "marsh", and *anthos,* a "flower".

Description: Meadow Foam grows only about 6 in. (15 cm) tall with comparatively large yellow flowers (1 in. (2 cm) across) with white margins. It blooms profusely and is very attractive when in full bloom.

Propagation and Culture: Seeds may be sown outdoors as soon as the soil is reasonably dry and warm. Seedlings should be thinned to a spacing of 5 to 6 in. (12 to 15 cm). Seeds may also be sown indoors about 4 to 5 weeks before the last frost is due. They germinate best at 50°F (10°C). Meadow Foam thrives only in sunny weather and must be grown in a spot fully exposed to the sunshine. Ordinary garden soil is suitable.

Use: Meadow Foam makes a good edging plant for beds and borders, especially near a pond or stream.

Limnanthes douglasii

Limonium sinuatum

Limonium sinuatum

Limonium sinuatum

Limonium sinuatum and *Limonium bonduellii superbum*
Statice, Sea Lavender

History: *Limonium* comes from the Greek *lemon*, meaning "meadow", and alludes to salt meadows where species of this genus often grow naturally.

Description: Both these species produce terminal compact clusters of 0.5-in. (1-cm) diameter, paper-textured blossoms on many-branched, 18-in. (45-cm) tall stems that arise from a ground-hugging rosette of leaves. *Limonium sinuatum* (sometimes called "Notchleaf Statice") produces blue, lavender, rose, or white blossoms. The color range is continually being expanded (e.g., Sunburst series of pastel colors including apricot-peach). *Limonium bonduellii* produces yellow flowers. Both these species are commonly called Statice or Sea Lavender. There is also a Yellow Statice in the trade called *Limonium aureum* 'Supernova'.

Propagation and Culture: Seeds may be sown indoors 8 weeks before all danger of frost has passed for early summer flowering, or seeded directly outside in the garden as early as the soil can be cultivated. Plants should be spaced 9 to 12 in. (23 to 30 cm) apart. For best results, Statice should be given full sun and fairly dry, well-drained soil.

Use: Statice makes an excellent cut flower, both fresh and dried for winter bouquets and arrangements. Both species can readily be dried by cutting the flowers when they are fully expanded and hanging them upside down in a shady place until completely dry. Statice is also an interesting addition to flower beds.

Linanthus androsaceus subsp. *micranthus* (*Gilia micrantha*, *Leptosiphon hybrida*)
Stardust

Description: Stardust grows 6 to 9 in. (15 to 23 cm) tall and is covered in a myriad of tiny star-like flowers of golden yellow, bright rose, cream, orange, or red.

Propagation and Culture: Stardust is easy to grow and can be seeded outdoors after all danger of frost has passed. However, with a short summer season it is advisable to start the seedlings indoors or in a coldframe 4 to 5 weeks before the last frost is due. Plants should be spaced about 8 to 12 in. (20 to 30 cm) apart. They thrive in full sun in dry to average soil. Seed is not widely available commercially.

Use: Stardust plants make a colorful addition to a flower bed or border and are low enough to serve as an edging plant. They withstand wind and thrive in balcony planters and window boxes.

Linanthus androsaceus subsp. *micranthus*

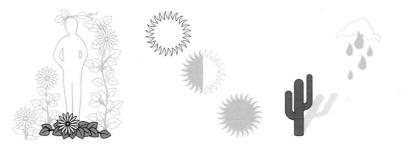

Linaria maroccana
Annual Linaria, Morocco Toadflax

History: Linaria, a close relative of the snapdragon, is found mainly in the Old World regions of the northern hemisphere temperate zones. The name is derived from *linon* meaning "flax" because of the resemblance of the leaves to those of flax plants.

Description: Annual Linaria forms mounds of dainty blossoms in shades of yellow, blue, lavender, pink, red, salmon, bronze, and white as well as multicolors. Individual blooms are about 0.5 in (1.3 cm) in diameter. Plants grow 9 to 12 in. (23 to 30 cm) tall.

Propagation and Culture: Seeds are sown outdoors as soon as the ground can be worked in the spring and plants spaced at 6 in. (15 cm) intervals. Seeds take about 2 to 3 weeks to germinate at 55°F (12°C). Linaria does well in ordinary soil but requires full sun and relatively cool weather.

Linaria maroccana 'Fairy Bouquet'

Brendan Casement

Use: Linaria is useful as an edging plant or an addition to the rock garden. It is also lovely and long-lasting as a cut flower for small indoor arrangements.

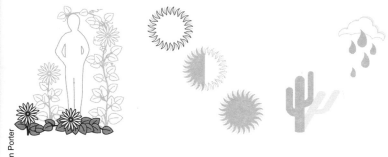

Linaria maroccana 'Northern Lights'

Linum grandiflorum rubrum

Linum grandiflorum
Flowering Flax, Scarlet Flax

History: Flowering Flax is an easily grown annual from North Africa. The common flax, *Linum usitatissimum,* a native of Europe, is also an annual and occasionally grown as a garden annual for its attractive blue flowers. It is the species grown commercially for its linen fiber and linseed oil.

Description: Flowering Flax grows to 18 in. (45 cm) in height and is topped throughout the summer with a succession of flowers nearly 2 in. (5 cm) in diameter. Most cultivars bear red blossoms but others are available in bluish-purple, pink, or white flowers.

Propagation and Culture: Since Flax is very difficult to transplant, it is best to plant the seed where the plants are to grow as early in the spring as possible, spacing the seed so that plants will stand 8 to 10 in. (20 to 25 cm) apart. Seeds germinate in 3 to 4 weeks at 54°F (12°C). Successive plantings can be tried at 2-week intervals since each plant blossoms for only a 3- to 4-week interval. Plants bloom most profusely in cool weather but require plenty of sunshine and a light, well-drained soil.

Use: Flowering Flax is a colorful border plant that appears to come and go as the succession of flowers open and drop their petals. Flax stalks can be harvested and dried as filler in dried arrangements. For this purpose, they are cut after the capsules are fully formed and hung upside down in a cool, shady place.

Linum grandiflorum

Lobelia erinus
Bedding or Edging Lobelia

History: *Lobelia* is named after Matthias de l'Obel, a Flemish botanist, author, and physician to James I of England. *Lobelia erinus,* from which the popular bedding Lobelias have been selected, comes from the Cape of Good Hope. The wild plant is somewhat straggly in habit with blue flowers.

Description: There are both trailing and compact bedding types of Lobelia with billowing masses of blossoms on plants that seldom exceed 6 in. (15 cm) in height. The 0.5- to 1-in. (1.5- to 2.0-cm) wide flowers, borne along each stem, are in shades of blue on the common cultivars; white and carmine colored types have also been developed.

Propagation and Culture: Seeds need to be sown about 3 months in advance of the last frost-free day in order to get flowering plants throughout the summer season. Seeds germinate in 2 to 3 weeks at 68 to 86°F (20 to 30°C), but seedling growth is slow. It is essential, therefore, to have greenhouse facilities for starting the plants. Therefore, most gardeners purchase young plants for putting in the garden after all danger of frost has passed. Plants are spaced about 4 to 6 in. (10 to 15 cm) apart. They do best in full sun and cool temperatures but tolerate partial shade, especially in hot weather. They prefer rich moist soil and should not be allowed to suffer stress from inadequate moisture.

Use: Trailing forms of Lobelia are prized for hanging baskets, window boxes, or raised planters. They can also serve as good ground covers. The compact types are excellent for edging beds and borders.

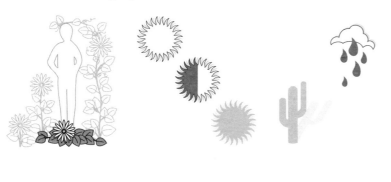

Lobelia erinus

Lobelia erinus 'Rainbow Mix'

Lobelia erinus 'Rainbow Mix'

Lobularia maritima
Sweet Alyssum

Lobularia maritima

University of Alberta Plant Science Collection

Lobularia maritima

Ed Toop

Lobularia maritima 'Carpet of Snow'

Ed Toop

History: *Lobularia maritima* is sometimes listed in catalogues under the invalid name *Alyssum maritimum.* It is a member of the Mustard family or *Brassicaceae (Cruciferae).*

Description: Sweet Alyssum is an old-time favorite summer garden border plant. It is native of the Mediterranean area but surprisingly hardy as an annual for northern gardens. The plants can vary in height from 4 to 10 in. (10 to 25 cm) depending on cultivars, but all form mounds of solid color broader than their height. The original selections were white, but clear pink and deep lavender types have been developed. All produce a honey-like fragrance.

Propagation and Culture: Seeds may be sown outdoors as early in the spring as the seed bed can be prepared or started indoors 4 to 6 weeks before the last spring frost is due. Seeds germinate in 1 to 2 weeks at 68°F (20°C) and flowers develop by 6 weeks. Plants should be set out in the garden 6 to 8 in. (15 to 20 cm) apart after the danger of frost has passed. Plants bloom rather quickly from seed and continue to flower until killed by frost. They often seed themselves in the garden, even with our harsh winter climate. They prosper in almost any soil and tolerate light shade.They may be attacked by flea beetles in areas where canola is grown.

Use: Sweet Alyssum provides fragrance in window boxes, patio planters, and hanging baskets as well as in its primary role as an edging plant. It does well in rock gardens, between flagstones, or as an early ground cover where spring flowering bulbs have faded.

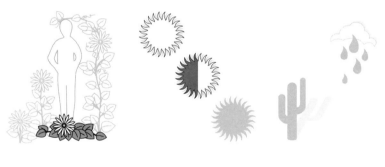

Lupinus Hybrids
Annual Lupine

History: The genus *Lupinus* includes many hardy annual or perennial herbaceous and shrubby plants of decorative value in the garden. They belong to the Pea family or *Fabaceae (Leguminosae)*. The name is derived from *lupus*, a "wolf", alluding to the erroneous thought that they impoverished the soil because of their deep-rooting character. Because of the short-lived nature of the herbaceous perennial lupines, they are not particularly popular. The annual types should be an interesting challenge for the prairie gardener.

Description: Several species of annual lupines have been involved in the development of hybrids, chiefly *Lupinus luteus, Lupinus pubescens, Lupinus hartwegii,* and *Lupinus hirsutus.* They bear graceful flower spikes 12 to 36 in. (30 to 90 cm) tall, depending on the strain. They produce blue, lavender, pink, yellow, white, or bi-colored flowers.

Propagation and Culture: The seeds should be planted in the garden as soon as the ground can be prepared in the spring, by placing the seeds about 4 in. (10 cm) apart and thinning plants later to a 8-in. (20-cm) spacing. Plants require a good deep rich soil and full sun to partial shade. They thrive in areas with cool spring and summer weather. They are susceptible to attack by aphids.

Use: Lupines have a short blooming period, a characteristic that is not in their favor when competing with the many other annual flowers that bloom throughout the summer. Nevertheless, they do make interesting garden plants as well as cut flowers. They are being introduced as a new dried commodity in the florist trade.

John Beedle

Lupinus hybrid

Ed Toop

Lupinus hybrid

Lupinus

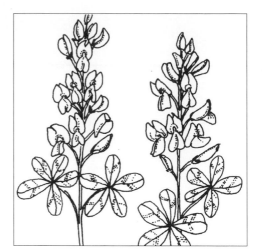

Lupinus texensis

Lupinus subcarnosus and *Lupinus texensis*
Texas Bluebonnet

Description: These very similar species of lupine are native to Texas and the latter is, in fact, the state flower. They grow to 12 in. (30 cm) in height with purplish-blue flowers with a white spot in their centers.

Propagation and Culture: The seeds should be planted in the garden as soon as the ground can be prepared in the spring, by placing the seeds about 4 in. (10 cm) apart and thinning plants later to an 8-in. (20-cm) spacing. Plants require a good deep rich soil and full sun to partial shade. They thrive in areas with cool spring and summer weather. They are susceptible to attack by aphids.

Use: Lupines have a short blooming period, a characteristic that is not in their favor when competing with the many other annual flowers that bloom throughout the summer. They do make interesting garden plants as well as cut flowers.

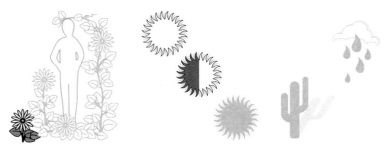

Machaeranthera tanacetifolia (*Aster tanacetifolius*)
Tahoka Daisy

History: This aster-like plant grows wild from South Dakota and Montana to Mexico and California. The name is derived from *machaira* meaning "a dragon" and *anthera* or "anther".

Description: This member of the Aster family bears long-lasting, pale blue flowers with yellow-orange centers (2 in. (5 cm) in diameter) and grows 12 to 24 in. (30 to 60 cm) tall. It has wispy thread-like foliage.

Propagation and Culture: Seeds may be sown indoors 6 to 8 weeks before the last frost is due or outdoors as early in the spring as the soil is workable. Plants should be spaced 6 in. (15 cm) apart in average soil. They thrive in full sun or partial shade and will withstand heat. Seed is not commonly available.

Machaeranthera tanacetifolia

Use: This is a good plant for summer borders because it will flower with little attention from mid-summer until frost.

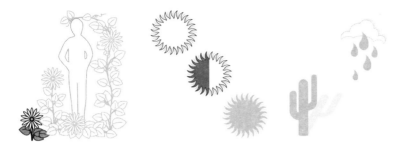

Malcolmia maritima *(Chieranthus maritimus)*
Virginia Stock or Virginian Stock

History: This plant's name commemorates William Malcolm, a London nurseryman of the 18th century. It comes into bloom quickly and is one of the most easily grown annuals. It is a member of the Mustard family *(Brassicaceae)*.

Description: The 1-in. (2-cm), four-petalled blossoms appear in great profusion on bushy plants that are 6 to 9 in. (15 to 23 cm) tall. The flowers range in color from lilac, red, pink to white, and occasionally yellow.

Propagation and Culture: Seeds are sown in the garden as early in the spring as possible. Plants should be thinned and transplanted to a spacing of 4 in. (10 cm). They thrive in any soil in full sun or light shade.

Use: Virginia Stock is useful for borders and edges and for added color in rock gardens. Like Sweet Alyssum, it is fast to develop and flower and can be used to fill in around spring bulb plantings to add color as the bulbs fade. It is a good companion for evening scented stock *(Matthiola longipetala bicornis)*.

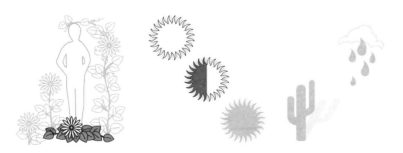

Malcolmia maritima

Malcolmia maritima

Malope trifida
Malope, Mallow-wort

Malope trifida

History: This is a hardy annual that grows wild in Spain and parts of northern Africa. It is a member of the Mallow family, *Malvaceae.*

Description: Malope develops into husky plants 30 to 36 in. (75 to 90 cm) tall with typical mallow flowers, 3 in. (7.5 cm) across, in clusters of rosy-purple, pink, red, or white.

Propagation and Culture: Seeds are started indoors 4 to 6 weeks before the last frost is due, or sown indoors as early as the garden soil can be prepared. Plants can be set out as soon as the danger of frost is past at a spacing of 9 to 12 in. (23 to 30 cm). They do best in full sun in a sandy loam soil.

Use: Malope flowers are excellent as middle to background material for flower beds. They also make attractive cut flowers.

Malva sylvestris zebrina and Malva sylvestris mauritiana
High Mallow, Cheeses

Malva sylvestris zebrina

History: *Malva* includes hardy annual, biennial, and perennial plants that grow wild in European countries and are members of the mallow family, *Malvaceae.*

Description: High Mallows are shrubby annuals growing to 36 in. (90 cm) or more in height with 5- to 7-lobed leaves and large purple-rose flowers. The variety *mauritiana* has broader, rounded leaf lobes and deeper colored flowers than the straight species. The variety *zebrina* has variable flowers, usually white-striped with purple. High Mallow produces somewhat similar plants to *Lavatera trimestris,* Annual Rose Mallow.

Propagation and Culture: Seeds are best sown outdoors where the plants are to grow as soon as the soil can be cultivated in the spring. Plants can be thinned as well as transplanted to a spacing of 18 to 24 in. (45 to 60 cm). They thrive in ordinary soil in a sunny to partially shaded location and self-seed readily.

Use: High Mallows make fine middle-height hedges or screens.

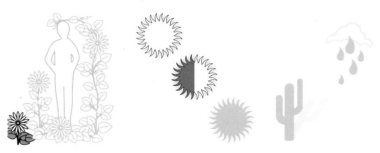

Malva sylvestris mauritiana

Matricaria grandiflora (Pentzia grandiflora, Pentzia 'Gold Button')
Gold Button, Gold Pompons, Pentzia

History: There are at least two distinct plants in the trade sold under names such as Gold Button (*Pentzia* 'Gold Button') and Gold Pompons (*Pentzia* 'Gold Butter'). It would appear that these and another sold as 'Harvest Moon' are all probably cultivars of the species *Matricaria grandiflora (Pentzia grandiflora)*. Pentzia is also sold under the name of *Cotula* or *Cotula turbinata*.

Description: Gold Button has fine, grayish green, cut-leaf foliage with a rather sweet scent. It grows 16 to 24 in. (40 to 60 cm) tall and is very bushy and floriferous. The golden-orange flower heads are 0.5 to 1 in. (1.0 to 2.0 cm) in diameter, button-like in appearance and held upright on long, strong stems. The Gold Pompons or *Pentzia* 'Gold Butter' has flower heads up to 10 in. (25 cm) in diameter in a rich, deep yellow color.

Propagation and Culture: Seed may be sown directly outdoors after all danger of frost is past and the soil is warm. Plants should be thinned to a spacing of about 18 in. (45 cm). They thrive in full sun in ordinary to dry soil and come into bloom quickly.

Matricaria grandiflora

Matricaria grandiflora

Use: *Matricaria grandiflora* is excellent as a cut flower, both fresh and dried. Dried blooms hold their color indefinitely and are perfect for use in long-lasting dried arrangements. For drying, the whole plant is usually harvested before the flower heads reach full maturity since the blossoms are subject to shattering if harvested too late. Flowers are dried by hanging them upside down in a cool, dry place. Gold Button also makes an attractive addition to flower beds and borders.

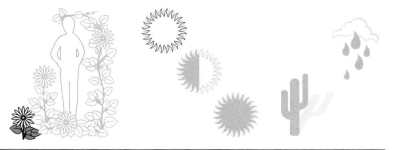

Matthiola incana annua

Matthiola incana annua 'Midget Mix'

Matthiola incana annua
Ten-weeks Stock, Common Stock

History: The genus *Matthiola* contains several plants which are scented garden favorites and known collectively as Stocks. The name commemorates an Italian botanist and physician, Pierandrea Matthioli, of the 16th century. The genus belongs to the Mustard family, *Brassicaceae (Cruciferae)*.

Description: Common Stocks including various strains such as Ten-week Stocks, Column Stocks, and Brampton Stocks vary in height from less than 12 in. (30 cm) up to 36 in. (90 cm). These delicately fragrant Stocks all have stems covered with flowers ranging in color from white through shades of cream and buff to pink, deep rose, lilac, and purple. There are both double-flowered and single-flowered plants with the doubles being more colorful with denser flower spikes.

Propagation and Culture: Seeds may be sown outdoors as soon as the soil can be prepared in the spring or started indoors 5 to 6 weeks before the last spring frost is expected. Seeds germinate in 2 weeks at 54 to 90°F (12 to 32°C) and may respond to light. Plants should be spaced about 8 in. (20 cm) apart in the garden. They grow well in moderately rich soil and cool temperatures with full sun to partial shade. They require abundant moisture.

Use: Common Stocks are excellent for flower beds and borders and their densely-flowered spikes also make excellent fragrant cut flowers. Their scent, however, can be overpowering in a confined space. Stocks can also be successfully dried for winter bouquets.

Matthiola longipetala bicornis (M. bicornis)
Evening Stock, Grecian Stock

Description: Evening Stocks grow about 12 to 14 in. (30 to 35 cm) tall with spikes of small, four-petaled lilac-colored flowers that open in the evening but are closed during the day. At night and even on dull or rainy days, they emit a tantalizing fragrance. Because of their lack of color during sunny days, they are often planted with colorful but unscented flowers such as their cousin *Malcolmia maritima,* Virginian Stock.

Propagation and Culture: Seeds may be sown outdoors as soon as the soil can be prepared in the spring or started indoors 5 to 6 weeks before the last spring frost is expected. Seeds germinate in 2 weeks at 55 to 90°F (12 to 32°C) and may respond to light. Plants should be spaced about 8 in. (20 cm) apart in the garden. They grow well in moderately rich soil and cool temperatures with full sun to partial shade. They require abundant moisture.

Use: Evening Stocks are best mixed with other more colorful plants of similar appearance and stature in beds, borders, or planters, especially close to the house or outdoor sitting areas.

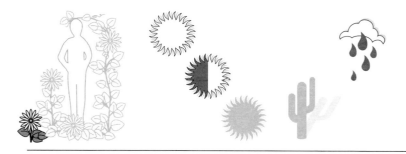

Matthiola longipetala bicornis

Matthiola longipetala bicornis

Mentzelia lindleyi (Bartonia aurea)
Bartonia, Blazing Star

History: This is a common wild flower in many parts of western North America. The species *Mentzelia decapetala* (Sand Lily or Evening Star) grows on dry eroded hillsides and banks across the southern part of prairie Canada south to Nevada, Texas and Oklahoma. *Mentzelia* belongs to the Loosa family *(Loosaceae).* The name commemorates Christian Mentzel, a German botanist.

Description: Bartonia grows about 18 in. (45 cm) in height and produces fragrant golden flowers about 2.5 in. (6 cm) in diameter that open in the evening and last until the afternoon of the next day. Their deeply divided leaves are also ornamental.

Mentzelia lindleyi

Mentzelia lindleyi

Propagation and Culture: Seeds are sown where the plants are to flower as soon as the ground can be prepared in spring and the young plants thinned to a spacing of about 8 to 10 in. (20 to 25 cm). They are difficult to transplant. Bartonia does well in windy spots with plenty of sunshine and a well-drained soil.

Use: Bartonias make gaudy borders and will do well in planters and balcony boxes. They are also attractive as cut flowers. Although open flowers are short-lived on cut stems, new buds quickly replace faded flowers with new ones.

Mesembryanthemum crystallinum

Mesembryanthemum
Fig Marigolds

Dorotheanthus bellidiformis (Mesembryanthemum criniflorum)
> Livingstone Daisy

Aptenia cordifolia 'Variegata' (Mesembryanthemum cordifolium 'Variegatum')
> Variegated Heartleaf Mesembryanthemum

Mesembryanthemum crystallinum (Cryophytum crystallinum)
> Ice Plant

Dorotheanthus tricolor (Mesembryanthemum tricolor)
> Tricolor Mesembryanthemum

History: There are thousands of species of South African succulents commonly known as Fig Marigolds that are grouped together under the name *Mesembryanthemum*. The cultivated species listed here all grow less than 6 in. (15 cm) tall and produce daisy-like flowers. They belong to the *Aizoaceae* family.

Description: Of the group of species listed, Livingstone Daisy is perhaps the most commonly grown as an outdoor annual. It produces flowers 1 to 2 in. (2.5 to 5 cm) across in rose, buff, pink, crimson, apricot, orange, or white. Ice Plants and variegated Heartleaf Mesembryanthemums are noted more for their foliage than flowers. The Ice Plant derives its name from its silvery-flecked eruptions on the leaves that look like ice. The Variegated Mesembryanthemum has green and white heart-shaped leaves and rose-colored flowers. The Tricolor species produces a profusion of pink, red, or white blossoms.

Dorotheanthus bellidiformis

ANNUALS FOR THE PLAINS AND PRAIRIES

Propagation and Culture: Seeds must be started indoors 10 to 12 weeks before the last frost is due, so it is recommended to purchase plants for bedding out. Seeds require high temperature to germinate (84 to 95°F (29 to 35°C)) and the seedlings are susceptible to damping-off. Plants should be spaced 6 in. (15 cm) apart. All species require full sun and warm temperatures as well as a light, well-drained dry soil.

Use: Fig Marigolds are good choices for hot, windy places and can be used in window boxes and planters where their blossoms cascade over the edges.

Dorotheanthus tricolor

Mimulus x *hybridus* 'Grandiflorus'
Monkey Flower

History: The genus *Mimulus* contains some 70 species of hardy and tender herbs, often with showy flowers, from various parts of the world, but many are indigenous to western America. They are members of the Figwort or Snapdragon family, *Scrophulariaceae.* The name *Mimulus* is derived from *mimus,* a "buffoon", an allusion to the shape of the flower.

Description: The Monkey Flowers are derived from the species *Mimulus luteus, Mimulus luteus variegatus,* and *Mimulus cupreus,* and are often sold under the name of *Mimulus* x *hybridus grandiflorus.* Many are actually tender perennials grown as annuals and get their name from the fancied resemblance of the flowers to that of the faces of grinning monkeys. The flowers are about 2 in. (5 cm) across and borne on low mound-shaped plants and look somewhat like small spotted Gloxinias. The color range includes bright shades of red as well as yellow with red, maroon, or purple spots. They grow 6 to 12 in. (15 to 30 cm) tall.

Propagation and Culture: Like Mesembryanthemums, monkey flowers take a long time to develop from seed so they should be started indoors 10 to 12 weeks before the last frost is due. Seeds will germinate in 1 to 2 weeks at 55°F (12°C), but seedling development is slow. Without greenhouse facilities, it is best to purchase plants for bedding out after all danger of frost has passed. They should be spaced about 6 in. (15 cm) apart.

Mimulus x *hybridus* 'Grandiflorus'

Mimulus x *hybridus* 'Grandiflorus'

Use: Monkey Flowers are among the few annuals that thrive in shady locations and wet soil. Plants can also be brought indoors at the end of the season and kept as house plants for winter flowering.

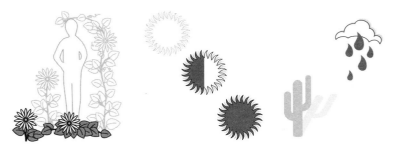

Mirabilis jalapa
Four-o'clock, Marvel-of-Peru

History: The name *Mirabilis* comes from its longer, older name *Admirabilis,* meaning "wonderful" or "strange", a reference to the beautiful colors of the flowers and the fact that they have no corolla (petals) but rather a colorful calyx that looks like a corolla. Species of this genus are for the most part natives of tropical America.

Description: Four-o'clocks are so called because fresh blossoms open late in the afternoon and remain open until the following morning – or longer on dull or rainy days. The trumpet-like flowers are about 1 in. (2.5 cm) in diameter and 1 to 2 in. (2.5 to 5 cm) long or deep. They are borne on plants 24 to 36 in. (60 to 90 cm) tall. A dwarf strain has been developed which grows only 18 to 20 in. (45 to 50 cm) tall. Colors include pink, red, yellow, violet, and white with more than one color appearing often on a single plant.

Propagation and Culture: Seeds may be sown indoors 4 to 6 weeks before the last frost is expected or directly in the garden as soon as the soil has warmed up and become dry enough to cultivate. Since the plants produce tuberous roots like Dahlia, these can be started overwinter the same way as Dahlias and planted in the garden again in spring. For best performance, Four-o'clocks require a sunny location and well-drained soil.

Use: Four-o'clocks are a colorful addition to flower beds and borders. They provide a changed look to the garden every late afternoon when the flowers open to present a display of fresh color.

Mirabilis jalapa

Gabe Botar

Mirabilis jalapa

Gail Rankin

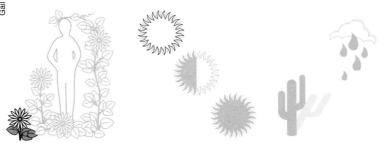

Moluccella laevis
Bells of Ireland, Molucca Balm, Shellflower,
Irish Bells

Moluccella laevis

History: This plant is native to the eastern Mediterranean and western Asia regions. The name is derived from the Moluccas, a group of islands in the Pacific Ocean, where one of the species was wrongly believed to have originated. The common names Bells of Ireland and Irish Bells were applied because of the green color of the "bells". *Moluccella* belongs to the mint family, *Lamiaceae (Labiatae)*.

Description: The white-veined green bells, 1 to 2 in. (2.5 to 5 cm) in diameter, that cling closely to the 24 to 30 in. (60 to 75 cm) tall stems of this annual, are the enlarged calyxes (sepals) of the flowers. The other parts of the flower, including the tiny white corolla, are deep within the bells and rather inconspicuous but fragrant.

Propagation and Culture: Bells of Ireland are difficult to transplant but should be started indoors, if possible, in order to get mature plants before late summer. Seeds should be started indoors, preferably in a greenhouse, about 10 to 12 weeks before the last frost is due. They should be planted directly into 3-in. (7.5-cm) peat pots or young seedlings transplanted to such pots for development to bedding-out size. There are conflicting recommendations on the best temperature for germination, ranging from 50 to 80°F (10 to 27°C). Some authorities recommend alternating the temperature between these two extremes; others suggest pre-chilling the seed (stratification) at 50°F (10°C). Germination may take up to 5 weeks. In the garden they should be spaced about 12 in. (30 cm) apart. If seeded directly outdoors, seed should be planted as soon as the soil can be worked in the spring, but seedlings will require protection from any frosts that may occur. Irish Bells have been successfully grown by direct seeding in southern Alberta for many years. It takes about 100 days from seed to flowering. They grow well in average soil if given a sunny location.

Moluccella laevis

Use: Bells of Ireland add another color dimension to flower beds with what appear to be green flowers. They make excellent, long-lasting fresh cut flowers as well as fair dried flowers for winter arrangements. Cut stems can easily be dried by hanging them in a cool, dark, airy location. If the sparse leaves are removed before drying, the bells will be more conspicuous; however, they are subject to shattering.

Nemesia strumosa

Nemesia strumosa 'Mello'

Nemesia strumosa
Nemesia

History: *Nemesia* is native to South Africa where cool summers prevail. It is a member of the Snapdragon family, *Scrophulariaceae.*

Description: Nemesia grows about 10 to 12 in. (25 to 30 cm) tall and becomes covered with masses of 1-in. (2-cm) wide, cup-like flowers in 3- to 4-in. (8- to 10-cm) wide clusters. Colors range from white through yellow, bronze, to pink, crimson, or lavender-blue.

Propagation and Culture: Nemesia is best started indoors about 4 to 6 weeks before the last frost is due. Seeds tend to germinate somewhat irregularly, so should be seeded rather thinly and seedlings pricked out as they become large enough to handle; the smaller ones should be left undisturbed until they too can be transplanted to other containers. Seeds germinate in 2 to 3 weeks at 55°F (13°C). Plants should be put in the garden after all danger of frost has passed at a spacing of 6 in. (15 cm). Nemesia thrives in full sun but cool summer temperatures (night temperatures below 65°F (18°C)) and moist soil enriched with compost or other organic material.

Use: Nemesia makes an attractive, jewel-like edging for borders as well as a good cut flower. It is also useful for planters and other types of containers provided it is kept adequately watered.

Nemophila menziesii

Nemophila menziesii
Baby Blue-eyes

History: This species is a wild flower in California. The botanical name comes from the Greek words *nemos,* or "grove", and *phileo,* to "love", alluding to the plant's preference for shady areas.

Description: These plants grow 6 to 8 in. (15 to 20 cm) tall in mounds about 12 in. (30 cm) across. The flower is 1 to 1.5 in. (2.5 to 4 cm) in diameter with 5 rounded petals forming an open cup that is sky blue with a white center.

Propagation and Culture: Seeds can be sown outdoors as soon as the soil can be worked in the spring and seedlings thinned to a spacing of 6 in. (15 cm). The plants do well in full sun or partial shade in a light, well-drained soil.

Use: Baby Blue-eyes are excellent for beds, borders, or planters as well as rock gardens. They are attractive but short-lived cut flowers.

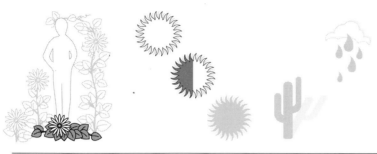

Nemophila menziesii

Nicotiana alata (N. affinis)
Flowering Tobacco, Jasmine Tobacco

History: *Nicotiana* includes the species *Nicotiana tabacum,* the commercial source of tobacco. The species listed here is one of the best known that is grown for its ornamental value.

Description: *Nicotiana alata* is the main source of the strains of Flowering Tobacco on the market. Cultivars come in a wide range of colors from white to scarlet including unusual off-shades of wine, chartreuse, and chocolate. The flowers are borne on 12 to 18 in. (30 to 45 cm) tall plants with each flower about 2 in. (5 cm) in diameter and similar in appearance to petunia flowers. Many are scented with a heavy, pleasant fragrance. Two other species of Flowering Tobacco are also grown, namely *Nicotiana sylvestris* and *Nicotiana langsdorffii.* The former grows 3 to 4 ft (90 to 120 cm) tall producing a candelabra of fragrant white blooms and lyre-shaped leaves. The latter grows 3 to 5 ft (90 to 150 cm) tall with branching stems and swooping sprays of greenish-yellow (chartreuse) flowers.

Propagation and Culture: The tiny seeds should be sown indoors about 8 to 10 weeks before the last frost or plants purchased ready for bedding out. Seeds germinate in 1 to 2 weeks at 68 to 86°F (20 to 30°C) and may respond to light. Cover seeds very lightly. Plants should be set out at a spacing of 9 to 12 in. (23 to 30 cm) when all danger of frost is past. Flowering Tobacco grows well in any soil in either full sun or light shade.

Nicotiana alata

Nicotiana alata

Use: The plants are particularly useful for beds and borders even along the north side of a building. The tall *Nicotiana sylvestris* makes an excellent "dot" plant or focal point in a flower bed. Flowering Tobacco is also useful as a fragrant cut flower.

Nicotiana alata 'Nicki Series'

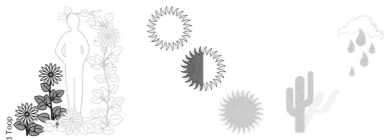

Nierembergia hippomanica 'Purple Robe'

Nierembergia hippomanica 'Mont Blanc'

Nierembergia hippomanica var. *violacea* (*N. caerulea*)
Cupflower, Nierembergia

History: Cupflowers are native to Argentina and members of the Nightshade family, *Solanaceae*. The genus is named for John E. Nieremberg, a Spanish Jesuit and first professor of natural history at Madrid in the early 17th century.

Description: Cupflowers grow about 6 to 8 in. (15 to 20 cm) tall, forming mounds covered with 1-in. (2.5-cm) diameter cup-shaped flowers. Flower color is a blue-violet. A white-flowered cultivar, 'Mont Blanc', was recently introduced.

Propagation and Culture: Seeds are sown indoors 8 to 10 weeks before the last spring frost is expected. Seeds germinate in 2 to 3 weeks at 68 to 86°F (20 to 30°C). Young plants are set out in the garden 6 to 8 in. (15 to 20 cm) apart when all danger of frost has passed. They require full sun and a moist rich soil but do not do well in high temperatures.

Use: Cupflowers make excellent edging plants for beds and borders. They are also successful in planters and window boxes as well as rock gardens if kept well watered.

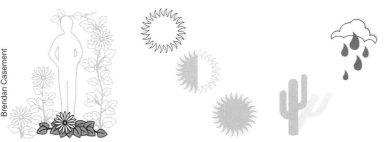

Nigella damascena
Love-in-a-mist, Devil-in-a-bush, Fennel Flower,
Nigella

History: This favorite annual grows wild in southern
Europe and is a member of the Buttercup family,
Ranunculaceae. The name is the diminutive of *niger*, "black",
and refers to the color of the seeds.

Description: The 1.5-in. (4-cm) blossoms of this plant are set
in the fringe of thread-like foliage and resemble Cornflowers
in shape and color. They may be blue, pure white, pink, rose,
mauve, or purple. They grow about 12 to 18 in. (30 to 45 cm)
tall. There are also dwarf cultivars in the trade that are 6 to 8
in. (15 to 20 cm) tall.

Propagation and Culture: Seeds may be sown outdoors in
the fall or as soon as the soil can be worked in the spring.
They may also be started indoors a few weeks before the last
frost is due. Plants should be spaced 8 in. (20 cm) apart in the
garden. Nigellas are difficult to transplant but do well in
ordinary soil provided there is full sunshine available.

Use: In addition to adding beauty to the garden flower beds,
Nigella is excellent for cut flowers. The blooms are replaced
with 1-in. (2.5-cm) diameter seed pods. These seed pods are
pale green with reddish-brown markings and are excellent
for winter bouquets and arrangements. To preserve the pods,
the stems are cut when the pods are mature and hung upside
down in a cool, dry place to cure.

Nigella damascena 'Moody Blues'

Nigella damascena 'Mulberry Rose'

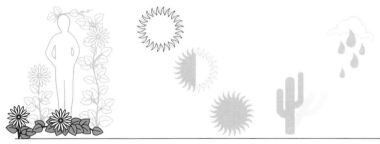

Nolana paradoxa (N. grandiflora)
Chilean Bellflower

History: *Nolana* is a genus of annual flowering plants from
Chile and Peru belonging to the family *Nolanaceae*. The name
is derived from *nola* meaning "little bell", and refers to the
bell-shaped flowers. They grow wild mainly as roadside
plants in their native habitat.

Description: Chilean Bellflowers are prostrate plants
growing 6 to 10 in. (15 to 25 cm) tall with oval to elliptical
leaves 2 to 6 in. (5 to 15 cm) long. The bell-like flowers are
pale blue, violet, or white, 1 to 2 in. (2.5 to 5 cm) in diameter,
borne singly in the axils of the leaves.

Nolana sp.

Nolana sp.

Propagation and Culture: Seeds may be sown directly outdoors in the spring as soon as the soil is sufficiently dry and warm to cultivate a smooth seed bed. For an earlier start, they may be seeded indoors about 8 to 10 weeks before the last frost is due. Plants should be spaced about 6 in. (15 cm) apart in the garden. They thrive in ordinary to poor, dry soil in full sun.

Use: Because of their tolerance of dry conditions and prostrate habit, Chilean Bellflowers do well in planters, hanging baskets, and sunny rock gardens.

Ocimum basilicum 'Dark Opal'

Ocimum basilicum
Dark Opal Basil, Sweet Basil

History: *Ocimum* includes annual and perennial plants, the leaves of which are used to flavor salads, stews, and soups. They are native to tropical Asia and belong to the Mint family, *Lamiaceae (Labiatae).*

Description: This species is the one grown as the culinary herb (Common Basil). There are various ornamental forms including some with a compact habit of growth, dark purplish foliage, or crimped or wavy leaves. Basils are tender and do well only when the weather is settled and warm. Sweet Basils grow about 16 in. (40 cm) tall and 12 in. (30 cm) broad and produce short 2-in. (5-cm) stalks covered with small white or purple-tinged flowers. The ornamental value of these plants is in their leaf color, shape, plant form, and fragrance.

Propagation and Culture: Seeds are sown indoors about 8 to 10 weeks before the last frost is expected. Plants are put in the garden only when all danger of frost is past and there is warm settled weather. Plants should be spaced 12 in. (30 cm) apart. They do well in light, sandy loam and full sun.

Use: Sweet Basil is striking in beds and borders as well as in planters and window boxes. Plants can be harvested and the leaves dried or even frozen for use as flavoring. Plants can be pruned back, moved into pots in late summer, and brought indoors to grow on a sunny window sill through the cold fall and winter months.

Ocimum basilicum 'Dark Opal'

Oenothera deltoides
Desert Evening Primrose, Hairy-calyx Sundrop

History: *Oenotheras,* or Evening Primroses as they are often referred to, are a large group of about 200 species, native mainly to North and South America. The perennial species, *Oenothera missouriensis,* is perhaps the best known, at least to prairie gardeners. All are members of the *Onagraceae* or Evening Primrose family.

Description: Hairy-calyx Sundrop grows to a height of 12 to 18 in. (30 to 45 cm) and produces a continuous supply of sweetly-scented cup-like flowers more than 2.5 in. (6 cm) in diameter throughout the summer. The flowers open as a pure white in the evening and stay open throughout the following day, turning pink as they fade.

Propagation and Culture: Seeds should be started indoors 6 to 8 weeks before the last spring frost is due and the young plants put into the garden after all danger of frost has passed. Seeds germinate in 1 to 3 weeks at 68 to 86°F (20 to 30°C). A spacing of about 6 in. (15 cm) should be used. They prefer a well-drained soil in full sun or partial shade.

Use: The flowers are freshest at night and are prized for their evening fragrance. To take advantage of this, planting them in borders or planters close to a patio, deck, or other sitting area is recommended.

Oenothera deltoides

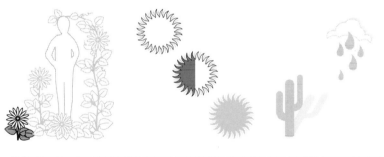

Papaver spp.
Annual Poppies

History: There are a number of species of *Papaver,* the true poppies, that can be grown as annuals or summer flowers. These include Corn Poppy and its more popular form, Shirley Poppy *(Papaver rhoeas),* Flanders Poppy *(Papaver commutatum),* Alpine Poppy *(Papaver alpinum),* and Tulip Poppy *(Papaver glaucum).*

Description:

Alpine Poppy *(Papaver alpinum)*
Alpine Poppy is a hardy dwarf species native to the high mountains of Europe. Its wiry stems rise 6 to 10 in. (15 to 25 cm) above the gray-green foliage and produce sweetly fragrant flowers, 1 to 2 in. (2.5 to 5 cm) in diameter, in orange, yellow, apricot, pink, white, and scarlet.

Papaver commutatum

Papaver rhoeas

Papaver rhoeas

Flanders Poppy (*Papaver commutatum*)
This species is very similar to Corn Poppy. The best known cultivar is 'Lady Bird'. It grows to 18 in. (45 cm) in height producing shiny crimson, single blooms about 2 to 3 in. (5 to 8 cm) in diameter, with each petal having a black blotch.

Tulip Poppy (*Papaver glaucum*)
Tulip Poppies, native to Asia Minor, produce blossoms that are 4 to 5 in. (10 to 13 cm) across with scarlet petals that stay erect to semi-erect, giving them the appearance of giant tulips. Each plant may produce 50 or more flowers over the summer. They grow to 20 in. (50 cm) in height.

Corn Poppy (*Papaver rhoeas*)
The wild field poppies of Europe, often called Corn Poppies, are usually attributed to this species rather than to *Papaver commutatum*, Flanders Poppy. Some authorities consider *Papaver commutatum* to be a variety of *Papaver rhoeas*. At any rate, the Shirley Strain was developed by the Reverend M. W. Wilks of Shirley, England, in 1880. Every Shirley Poppy has white-based petals in the blooms which range in color from white to shades of pink, orange, and red. The original Corn Poppies are shades of red and sometimes dark spotted. Flowers are about 2 to 3 in. (5 to 7 cm) in diameter on plants 18 to 30 in. (45 to 75 cm) tall.

Propagation and Culture: None of the species of poppies transplant well, so they should be seeded directly where they are to bloom. Seeds may be sown in the fall, late enough that no germination will take place until spring, or in the spring as early as the soil can be prepared for seeding. Seeds germinate in 1 to 2 weeks at a temperature of 55°F (13°C). The tiny seed may be sown in rows or broadcast and barely covered with soil. Fine sand may be mixed with the seed to provide a more even and thinner distribution. Seedlings should be thinned to a spacing of 6 to 12 in. (15 to 30 cm). Poppies do best in full sun and ordinary, well-drained soil.

Use: Poppies are most effective when planted in masses in beds by themselves. The Alpine Poppy requires good drainage and flourishes in rock gardens. Most poppies can also be used as cut flowers if harvested when the nodding buds become erect, just before the flowers open into full bloom. The cut ends should be seared with a flame or dipped into boiling water to prevent bleeding. The capsular fruit is useful in fresh-flower arrangements but is more popular as a dried item.

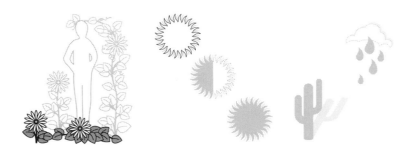

Pelargonium x domesticum
Lady Washington Geranium, Royal Geranium, Fancy Geranium, or Show Geranium

History: There are many species of *Pelargonium* grown as tender perennial house plants or outdoor summer bedding plants or "annuals". They are natives of South Africa and known and cherished by more people than any other flower in the world. The name is derived from *pelargos*, a "stork", and refers to the shape of the fruit which somewhat resembles the beak of a stork. These plants are close relatives of the *Geranium* spp. or Cranesbills, a number of which are hardy perennials that thrive in prairie gardens.

Description: Lady Washington Geraniums grow about 12 in. (30 cm) tall as summer season bedding plants producing huge clusters of 2- to 4-in. (5- to 10-cm) single and double blossoms, sometimes blotched with a darker shade on the two upper petals. These flower clusters are often azalea-like in appearance and range in color from various reds and pinks to purple and white. The leaves are palmate, toothed at the margins, and wrinkled.

Propagation and Culture: Show Geraniums are primarily propagated from cuttings and require considerable skill in handling. They do not endure hot summer sun and require cool night temperatures below 60°F (15°C) in order to set buds. It is recommended to buy plants ready for bedding out or already established in hanging baskets or planters. They will grow in ordinary well-drained soil with a good organic matter content. Plants should be spaced about 12 in. (30 cm) apart.

Use: Show Geraniums are traditional gift plants for Mother's Day. Their beauty can be enjoyed throughout the summer by placing them on the patio or deck, or by putting them in a garden bed or planters for the rest of the summer season. They make excellent specimen plants in window boxes or hanging baskets provided they are protected from the sun during the heat of the day.

Pelargonium x *domesticum*

Pelargonium x *domesticum* 'Peggy'

Pelargonium x *domesticum*

Pelargonium x *hortorum* 'Picasso'

Pelargonium x *hortorum* 'Frank Headley'

Pelargonium x *hortorum* 'Rose Diamond'

Pelargonium x *hortorum*
Common Bedding Geranium, Zonal Geranium

History: *Pelargonium* x *hortorum* is the species from which all the popular types and cultivars of bedding geraniums have been developed. Within the last 20 to 25 years, "hybrid geraniums from seed" have been developed and have superseded the old cultivars that could only be propagated from cuttings. Common Bedding Geraniums often show a zonal pattern of light and dark areas in concentric rings on the leaves and hence the name Zonal Geraniums.

Description: Common Bedding Geraniums grow 12 to 18 in. (30 to 45 cm) tall. The single or double flowers develop in hemi-spherical or spherical clusters in a wide range of colors including crimson, red, scarlet, rose-pink, salmon-pink, purple, and white.

Propagation and Culture: Common Bedding Geraniums are usually purchased as plants in bloom or ready to bloom that can create instant color in flower beds and borders as soon as danger of frost is past. Plants can be started from cuttings or from seed, but good environmental control such as that provided by a greenhouse is highly recommended. Seeds should be sown indoors about 4 months before the last frost is due. Seeds germinate best at about 72°F (22°C) in a soilless medium. Common Bedding Geraniums can be kept overwinter as house plants but require high light levels to prevent spindly growth. Plants can be stored in a dormant state in a dark cool place through the short days of winter and encouraged to start new growth by providing light, warmth, and water by mid-February. The new shoot growth can then be removed as cuttings and rooted to produce bedding plants for setting out in the garden. Geraniums flower well in either full sun or partial shade and a well-drained average soil. Plants should be spaced about 12 in. (30 cm) apart.

Use: Common Bedding Geraniums make excellent garden plants for use in beds, borders, planters, window boxes, or hanging baskets. They are often grown in combination with Spike-grass Dracaena (*Cordyline australis*) and Lobelia.

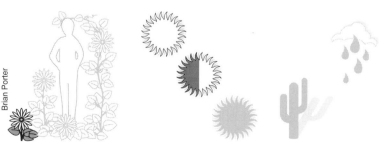

Pelargonium peltatum
Ivy Geranium

Description: Ivy Geranium is so called because of its ivy-like leaves and trailing growth. Its graceful stems, which may reach a length of 40 in. (100 cm), will creep along the ground or trail down from hanging baskets or planters. The range of flower color is similar to that of other species of *Pelargonium*, but pink and mauve are perhaps the most common.

Propagation and Culture: Like other species of *Pelargonium*, Ivy Geraniums are usually purchased as plants in bud ready to flower. They may be started from cuttings or from seeds as indicated for Common Bedding Geraniums. Ivy Geraniums thrive in either full sun or partial shade and a well-drained average soil.

Use: Ivy Geraniums are particularly adapted for use in raised planters, window boxes, or hanging baskets.

Pelargonium peltatum 'Rouletta'

Pelargonium peltatum 'Princess Belcon'

Pelargonium spp.
Scented Geranium

History: There are many species of Scented Geranium, a few of which are *Pelargonium crispum* (lemon-scented), *Pelargonium* x *fragrans* (nutmeg-scented), *Pelargonium graveolens* (rose-scented), *Pelargonium odoratissimum* (apple-scented), *Pelargonium tomentosum* (peppermint-scented), and *Pelargonium* x *citrosum* (orange-scented). In each case, the scent is produced by crushing the leaves. In recent years, there has been much interest in a new plant called Citrosa *(Pelargonium* x *citrosum* 'Van Leenii'), whose volatile scent can be used to repel mosquitoes. However, the plant is only available through vegetative propagation and there is controversy over its effectiveness against mosquitoes.

Pelargonium sp.

Pelargonium sp.

John Beedle

Description: Scented Geraniums, being a collection of different species, will vary in height, leaf shape, and flower size and color. In general they are grown primarily for their scented leaves and not for the flowers, which are often of little ornamental value.

Propagation and Culture: Scented Geraniums can be started from cuttings or from seed, but good environmental control such as that provided by a greenhouse is highly recommended. Seeds should be sown indoors about 4 months before the last frost is due. Plants can be kept overwinter as house plants but require high light levels to prevent spindly growth. Scented Geraniums can be stored in a dormant state in a dark, cool place through the short days of winter and encouraged to start new growth by providing light, warmth, and water by mid-February. The new shoot growth can then be removed as cuttings and rooted to produce bedding plants for setting out in the garden. Scented Geraniums do well in either full sun or partial shade and a well-drained average soil. Plants should be spaced about 12 in. (30 cm) apart.

Use: Scented Geraniums are grown primarily for their scented foliage.

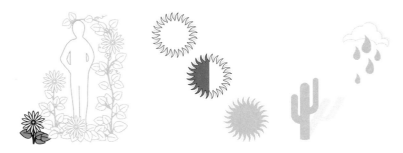

Pennisetum setaceum (P. ruppelii)
Fountain Grass

History: The genus *Pennisetum* includes about 80 species of annual and perennial grasses in tropical regions. Fountain Grass is native to Africa and is grown for its ornamental qualities. The name *Pennisetum* is derived from *penna*, a "feather", and *seta*, a "bristle", and refers to the feathery bristles or awns.

Description: Fountain Grass is perennial but grown as an annual in colder climates. It grows to about 40 in. (100 cm) in height with clustered stems bearing inflorescences up to 14 in. (35 cm) long, nodding, loose, and pink or purple in color. The cultivar 'Atrostanguineum' has both purple leaves and purple spikes. The cultivar 'Cupreum' produces reddish foliage and copper-colored spikes whereas the cultivar 'Rubrum' has both foliage and spikes that are rose colored.

Pennisetum setaceum

Brian Porter

Propagation and Culture: Seed may be started indoors 4 to 6 weeks before the last frost is due, or sown outdoors as soon as the soil is warm and danger of frost is past. Plants thrive in full sun in a deep, well-prepared loam garden soil. When the seedlings are 2 in. (5 cm) tall, they should be thinned to a spacing of 6 in. (15 cm) in the garden.

Use: Fountain Grass is a most attractive ornamental grass for use as a background material in flower beds or borders, or as a specimen or "dot" plant. The plumes are useful for winter decoration and should be cut for this purpose when fully expanded. The cut stems can be tied in small bundles and hung upside down in a cool, airy place to dry.

Pennisetum setaceum

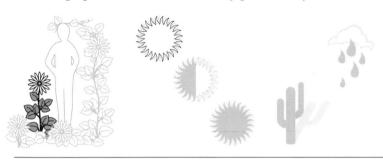

Perilla frutescens 'Crispa' (*P. frutescens* var. *nankinensis*)
Perilla, Beefsteak Plant

History: *Perilla* is a member of the Mint family *(Lamiaceae)* and native to India and China. Throughout the Orient, Perillas are grown commercially for their small nut-like seeds that are pressed to yield a drying oil (perilla oil) used in the manufacture of paint and varnishes.

Description: Perillas are grown for their reddish-purple foliage with its metallic, bronzy sheen but also may produce flower stalks late in the summer that are covered with tiny pale lavender-pink or white blossoms. The leaves grow in crisp fringed pairs each 2 to 3 in. (5 to 8 cm) long. If the leaves are rubbed or bruised, they emit a spicy cinnamon-like fragrance. Plants grow about 18 in. (45 cm) tall or taller if flower stalks develop. They are similar in form and leaf shape to their close relative, Coleus.

Propagation and Culture: Seed may be sown indoors 4 to 6 weeks before the last spring frost is expected or sown outdoors after danger of frost is past. Plants should be spaced about 12 to 16 in. (30 to 40 cm) apart in the garden. Several weeks before the season is over, cuttings may be taken and rooted for use as house plants over winter. Tough and pest-free, perillas withstand wind or wind-driven rain and thrive in almost any dry to average soil in a sunny location.

Louis Lenz

Perilla frutescens 'Crispa'

Perilla frutescens 'Crispa'

Use: Perillas are excellent as a contrast or backdrop to white and brightly-colored flowers in beds or borders. They can be used as hedges or as specimen pot plants, either indoors or out.

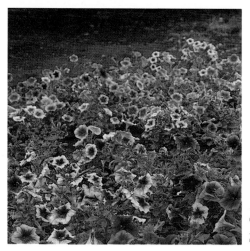

Petunia 'Strawberry Daddy'

Petunia 'Plum Pudding'

Petunia x *hybrida*
Petunia

History: The *Petunia* genus includes an indispensable array of hybrids which adapt to almost every climate. They are members of the Nightshade family, *Solanaceae,* and are native to South America. Until the mid 1950s, most Petunia seeds came from established hybrid strains that were inbred and standardized to the extent of being self-perpetuating for many generations. The seed offered today is produced by crossing inbred lines to produce so-called F1 hybrids that produce blossoms often more than twice the size of those of the parents. These hybrids consistently produce vigorous plants in the desired colors. However, these qualities seldom carry over to their offspring. Seeds produced from F1 hybrid plants are called F2 hybrids and these produce flowers that are generally superior to the old inbred strains but are not as good as those of the F1 hybrids. F1 hybrid seed can be very expensive because of the need to maintain the parent lines in order to produce the F1 seed.

Description: The beautiful blooms produced by F1 hybrids have been categorized into four major groups:

Double Multifloras
great quantities of double blossoms about 2 in. (5 cm) across.

Double Grandifloras
fewer but larger double flowers than the multifloras, some more than 3 in. (8 cm) across.

Single Multifloras
large numbers of single blooms 2 to 3 in. (5 to 8 cm) across.

Single Grandifloras

huge single blooms up to 5 in. (12 cm) or more in diameter, some with ruffled or fringed petals.

Many Petunias are fragrant, especially during the cooler evening hours. Plant height ranges from 6 to 8 in. (15 to 20 cm) for the compact dwarf cultivars, and 12 to 15 in. (30 to 38 cm) for the others. Flower colors include solid red, crimson, pink, rose, coral, salmon, blue, purple, orange, cream, yellow, and white as well as various bi-color combinations.

Propagation and Culture: Petunias have very fine seed that requires considerable time to germinate and develop seedlings to the flowering stage. Therefore, most gardeners purchase plants ready for bedding-out from the great selection of types and colors of blooms that is available at garden centers. To start your own, seed should be sown indoors, preferably in a greenhouse, at least 8 to 10 weeks before the last frost is due. For double-flowering cultivars it is advisable to plant the seed 10 to 12 weeks before the last frost is expected. Seeds germinate in 1 to 2 weeks at 68°F (20°C) but some cultivars require a high temperature of 80 to 85°F (27 to 29°C) (especially double-flowered cultivars and some F1 hybrids). Many cultivars also require light for germination. When seedlings develop 3 to 4 leaves, they should be transplanted to individual 2- to 3-in. (5- to 8-cm) pots or comparable size "cell paks." Petunias do better in cool temperatures, and hence the need for a greenhouse or cold frame to grow the young seedlings on to the budding stage. A night temperature of about 54 to 55°F (12 to 13°C) is ideal. Plants are put into the garden after all danger of frost has passed at a spacing of 8 to 12 in. (20 to 30 cm). Petunias require a well-fertilized loam soil and plenty of moisture. They will tolerate several hours of light shade provided they receive full sunshine for at least 3 hours each day.

Use: Single-flowered Petunias withstand strong rain better than double-flowered kinds and hence are better choices for beds and borders. The double-flowered multifloras and grandifloras are better suited to planters, window boxes, and hanging baskets where they can effectively trail over the edges and can be appreciated at or near eye level. However, with the wide selection of types on the market today, including for instance, single-flowered cascading cultivars, designating a particular category for a particular use in the landscape is really not possible. Generally the multiflora singles make the most colorful displays when grown as a mass planting.

Petunia 'Ultra Red'

Petunia

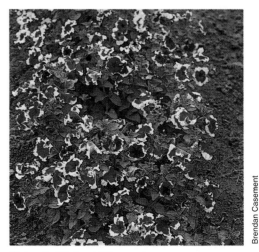

Petunia 'Velvet Picotee'

Brian Porter

Phacelia campanularia
California Bluebell

History: *Phacelias* are a group of plants native to South and North America belonging to the family *Hydrophyllaceae*. The word *Phacelia* is derived from *phakelos*, a "bundle" or "fascicle", and refers to the way in which the flowers are arranged. *Phacelia campanularia* is native to California and is the favorite species of *Phacelia* grown in gardens. Two other species, also native to the western U.S., *Phacelia viscida* (Sticky Phacelia) and *Phacelia tanacetifolia* (Wild Heliotrope or Tansy Phacelia), are also attractive garden annuals.

Description: California Bluebells grow 8 to 10 in. (20 to 25 cm) tall producing clusters of bright blue, bell-shaped blossoms that are 0.5 to 1 in. (2 to 2.5 cm) in diameter. Sticky Phacelia has hairy, sticky (viscous) leaves and deep blue flowers with blue-speckled white throats. Wild Heliotrope has lavender-blue flower heads. Both of these latter species grow 18 in. (45 cm) or taller.

Propagation and Culture: Seed is sown outdoors after all danger of frost is past or started indoors 4 to 6 weeks before the last frost is due. Phacelias do not transplant well beyond the "pricking out" stage, so should be grown in cell packs or individual small pots. They take 6 to 7 weeks from germination to flowering stage. Full sun and hot, dry days followed by cool nights are needed for best results. California Bluebells, in particular, require rather poor, sandy loam in a very dry location. Sticky Phacelia and Wild Heliotrope need not be kept quite so dry. Plants should be spaced 6 to 8 in. (15 to 20 cm) apart for California Bluebells and 12 to 15 in. (30 to 38 cm) for the other two taller species.

Use: Phacelias make extremely effective mass plantings in low borders. They are also successful in rock gardens. They do not make good cut flowers and the leaves may cause dermatitis when handled by people who are prone to allergic reactions.

Brian Porter

Phacelia campanularia

Brendan Casement

Phacelia campanularia

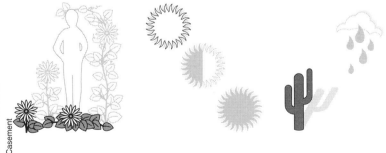

Phalaris canariensis
Canary Grass

Description: Canary Grass is an annual grass that grows 28 to 60 in. (70 to 150 cm) in height and has green leaves but bears variegated flowering spikes 1 to 2 in. (2 to 5 cm) long that are very ornamental. It is naturalized in parts of the United States and is grown chiefly for its seeds which are used as food for tame birds.

Propagation and Culture: Seeds are sown in the garden as soon as the soil can be worked in the spring. Seedlings are later thinned to a spacing of 4 in. (10 cm). Canary Grass will thrive in ordinary soil, in sun or shade, but must have a sunny location for production of flower spikes.

Use: Canary Grass may be used as a ground cover or in small clumps in the flower border for the beauty of its small, compact spikes of variegated flowers. The flower spikes, when fully expanded, may be cut and dried for use in winter bouquets and arrangements.

Phalaris canariensis

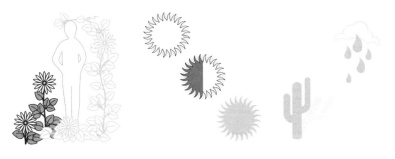

Phalaris canariensis

Phaseolus coccineus (P. multiflorus) and Phaseolus coccineus 'Albus'
Scarlet Runner Bean and White Dutch Runner Bean

History: These climbers are an old-time favorite from the South American tropics and members of the Pea family, *Fabaceae (Leguminosae).*

Description: Scarlet Runner Bean and its cultivar, White Dutch Runner Bean, produce brilliant red or white blossoms about 1 in. (2 cm) in diameter borne in clusters similar to Sweet Peas. Plants usually will climb 6 to 8 ft (2 to 2.5 m) high, although there are dwarf cultivars that form mounds of deep green leaves less than 12 in. (30 cm) tall, which are covered by flower clusters. The large beans that develop as the flowers fade are attractive and edible as well.

Phaseolus coccineus 'Scarlet Emperor'

Phaseolus coccineus 'Scarlet Emperor'

Brian Porter

Propagation and Culture: Seeds are sown directly where the plants are to develop at a depth of 2 in. (5 cm) about a week before the last frost is due and the soil is warm. If planted at the base of a post or pole they will twine around it naturally provided the seeds are no further than 3 in. (7 cm) from the support. They will also climb on a lattice screen, trellis, or strings, but may need a little assistance to provide even coverage over the surface area. Five or 6 seeds per pole will suffice. When planted to cover a screen, seeds should be planted about 4 in. (10 cm) apart along its base. Plants require a moderately rich, well-drained soil with plenty of water and full sun.

Use: Runner beans are very decorative entwining the posts of a porch or arbor or as a covering for walls or screens. They also attract humming birds. An added advantage is that the beans can be harvested and eaten in the same fashion as snap beans.

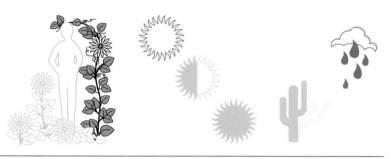

Phlox drummondii 'Globe Mix'

Ed Toop

Phlox drummondii
Annual Phlox, Drummond Phlox

History: *Phlox drummondii* is a beautiful annual that is native to Texas and is known in the U.S. as "Texas Pride".

Description: One of the strains of Drummond Phlox grows 15 to 18 in. (38 to 45 cm) tall, but the dwarf cultivars reaching only 6 to 8 in. (15 to 20 cm) in height are considered more desirable since they form compact mounds covered with flowers. Blooms are 1 to 1.5 in. (2.5 to 4 cm) in diameter and colors range from white to many shades of pink, red, scarlet, yellow, and lavender, as well as bi-colors. Some of the newer cultivars have sharply-lobed petals that make the blooms look like painted stars.

Propagation and Culture: Seeds should be sown indoors 4 to 6 weeks before the last frost is due in order to get early flowering, but they can also be seeded directly in the garden after the last frost is expected. Seeds germinate in 2 to 3 weeks at 68°F (20°C). Plants should be spaced 6 in. (15 cm) apart in the garden. If plants get straggly, the stems can be cut back to within 2 in. (5 cm) of the ground and new flowering shoots will soon develop. Annual Phlox grows in any good, well-drained garden soil with full sun or light shade.

Use: Annual Phlox makes attractive displays in mass border plantings or in planters, window boxes, and even rock gardens. The large compact flower clusters make good short-stemmed cut flowers.

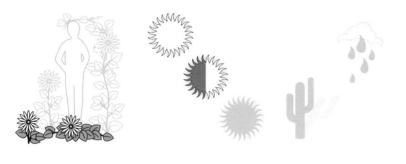

Brendan Casement

Phlox drummondii 'Petticoat Mix'

Polygonum capitatum
Polygonum, Knotweed

History: The genus *Polygonum* or Knotweed is widely distributed around the world. The name comes from the Greek, *poly*, "many", and *gonu*, a "knee joint", and refers to the swollen-jointed stems. Many of the species are rather coarse growing and weedy in habit.

Description: *Polygonum capitatum* is a prostrate plant from the Himalayas. It has heart-shaped leaves that are mainly green with a broad brownish zone in the middle of the blades and a reddish mid-rib and margin. The delicate pink color of the flowers is highlighted by their clustering in clover-like heads on short slender stalks. It will flower in summer if started early enough from seed and reaches a height of about 4 to 6 in. (10 to 15 cm).

Propagation and Culture: Seed should be sown indoors 4 to 6 weeks before the last frost is due and plants put in the garden after all danger of frost is past. Polygonum thrives in ordinary, well-drained garden soil in full sun or light shade. Plants should be spaced about 6 to 8 in. (15 to 20 cm) apart.

Use: This plant does well in the rock garden or in planters. It can also serve as an edging plant for borders or even as a ground cover.

Brian Porter

Polygonum capitatum 'Magic Carpet'

Louis Lenz

Polygonum capitatum 'Magic Carpet'

Portulaca grandiflora 'Sundance'

Portulaca grandiflora

Portulaca grandiflora

Portulaca grandiflora
Portulaca, Rose Moss

History: For the prairie gardener the common name for this genus, "Purslane", brings to mind the common annual weed, *Portulaca oleracea,* that is so difficult to control with ordinary cultivation. However, the species *Portulaca grandiflora*, that is grown as an ornamental is non-invasive and makes a very colorful carpet plant for hot, dry areas. It is native to Brazil.

Description: Rose Moss, or Sun Moss as it is also called, grows 6 in. (15 cm) or less in height and produces rose-like double or single blossoms that open every morning in the sunshine but not on cloudy days. However, some of the newer strains such as Cloudbeater stay open on cloudy days. Portulaca forms a carpet of color in shades of rose, salmon, pink, scarlet, orange, yellow, and white. Its narrow fleshy leaves are almost hidden by the open blooms.

Propagation and Culture: Plants may be started indoors by sowing seed 4 to 6 weeks before the last frost is due. Seeds germinate in 2 to 3 weeks at 68 to 86°F (20 to 30°C) and they respond to light. Seed may also be sown outdoors by broadcasting the very fine seed (mixed with dry sand) and leaving the seedlings to develop a carpet that does not require any thinning. If plants are purchased or started indoors, then the spacing in the garden should be close, about 4 in. (10 cm) between plants, in order to produce a solid mass or carpet of bloom. Young plants will transplant successfully. In sheltered areas or milder parts of the prairies some self-seeding is possible. To thrive and produce a blanket of color, Rose Moss needs full sun and rather poor soil, even soil that is predominantly sand.

Use: Portulaca is the answer for that hot, dry location where nothing else can survive. They are ideal for dry banks, along a driveway, in a rock garden, as a ground cover, or in patio pots or planters.

ANNUALS FOR THE PLAINS AND PRAIRIES

Proboscidea louisianica (Martynia proboscidea)
Unicorn Plant, Proboscis Flower, Ram's Horn

History: Unicorn Plants are grown in gardens for their large flowers, abundant foliage, and odd-shaped pods. The pods, when small and tender, can be pickled the same as cucumbers. The thick fleshy root of the unicorn plant is preserved in sugar and eaten in some parts of the world. This plant is native to the southeastern United States and Mexico.

Description: The Unicorn Plant produces rather coarse ascending or prostrate branches 24 to 36 in. (60 to 90 cm) long with rounded leaves 4 to 12 in. (10 to 30 cm) wide. The 5-lobed flowers, which are 1 to 2 in. (3 to 5 cm) long and just about as broad, are dull white or yellowish in color with mottles of purple or yellow within the throat. The fruits (pods) are 4 to 6 in. (10 to 15 cm) long at maturity with a beak equaling or exceeding the "body" portion where the seeds are located. The plant produces a rather strong odor that is offensive to some people.

Propagation and Culture: Seeds may be sown indoors about 1 in. (2.5 cm) deep in pots or flats of sandy soil about 6 to 8 weeks before the last spring frost is due. When seedlings have produced the first pair of leaves, they should be potted separately into 3 in. (8-cm) peat pots. Plants are gradually hardened off and planted out of doors about the same time as tomatoes are set out. Plants require a sunny location and a fertile, evenly moist soil at a minimum spacing of about 18 in. (45 cm). They greatly benefit from a surface mulch to keep even moisture at the roots.

Use: Because of its rank growth, the Unicorn Plant requires considerable space. It can be used as a ground cover. The pods can be harvested for pickling (young) or for artistic purposes (mature).

Proboscidea louisianica

Psylliostachys suworowii

Psylliostachys suworowii

Psylliostachys suworowii
(Limonium suworowii)
Pink Poker Statice, Russian Statice, Rat-tail Statice

History: Russian Statice is native to Turkestan. *Psylliostachys* is closely related to *Limonium.* Both are members of the *Plumbaginaceae* family, the Plumbago or Leadwort family.

Description: Russian Statice produces pencil-thin spikes of tiny lilac-colored to rich pink blossoms which last for many weeks in the garden. It grows to 18 in. (45 cm) in height.

Propagation and Culture: Seeds may be sown indoors 8 weeks before all danger of frost has passed for early summer flowering, or seeded directly outside in the garden as early as the soil can be cultivated. Plants should be spaced 9 to 12 in. (23 to 30 cm) apart. For best results, Statice should be given full sun and fairly dry, well-drained soil.

Use: Russian Statice makes an interesting addition to the summer garden, and as a cut flower adds an airy grace to summer bouquets. It is not particularly desirable for use in winter bouquets because of its fragility when dried.

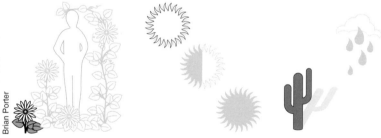

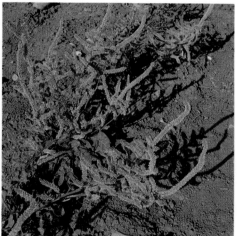

Reseda odorata

Reseda odorata
Mignonette

History: Mignonette, a member of the Mignonette family, *Resedaceae,* is native to north Africa and considered one of the most fragrant of all annual flowers. The name is derived from *resodo,* to "calm", and refers to the supposed medicinal virtues of the plant.

Description: Mignonettes stand about 12 to 18 in. (30 to 45 cm) tall, have thick stems and 6 to 10 in. (15 to 25 cm) long spikes of rather drab small greenish-yellow, yellowish-brown, or brownish-red flowers. The cultivar 'Grandiflora' found in the trade is a larger-flowered garden form.

Propagation and Culture: Seeds may be sown outdoors in early spring after the soil is warm and danger of frost has passed. Seed should not be covered since light is required for germination. Germination takes 2 to 3 weeks at 55°F (12°C). In very hot, dry weather, they have a short flowering period, so seed may be sown indoors a few weeks (3 to 4) before the last frost is due and seeded successively outdoors at 2 week intervals to ensure a continuous production of scented flowers. They do best in high lime soils that are firm, dry, and fertile. Plants should be thinned or transplanted to a spacing of 4 in. (10 cm). Mignonette does not transplant well so any indoor-grown plants should be in small peat pots or "cell paks". They should have shade for at least part of the day and preferably cool weather.

Use: Mignonettes can be grown in flower beds, borders, or planters as a source of fragrance, preferably close to the house or the patio. It can be added to bouquets as a source of fragrance.

Reseda odorata

Ricinus communis
Castor Bean, Castor Oil Plant

History: Castor Beans are believed to have originated in tropical Africa. They are grown as an annual for their handsome leaves. *Ricinus* is a member of the Spurge family, *Euphorbiaceae.* The name ricinus means "tick" and refers to the resemblance of the seed to that insect. The "beans" yield castor oil and are grown commercially for that purpose in India.

Description: The huge palm-like leaves of Castor Bean create an exotic effect, but they can be entirely out of scale for use in a small city lot. The plant may grow up to 8 ft (2.5 m) in height by the end of the summer with leaves up to 24 in. (60 cm) across, each having 5 to 12 deeply cut lobes. Young leaves have a distinct red and bronze coloration. There are cultivars with more pronounced coloration in the older leaves ranging from reds to purples. The flowers are unimpressive, petal-less, reddish-brown in color, and borne in spike-like clusters. The prickly seed husks contain large shiny seeds that are poisonous but flowers, if formed, are unlikely to produce any seeds in our short summer season. Some people are allergic to the spiny seed pods or to the leaves.

Propagation and Culture: Seeds should be sown indoors 6 to 8 weeks before the last frost is expected. The hard-coated seeds should be nicked with a file or soaked in water overnight before planting. Seeds are best planted in individual 3-in. (8-cm) peat pots and the seedlings put into the garden, pot and all, at a spacing of 36 in. (90 cm) when all danger of frost is past. Plants require a rich, friable soil, good drainage, full sun, and plenty of heat and moisture.

Ricinus communis

Ricinus communis 'Zanzibarensis'

University of Alberta Plant Science Collection

Brian Porter

Ricinus communis

Use: Castor Beans provide excellent quick growing background plantings to hide unsightly areas or as broad temporary hedges. Because of their size and coarse texture, they tend to be out of scale for the average urban yard. However, they are excellent for defining more intimate spaces in large landscape areas such as residential acreages.

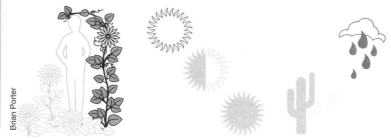

Rudbeckia hirta burpeei

Rudbeckia hirta 'Marmalade'

Rudbeckia hirta
Gloriosa Daisy, Black-eyed Susan

History: Black-eyed Susan *(Rudbeckia hirta)* is an introduced species that is seen growing wild occasionally in waste places and roadsides in parts of the plains region. The popular garden plants, which are better known as Gloriosa Daisies, are actually tetraploid selections and cultivars of the species, and are sometimes listed as *Rudbeckia hirta* 'Gloriosa Daisy' and 'Double Gloriosa Daisy'. These plants are actually perennial but can be treated as annuals since they will bloom the first year from seed.

Description: Gloriosa Daisies grow 24 to 36 in. (60 to 90 cm) tall producing glorious flower heads 6 in. (15 cm) in diameter with a typical cone-shaped, dark, blackish-brown center surrounded by yellow, gold, or mahogany "petals". They may have single to double blossoms. Some of the newer dwarf selections such as 'Becky', 'Goldilocks', and 'Marmalade' are often under 24 in. (60 cm) in height.

Propagation and Culture: Seeds may be sown outdoors as early in the spring as the soil can be prepared or started indoors 6 to 8 weeks before the last frost is due. Seeds germinate in 2 to 3 weeks at 68 to 86°F (20 to 30°C). Plants should be spaced 12 to 15 in. (30 to 38 cm) apart in the garden. They will thrive in ordinary garden soil in either full sun or partial shade.

Use: Gloriosa Daisies make an interesting addition to flower beds and borders. They also make excellent long-lasting cut flowers, and the cutting of blooms encourages the production of more blossoms.

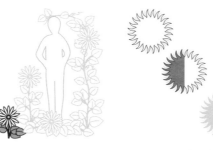

ANNUALS FOR THE PLAINS AND PRAIRIES

Salpiglossis sinuata
Salpiglossis, Painted Tongue

History: Painted Tongues are close relatives of the Petunia and originated in Chile. The name is derived from *salpinx*, a "tube", and *glossa*, a "tongue", and refers to the shape of the style of the flowers. It is offered in the trade under a variety of names such as *Salpiglossis gloxiniflora*, *Salpiglossis grandiflora*, *Salpiglossis superbissima*, and *Salpiglossis variabilis*.

Description: Salpiglossis grows 16 to 36 in. (40 to 90 cm) tall with slender, wiry stems topped with trumpet-shaped flowers 2 to 2.5 in. (5 to 6 cm) across. The blossoms have a rich velvety texture and a delicate veining that enhances their appearance. They come in muted tones of gold, scarlet, rose, crimson, mahogany, and blue. Some of the newer cultivars are dwarfs (12 in. (30 cm)) and are compact, giving the appearance of being more floriferous.

Propagation and Culture: Like Petunia, Salpiglossis grows slowly in the early seedling stages so should be started indoors at least 8 weeks before the last frost is due or young plants purchased for bedding out. Seeds germinate, however, in only 1 to 2 weeks at 68 to 86°F (20 to 30°C). Plants should be set out in the garden after all danger of frost has passed at a spacing of 12 in. (30 cm). The taller growing cultivars in particular should be given some support such as wire hoops or pieces of brush. Painted Tongues require a fertile soil, protection from wind, and full sun.

Use: Salpiglossis is useful as background material in borders or as a filler among perennial flowers in the perennial border. The plants make excellent cut flowers as well, although their sticky leaf and stem surfaces tend to trap small insects and bits of debris.

Salpiglossis sinuata

Brendan Casement

Salpiglossis sinuata

Ed Toop

Salpiglossis sinuata

University of Alberta Plant Science Collection

Salvia farinacea 'Catima'

Salvia farinacea

Salvia farinacea
Mealycup Sage

History: Mealycup Sage is native to Texas and, like all Salvias, is a member of the Mint family, *Lamiaceae (Labiatae).* It is a tender perennial but flowers from seed the first season.

Description: Each lavender flower, about 1 in. (2 cm) in diameter, is held on a calyx or leafy cup under the petals that looks as if it has been dusted with flour, and hence the common name, Mealycup. The flower stems arise from mounds of silvery foliage reaching heights of about 30 in. (75 cm).

Propagation and Culture: Mealycup Sage seeds should be sown indoors 8 to 10 weeks before the last frost is due and plants set out in the garden when all danger of frost is past. Seed germinates best at a temperature of 65 to 68°F (18 to 20°C), and may respond to light, but seedling development is best at a night temperature of 53 to 55°F (12 to 13°C). Plants should be spaced 12 in. (30 cm) apart in the garden. All Salvias will thrive in fertile, well-drained soil and full sun or very light shade.

Use: Mealycup Sage is attractive in flower beds or in foundation plantings as accent plants. Some of its cultivars are excellent in mass plantings or as cut flowers.

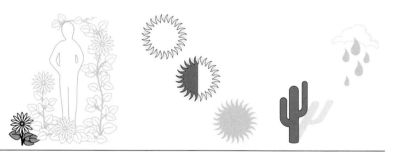

Salvia splendens
Scarlet Sage, Salvia

History: *Salvia splendens* is the best known of the sages and is commonly referred to as Salvia. It is sometimes called St. John's Fire and is available in a wide range of heights from 8 in. (20 cm) (dwarf) to 30 in. (75 cm). This species of Sage is native to Brazil. A similar species, *Salvia coccinea,* native to parts of the U.S., including Texas, produces scarlet blooms on black stems. Much of what is offered in the trade under this name could very well be a strain of *Salvia splendens.*

Description: The flowers of Scarlet Sage are firm, dense tubes of brilliant scarlet with equally vivid scarlet bracts in terminal spikes. The individual flowers themselves are often 1 in. (2.5 cm) long. Some of the strains of "scarlet" sage are in other colors including pink, purple, and white.

Propagation and Culture: Salvia seeds should be sown indoors 4 to 6 weeks before the last frost is due and plants set

Salvia splendens

out in the garden when all danger of frost is past. Seed germinates best at a temperature of 65 to 68°F (18 to 20°C), but seedling development is best at a night temperature of 53 to 55°F (12 to 13°C). Plants should be spaced 12 in. (30 cm) apart in the garden. All Salvias will thrive in fertile, well-drained soil and full sun or very light shade.

Use: Like the other Salvias, Scarlet Sage makes a handsome addition to flower beds or as accent plants in a foundation planting of shrubs. The vivid red of the "scarlet" cultivars can be overpowering when mixed with other colors, so is better combined with white flowers or massed for brilliant splashes of color. As cut flowers, their color fades rapidly.

Salvia splendens 'Empire Series'

Salvia viridis (S. horminum)
Clary Sage

History: Clary Sage is native to southern Europe and is a true annual species.

Description: Clary Sage grows about 20 to 24 in. (50 to 60 cm) tall and produces prominent blue, pink, purple, or white bracts beneath the less conspicuous small tubular flowers (1 in. (2 cm) long). The flowers appear in spike-shaped clusters at the tops of the stems.

Propagation and Culture: Clary Sage seeds should be sown indoors 4 to 6 weeks before the last frost is due and plants set out in the garden when all danger of frost is past. Seed germinates best at a temperature of 65 to 68°F (18 to 20°C) and may respond to light, but seedling development is best at a night temperature of 53 to 55°F (12 to 13°C). Plants should be spaced 12 in. (30 cm) apart in the garden. All Salvias will thrive in fertile, well-drained soil and full sun or very light shade.

Use: In addition to their use in flower beds and borders, Clary Sage flower stalks make useful cut flowers, both fresh or dried for winter bouquets. For drying, the stems should be cut when the blooms are at their peak and hung upside down in a cool, dry, shady place.

Salvia viridis

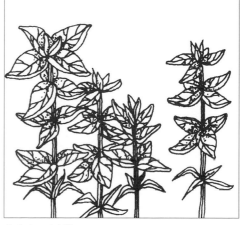

Salvia viridis

Sanvitalia procumbens
Creeping Zinnia

Sanvitalia procumbens 'Gold Braid'

Sanvitalia procumbens 'Lollipop'

Ed Toop

Brian Porter

History: This hardy annual grows wild in Mexico and is a member of the Daisy family, *Asteraceae (Compositae)*.

Description: This Zinnia-like plant bears small (1 in. (2.5 cm) diameter) flower heads with purple centers and yellow ray florets. They may be double or single. The plants, which rarely exceed 6 in. (15 cm) in height, have stems that tend to trail along the ground.

Propagation and Culture: Creeping Zinnias do not transplant well so are best seeded in the spring where they are to bloom as soon as the soil is dry and warm enough to work. They may be started indoors 3 weeks before the last frost is due and seeded into 3-in. (8-cm) peat pots or "cell paks" to minimize transplant shock when transferred to the garden. Seeds germinate in 1 to 2 weeks at 68°F (20°C) and may respond to light. Plants should be spaced 5 to 6 in. (12 to 15 cm) apart. They require a light, well-drained soil and plenty of sunshine for maximum performance.

Use: Creeping Zinnias are especially suited for edgings and filling in empty spots in the rock garden during the summer. They make good ground covers as well, especially in dry, exposed areas.

Scabiosa atropurpurea
Pincushion Flower, Sweet Scabious, Mourning Bride

Scabiosa atropurpurea 'Imperial Giants'

Brian Porter

History: Pincushion Flower is native to southern Europe and is a member of the Teasel family, *Dipsaceae*. The name *Scabiosa* is derived from *scabies*, "itch", referring to the fact that it was once thought to be a cure for itching. It is also called Sweet Scabious because of its sweet fragrance.

Description: The huge (up to nearly 3.5 in. (8 cm) diameter) rounded flower heads of Pincushion Flower resemble pincushions with their dozens of silvery stamens sticking out like pins. Flower color ranges from near black through maroon, red, rose, coral, salmon, pink, and blue to white. It grows 12 to 30 in. (30 to 75 cm) in height.

Propagation and Culture: Pincushion Flower seeds may be sown indoors 5 or 6 weeks before the last spring frost is due. The seedlings can then be acclimatized in cold frames for a week to 10 days and then bedded out in the garden after all danger of frost is past. Seeds germinate in 2 to 3 weeks at 68 to 86°F (20 to 30°C). Plants should be spaced about 10 in. (25 cm) apart. Seed may also be sown directly in the garden after the soil is warm and chances of a frost are remote. Plants require a fertile, well-drained soil and full sunlight.

Use: Sweet Scabious is beautiful among other flowers in a border or massed alone. Their unusual color range, fragrance, and long-lasting properties make them prime candidates as cut flowers for handsome bouquets.

Scabiosa atropurpurea

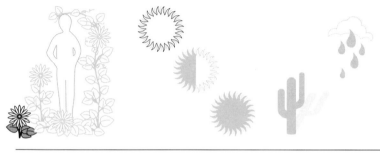

Scabiosa stellata
Papermoon, Starflower

Description: Papermoon produces globe-shaped flower clusters on long stalks. The flowers are powder blue maturing to a bronze cast in hemispherical heads up to 1.5 in. (3 cm) in diameter. The seed heads make attractive everlastings for winter bouquets. Depending on the cultivar grown, the height may range from 6 to 18 in. (15 to 45 cm).

Propagation and Culture: The propagation and culture of *Scabious stellata* is very similar to that for Pincushion Flower, *Scabiosa atropurpurea* (see page 164).

Use: Both the flower heads and the subsequent seed heads of Papermoon make attractive additions to the flower garden. The seed heads can be cut and dried for use in winter arrangements if picked as soon as the petals fall.

Scabiosa stellata

Scabiosa stellata

Scaevola aemula
'Weidner's Blue Wonder'

Brian Porter

Scaevola aemula
Australian Blue Fan-flower, Fairy Fan-flower

History: *Scaevola* is a genus in the *Goodeniaceae* (Goodenia and Fan-flower) family. The Fairy Fan-flower is native to Tasmania and parts of Australia. The word *Scaevola* is a Roman family name meaning "left-handed", alluding to the appearance of the flower.

Description: *Scaevola aemula* is a spreading to upright plant with toothed green leaves and purple, blue, or white flowers. The five-winged petals are united at the base and arranged in a one-sided manner, similar to an outstretched hand or a tiny fan. Flowers are 0.5 to 1 in. (1.3 to 2.5 cm) across. It can reach heights of 18 in. (45 cm), but most cultivars are 8 to 10 in. (20 to 25 cm) tall.

Propagation and Culture: Australian Blue Fan-flowers take 12 to 16 weeks from seed to full bloom, so are best purchased as bedding plants unless they can be started in a greenhouse. They require warm temperatures during daylight hours and night temperatures above 50°F (10°C) for optimum growth. They do well in full sun to partial shade in ordinary to dry soil. They are tolerant of drought conditions but perform best in hot temperatures with regular watering.

Use: Australian Blue Fan-flowers are excellent plants for hanging baskets as well as ground covers for hot sunny locations.

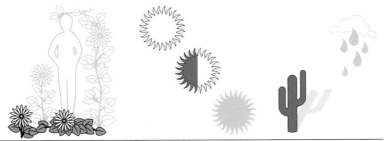

Schizanthus x *wisetonensis*
Butterfly Flower, Poor Man's Orchid, Schizanthus

History: *Schizanthus* x *wisetonensis* is a hybrid species that is intermediate between its parents, *Schizanthus pinnatus* and *Schizanthus retusus* 'Grahamii'. It is a member of the *Solanaceae* family. It has a beautifully incised corolla; hence its name *Schizanthus,* which literally means "split flower". The appearance of the incised corolla accounts for its common name of Poor Man's Orchid.

Description: Depending upon cultivars, the ultimate height for Butterfly Flower varies from 12 to 24 in. (30 to 60 cm). The flowers are about 1.5 in. (4 cm) across and are usually bi-colored in combinations of pink, crimson, violet, and purple as well as white, all heavily veined with gold.

Schizanthus x *wisetonensis*

University of Alberta Plant Science Collection

ANNUALS FOR THE PLAINS AND PRAIRIES

Propagation and Culture: Seeds may be started indoors 6 to 8 weeks before the last spring frost is expected. Seeds germinate in 1 to 2 weeks at 53°F (12°C) and are sensitive to high temperatures. Plants are put into the garden after all danger of frost has passed, spacing them about 12 in. (30 cm) apart. They do best in a moist soil in cool weather, especially cool nights, and either full sun or light shade.

Use: Butterfly Flowers are very effective in beds or borders because of their profuse flowering and surprising colors. In window boxes, planters, and hanging baskets, they trail over the edges in a colorful display. However, when grown in small containers such as hanging baskets, it is important to keep them well watered.

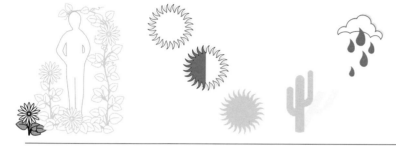

Schizanthus x *wisetonensis* 'Star Parade' (left) 'Angel Wings' (right)

Senecio cineraria (Cineraria maritima)
Dusty Miller

History: The Dusty Miller *Senecio* is native to southern Europe and a perennial in warm tropical or semi-tropical climates.

Description: *Senecio cineraria* is grown as an annual garden plant because of its handsome woolly-white, first-year foliage. The cultivars available range in height from 8 to 15 in. (20 to 38 cm) when grown as annuals. There are several other kinds of plants, also known as Dusty Miller, which are grown for their whitish foliage.

Propagation and Culture: Dusty Miller can be seeded indoors 10 to 12 weeks before the last frost is due. Seeds germinate in 2 to 3 weeks at 68°F (20°C). Plants should be set out in the garden after all danger of frost is past at a spacing of 10 to 12 in. (25 to 30 cm). They flourish in dry to average soil and full sun.

Use: Dusty Miller lends a distinctive beauty to flower beds because of its silvery foliage. It is useful in planters and window boxes as well.

Senecio cineraria

Senecio cineraria

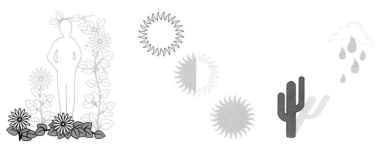

Senecio elegans

Senecio elegans (Jacobaea elegans)
Purple Groundsel, Purple Ragwort

Description: Purple Groundsel is native to South Africa and grows about 18 in. (45 cm) tall. Each stem is topped with single or double daisy-like blossoms 1.5 to 2 in. (3 to 5 cm) across. Colors include purple, mauve, crimson, rose, or white, with yellow centers.

Propagation and Culture: Purple Groundsel may be sown indoors about 8 to 10 weeks before the last spring frost is expected. Young plants should be set out in the garden after all danger of frost is past at a spacing of 6 in. (15 cm). They grow best in a light, sandy loam and full sun. Seed may be difficult to obtain commercially.

Use: Purple Groundsel provides masses of color in the garden. They are also excellent as cut flowers.

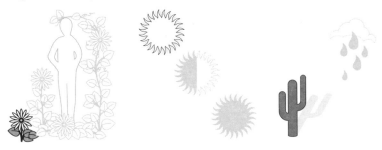

Silene armeria 'Royal Elektra'

Brian Porter

Silene armeria and *Silene pendula*
None-so-pretty, Sweet William Catchfly and Nodding Catchfly

History: The leaves of most *Silene* species have a sticky fluid on the leaves in which flies and other small insects are often entrapped; hence the name catchfly. The genus name *Silene* comes from *sialon*, "saliva", referring also to the sticky fluid on the leaves. Catchflies are members of the Pink or Carnation family, *Caryophyllaceae*.

Description: Sweet William Catchfly grows about 15 in. (38 cm) tall with rose pink flowers, each about 1 in. (2 cm) across, but grouped in globular clusters 2 to 3 in. (5 to 8 cm) across. Nodding Catchfly grows only about 6 in. (15 cm) tall with great quantities of flowers, usually 0.5 in. (1.3 cm) across, borne in drooping sprays of pink, salmon, scarlet, or white.

Propagation and Culture: Seed should be sown as early in the spring as the soil can be cultivated. Seedlings should be thinned and transplanted to a spacing of 6 to 9 in. (15 to 23 cm). Plants do best in full sun and a well-drained ordinary soil.

Use: Sweet William Catchfly and Nodding Catchfly are good additions to flower beds and borders as well as the rock garden. They are not long-lasting as cut flowers.

Silene armeria 'Royal Elektra'

Tagetes erecta; Tagetes patula and *Tagetes tenuifolia (T. signata)* Hybrids
African Marigold or Aztec Marigold; French Marigold and Dwarf Signet Marigold

History: Marigolds are among the most popular and rewarding flowers for the gardener. They are natives of Mexico and South America and members of the Daisy family, *Asteraceae (Compositae)*. The genus name *Tagetes* is said to have been derived from a mythological deity, Tages. The garden marigolds have been derived from three main species, but these have been crossed by plant breeders over the years to the extent that many cultivars in the market have characteristics common to all three.

Tagetes erecta 'Orange Lady'

Description:

African Marigolds *(Tagetes erecta)*
These are the tallest of the marigolds, growing 18 to 36 in. (45 to 90 cm) in height with globe-shaped, 3.5- to 5-in. (9- to 12-cm), double blossoms, mostly in off-white, yellow, or shades of orange. There are several flower types with some resembling carnations and others resembling chrysanthemums.

French Marigolds *(Tagetes patula)*
These are relatively low growing plants, 6 to 18 in. (15 to 45 cm) tall with 1 to 2 in. (2.5 to 5 cm) diameter single or double flowers. Flower colors include shades of yellow, orange, mahogany, red, and combinations of these colors.

Hybrids of African and French Marigolds
These cultivars display the combined colors of the two common species with 2- to 3-in. (5- to 8-cm) diameter double flowers on sturdy plants whose height and spread varies from 12 to 18 in. (30 to 45 cm).

Tagetes erecta

Dwarf Signet Marigolds *(Tagetes tenuifolia)*
This species is typified by having fern-like foliage that is much more finely divided than that of the other species and hybrids.

Tagetes patula 'Firelight'

Tagetes tenuifolia 'Lemon Gem'

The stems are topped by masses of single yellow or golden-orange flowers about 1 in. (2.5 cm) across. Plants that reach 12 in. (30 cm) or less in height are preferred and are given the group name of "pumila".

Propagation and Culture: Marigolds are very easy to grow from seed. Seeds should be sown indoors about 4 to 6 weeks before the last frost is due and plants set in the garden after all danger of frost has passed. Seed can be sown directly outdoors when the soil is warm and danger of frost is past. Seeds germinate readily in 1 week at 68 to 86°F (20 to 30°C) and sometimes respond to light. The taller kinds should be spaced about 12 to 18 in. (30 to 45 cm) apart whereas the dwarf kinds can be as close as 6 in. (15 cm) from each other. Marigolds flourish in ordinary soil in sunny locations.

Use: Marigolds in their diversity can serve every garden purpose from mass plantings and ground covers, to mixing with other annuals in beds or borders. They are attractive in planters, patio pots, or even hanging baskets. They stand up well to wind and rain and provide brilliant, long-lasting color as cut flowers. However, their foliage when crushed or bruised emits a strong odor which is unpleasant to some people. Nevertheless, it is probably this ingredient that makes marigolds virtually free of any pests. By planting marigolds in among other plants, including vegetables, they can protect these plants from infestation as well. Under certain weather conditions, they may be attacked by spider mites or leafhoppers as minor pests.

Thunbergia alata

Thunbergia alata
Black-eyed Susan Vine, Thunbergia

History: Thunbergias, or Clock Vines as they are sometimes called, are mostly tender perennial climbing vines of beauty from tropical areas of the world. Black-eyed Susan Vine comes from tropical Africa and will bloom from seed the first year. Another lesser known species, *Thunbergia gregorii*, Orange Clock Vine, is also from Africa and has somewhat larger blossoms in a glowing orange color.

Description: Black-eyed Susan Vines are low, twining climbers that seldom reach more than 40 to 60 in. (100 to 150 cm) when grown as annuals in the prairie climate. They bear attractive arrow-shaped leaves and individually borne flowers that are 1 to 2 in. (2.5 to 5 cm) in diameter. Most blooms have a black or dark purple center and five clearly defined rounded segments to the tubular corolla in either white, buff, yellow, or orange.

Propagation and Culture: Seeds should be started indoors 4 to 6 weeks before the last spring frost is expected. Germination will occur in 2 to 3 weeks at 68 to 86°F (20 to 30°C), but early seedling development is slow. Plants should be set outdoors when all danger of frost is past. Even mature plants are easily killed with the slightest frost. Since Thunbergias climb by twining, strings or netting make suitable trellises. They require fertile, moist soil and either full sun or partial shade.

Use: These vines make excellent additions to window boxes, planters, or hanging baskets because of their trailing habit. They can also be trained to climb a low trellis, wall, or fence. They make good ground covers.

Thunbergia alata

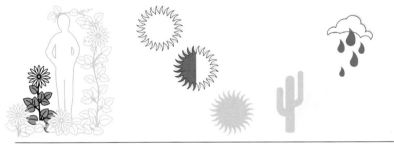

Torenia fournieri
Wishbone Flower, Torenia

History: *Torenia* commemorates the name of Olaf Toren who discovered one of the species in this genus in China. Wishbone Flower is used both as a garden annual and as a house plant. A pair of stamens in the throat of the flower are bent in the shape of a chicken's wishbone, and hence the common name, Wishbone Flower. It is a plant from Vietnam and is common in the tropics and subtropics.

Description: Most Wishbone Flowers grow about 12 in. (30 cm) tall and bear a host of trumpet-shaped, bi-colored blossoms about 1 in. (2.5 cm) in diameter. The upper lip is light violet and the lower one is dark purple. Some types have white blooms with yellow throats or yellow blooms with purple throats. The new 'Clown Mix' grows only 8 in. (20 cm) tall and has a wider color range.

Propagation and Culture: Seeds may be sown indoors about 10 to 12 weeks before the last frost is due. Seeds germinate in 2 weeks at 68 to 86°F (20 to 30°C). Many gardeners will prefer to buy plants ready for bedding-out. Plants should be spaced about 6 to 8 in. (15 to 20 cm) apart in the garden after all danger of frost has passed. They require warm, moist soil and partial shade. They will tolerate full sun in cool weather and cool night temperatures.

Torenia fournieri 'Clown Mixture'

All-America Selections

Use: These small plants are attractive in garden borders, planters, pots, and hanging baskets. They also make unusual and attractive house plants. Plants may be taken from the garden and potted for use as house plants a few weeks before the end of the summer season.

Torenia fournieri

Trachymene caerulea

Brian Porter

Trachymene caerulea

Trachymene caerulea (Didiscus caeruleus)
Blue Lace Flower

History: Blue Lace Flower is a native of Australia and a member of the Parsley or Carrot family, *Apiaceae (Umbelliferae)*. The name *Trachymene* is derived from *trachys*, "rough", and *hymen*, a "membrane", and refers to the rough seed coats.

Description: Blue Lace Flower is like a glorified version of Queen Anne's Lace *(Daucus carota carota)*. It produces tiny sky-blue flowers in sweet-scented clusters (2 to 3 in. (5 to 8 cm) in diameter) resembling umbrellas at the top of stems that are about 24 in. (60 cm) tall.

Propagation and Culture: Seeds should be sown indoors 6 to 8 weeks before the last frost is due or directly outside as early in the spring as the soil can be cultivated. Seeds germinate in 2 to 3 weeks at 68°C (20°C). Plants should be spaced about 12 in. (30 cm) apart in the garden. The placement of brush or similar support material among the half-grown plants is recommended to help them from being toppled over in the wind. They do best in light soil and full sun but do not tolerate hot weather, especially hot night temperatures.

Use: Blue Lace Flowers make interesting additions to some flower beds. They also make long-lasting cut flowers.

Tricholaena rosea (Rhynchelytrum repens)
Ruby Grass, Natal Grass

Description: This African grass is perennial but is customarily grown from seed and treated as an annual. It grows 36 to 48 in. (90 to 120 cm) tall bearing pyramidal clusters of silky spikelets that look the color of red wine but later darken to a purple color.

Propagation and Culture: Seeds should be sown outdoors at a spacing of 12 to 18 in. (30 to 45 cm) as early in the spring as the soil can be prepared . The seedlings will quickly develop into attractive clumps. Ruby Grass will grow in any garden soil in full sun but does best in a light, well-drained soil.

Use: Ruby Grass makes an attractive background for a flower border. Stems may be dried for use in winter bouquets, both upright in a vase to dry in graceful curves and hung upside down in a dry, shady place for straight stems.

Tricholaena rosea

Tropaeolum majus
Common Nasturtium, Garden Nasturtium

History: Species of *Tropaeolum* are native to the Americas from Mexico to Chile. The name is from *tropaion*, a "trophy", from the resemblance of the leaves to a buckler (shield) and the flowers to a helmet.

Description: Common Nasturtium comes in single and double flowering cultivars of both climbing vines and dwarf bushy plants. Dwarf types, which should probably be listed as *Tropaeolum minus*, seldom grow more than 12 in. (30 cm) tall whereas the climbers can climb or trail to a height or length of more than 80 in. (200 cm). The spurred flowers are generally about 2 in. (5 cm) across in a wide variety of colors: creamy white, salmon, golden yellow, orange, scarlet, cerise, mahogany, and deep red. They all have a tart fragrance, with the doubles being more scented than the singles. The bright green leaves are shaped like small shields.

Tropaeolum majus 'Whirlibird Scarlet'

Brian Porter

Tropaeolum majus

Ed Toop

Tropaeolum majus 'Whirlibird'

Brian Porter

Propagation and Culture: Seed should be sown outdoors where the plants are to be grown as soon as the danger of frost has passed, since the plants do not transplant easily. Dwarf types should be spaced 6 in. (15 cm) apart and the vine types 12 in. (30 cm) apart. Nasturtiums, including Canary-bird Vine, tend to be attacked by aphids and also flax beetles late in the season, especially in areas where canola is grown. A light, dry sandy soil is preferred for growing Nasturtiums since they tend to produce an abundance of leaves which completely hide the blossoms under conditions of a well-watered, rich soil. They flower best in full sun but tolerate partial shade. They perform best when night temperatures drop below 65°F (18°C).

Use: Common Nasturtiums make excellent cut flowers. Dwarf cultivars are good as edging plants for flower beds or even vegetable gardens and trail attractively from hanging baskets and planters. The vining types will cover old stumps, rocks, trellises, or fences very attractively. The young leaves have a flavor like watercress and may be used in salads as a substitute for watercress. The young seeds may also be pickled as a substitute for capers.

Tropaeolum peregrinum

Brian Porter

Tropaeolum peregrinum
Canary-bird Flower, Canary-bird Vine, Canary Creeper

History: This species of *Tropaeolum* is native to Peru and Ecuador.

Description: Canary-bird Vine is a fast-growing annual climber with 5-lobed leaves and yellow flowers with feathery lacerated petals, about 1 to 1.5 in. (2 to 4 cm) in diameter. It reaches heights of 80 in. (200 cm) or more.

Propagation and Culture: Seeds should be sown outdoors where the plants are desired as soon as the threat of frost has passed. Plants should be spaced about 12 in. (30 cm) apart with some sort of support for the vines to grow on. They may also be allowed to trail on the ground to form a ground cover. Plants require a light, sandy loam (poor in nutrients) and sunshine for at least part of the day.

Use: These vines will quickly cover fences, trellises, stumps, or rocks with their attractive lobed foliage and scatterings of canary-like flowers.

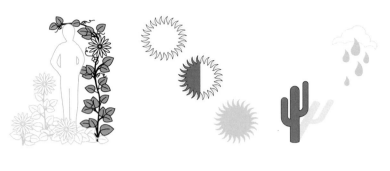

Tropaeolum peregrinum

John Beedle

Ursinia anethoides
Dill-leaf Ursinia

History: Ursinias are native to South Africa but are not very well known on this continent. The most popular kind is the annual, *Ursinia anethoides*. It is a member of the Daisy family, *Asteraceae*. The name *Ursinia* commemorates John Ursinus, a botanist.

Description: Dill-leaf Ursinia reaches a height of 10 to 18 in. (25 to 45 cm) and bears brilliant daisy-like blooms, 2 to 3 in. (5 to 8 cm) across, in orange or yellow with a center ring of purple. Flowers tend to close at night or on cloudy days. They have richly scented, feathery foliage that may be totally hidden with the profusion of brilliant flowers. The stems are thin but wiry.

Propagation and Culture: Seed should be sown indoors 4 to 6 weeks before the last frost is expected and the plants put outdoors when all danger of frost is past. They should be spaced 6 to 9 in. (15 to 23 cm) apart in the garden. They require full sun and a light, well-drained, rather low-fertility soil. Seed is not readily available from commercial sources.

Use: Ursinias are very colorful additions to the flower garden and make splendid cut flowers.

Ursinia anethoides

Gail Rankin

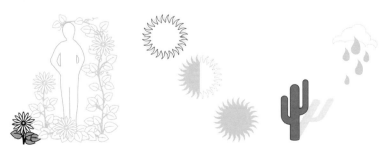

Ursinia anethoides

Brendan Casement

Venidium fastuosum

Venidium fastuosum

Venidium fastuosum
Cape Daisy, Monarch-of-the-veldt

History: This annual from South Africa belongs to the Daisy family, *Asteraceae (Compositae)*.

Description: Cape Daisy reaches a height of 24 in. (60 cm) or more with silver-white, feather-like, hairy leaves that shimmer as if covered with finely spun cobwebs. Its buds open into 4- to 5-in. (10- to 13-cm), daisy-like flower heads of brilliant orange with an inner zone of purplish black and a center of shiny black. Pale colored cultivars are also available in ivory, cream, and shades of lemon yellow as well as white.

Propagation and Culture: Seedlings should be started indoors 6 to 8 weeks before the last frost is expected and plants set outdoors after all danger of frost has passed. Seeds take 4 to 6 weeks to germinate (68 to 86°F (20 to 30°C)). Plants should be spaced about 12 in. (30 cm) apart in the garden. This annual requires well-drained, light, sandy loam and plenty of sunshine.

Use: Cape Daisy is a colorful addition to any flower bed and an excellent cut flower, although like many flowers from South Africa, the blossoms tend to close at night and on cloudy days.

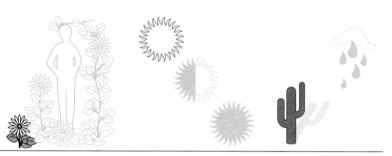

Verbena x *hybrida* 'Ideal Florist'

Verbena x *hybrida (V. x hortensis);Verbena peruviana (V. chamaedriyolia),* and *Verbena rigida (V. venosa)*
Verbena or Vervain; Scarlet Verbena or Creeping Verbena, and Brazilian Verbena or Tall Verbena

History: *Verbena* includes a group of about 80 hardy and tender annual or perennial herbs or shrubs, mostly native to the Americas.

Description: The common Verbena or Vervain, usually listed as *Verbena* x *hybrida,* is of hybrid origin and perennial in habit but treated as an annual. There are both upright growing strains forming mounds about 12 in. (30 cm) in height as well as carpeting cultivars that creep along the ground. The flowers are fragrant and bloom in flat clusters 2 to 3 in. (5 to 8 cm) across and range in color from white to pink, apricot-salmon, red, blue, lavender, and purple. Many of the colored flowers have contrasting white centers. Scarlet Verbena *(Verbena peruviana)* is a creeper with intensely brilliant scarlet flowers. In effect, it is a smaller edition of the regular Verbena. Tall Verbena *(Verbena rigida)* from southern Brazil, is an extremely handsome plant growing 18 to 24 in. (45 to 60 cm) tall with clusters of bright reddish-violet flowers about 2 in. (5 cm) in diameter. Leaves are dark green and blooms are fragrant.

Propagation and Culture: Seed may be sown indoors 10 to 12 weeks before the last frost is due or plants may be purchased ready for bedding-out. Seeds germinate in 3 to 4 weeks at 68 to 86°F (20 to 30°C) and are sometimes promoted by light. The plants should be put into the garden after all danger of frost has passed at a spacing of 12 in. (30 cm). They require full sun and a fertile soil.

Use: Common Verbenas produce masses of color and are therefore useful as ground covers, for mass plantings to produce splashes of color, for edging, or for any location where a low carpet of color is needed. They are attractive additions to the rock garden or window boxes. The Scarlet Verbena, an excellent creeping rock garden plant, provides carpets of scarlet color in flower borders. The tall-growing Brazilian Verbena is effective for massing in beds or borders. It also makes a good cut flower.

Verbena x *hybrida*

Verbena 'Imagination'

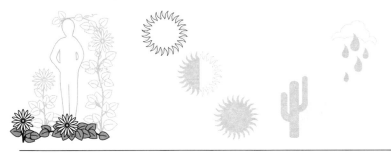

Verbesina encelioides
Butter Daisy, Golden Crownbeard

History: This daisy flower is native to the western U.S. from Montana to Mexico and belongs to the Daisy family, *Asteraceae (Compositae)*.

Description: Butter Daisy ranges in height from 24 in. (60 cm) to more than 36 in. (90 cm) and bears golden flower heads that are about 2 in. (5 cm) in diameter.

Propagation and Culture: Seeds should be sown outdoors where the plants are to grow as early in the spring as the soil can be cultivated. The seedlings should be thinned to a spacing of about 18 in. (45 cm). Butter Daisies do not transplant well. They thrive in well-drained, ordinary soil in a sunny location. Seed is not commonly available.

Verbesina encelioides

Use: These large, flamboyant daisies are best planted towards the back of a border, in a wild flower garden or even as a low hedge. They make fine cut flowers also.

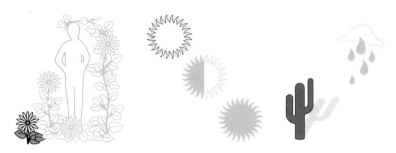

Vinca major 'Variegata'

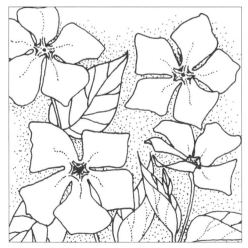

Vinca major

Vinca major 'Variegata'
Variegated Periwinkle

Description: Periwinkle, native to Europe, is a tender perennial evergreen vine treated as an annual because it will flower the first year from seed. The variegated variety makes a good annual trailing vine because of its attractive leaves and 1- to 2-in. (2.5- to 5-cm), lavender-blue flowers with round-edged petals. The trailing stems will root if they come in contact with the soil. The leaves are dark green marked with white and about 2 in. (5 cm) long and 1 in. (2.5 cm) wide.

Propagation and Culture: Variegated Periwinkles are propagated from cuttings rather than from seeds. Therefore, most gardeners will purchase plants at a garden center. Plants are set out in the garden after all danger of frost has passed at a spacing of 8 to 10 in. (20 to 25 cm). They thrive in almost any soil and prefer some shade.

Use: Variegated Periwinkle is valued as a trailing plant for use in window boxes, patio pots, planters, and hanging baskets. In milder climates with a long growing season, it is used as a perennial ground cover.

Viola x *wittrockiana and Viola* x *williamsii*
Pansy or Heartsease and Viola or Tufted Pansy

History: Pansies are hybrids originally created in Europe from *Viola lutea, Viola altaica,* and the small-flowered *Viola tricolor* (Johnny-jump-up) which is biennial in nature but a prolific self-seeder. *Viola* x *williamsii,* a hybrid species descended from *Viola cornuta* and others, has smaller, more violet-like blooms and is usually referred to as Viola or Tufted Pansy.

Description: The wonderful diversity of colors and markings of Pansies has made them one of the most popular of all garden flowers. They grow about 8 in. (20 cm) tall with delicately fragrant 2- to 3-in. (5- to 8-cm) wide flowers of 5 overlapping petals resembling gigantic violets. However, colors include almost black to purple, blue, dark red, rose or yellow as well as white combined in endless variations of stripes and blotches. Often the patterns resemble small smiling faces. Violas, on the other hand, grow 6 to 8 in. (15 to 20 cm) tall, and bear flowers about 1.5 in. (3.5 to 4 cm) across, each with a slender spur. They come in a variety of solid colors including blue, yellow, apricot, ruby red, and white.

Propagation and Culture: It is usual to buy started plants of Pansies and Violas but they can be started indoors about 10 to 12 weeks before the last frost is due. Seeds germinate in 2 to 3 weeks at 54 to 90°F (12 to 32°C). Seeds of some cultivars may need light. The plants will tolerate frost if "hardened off" beforehand. They flourish in cool weather in moist, fertile soil in either full sun or partial shade.

Use: Pansies and Violas provide brilliant masses of color in borders and edgings. They are great for window boxes, pots, planters, and as small cut flowers. Keeping faded flowers picked off encourages new flower growth.

Viola x *wittrockiana* 'Padparadja'

All-America Selections

Viola x *wittrockiana* 'Maxim Marina'

All-America Selections

Viola x *wittrockiana* 'Universal Mix'

Brian Porter

Xanthisma texana

Xanthisma texana
Sleepy Daisy, Star-of-Texas

History: This is a little known annual that is native to the state of Texas.

Description: Sleepy Daisy grows 18 to 30 in. (45 to 75 cm) tall and bears 2- to 3-in. (5- to 8-cm) diameter citron-yellow flower heads with daisy-like ray florets fanning out from the center in a star-like fashion. Flowers tend to close at night.

Propagation and Culture: Seed should be sown outdoors in spring as early as the soil can be prepared for planting. Seedlings should be thinned to a spacing of 6 in. (15 cm). Some sort of support is recommended to keep the flower stalks upright. Plants do well in poor dry soil under a hot sun.

Use: This plant will brighten dry, open spaces or wild gardens. The blooms make excellent cut flowers.

Xeranthemum annuum

Gabe Botar

Xeranthemum annuum
Common Immortelle

History: Common Immortelle is a native of the meadows of the Mediterranean region. It is a member of the Daisy family, *Asteraceae (Compositae)*. The name *Xeranthemum* is from the Greek *xeros*, "dry", and *anthos*, "flower".

Description: The plants reach a height of 24 to 36 in. (60 to 90 cm) producing 1.5-in. (3.5- to 4-cm) diameter single and double flower heads. The "petals" are of a papery nature ranging in color from shades of rose and pink to purple as well as white. It is an attractive strawflower or everlasting and as such is ideal for cutting and drying.

Propagation and Culture: Since this plant is difficult to transplant, it is best seeded outdoors after all danger of frost is past. However, because of our short growing season it could be started indoors in individual small peat pots 4 to 6 weeks before the last frost is due. Plants should be put into the garden after all danger of frost has passed at a spacing of 12 in. (30 cm). Twiggy brush or similar support is suggested to be placed among the half-grown plants to keep them upright. Plants do best in a sandy garden soil and full sunlight.

Use: Common Immortelle is an eye-catching addition to the garden border but is usually grown for its excellence as a cut flower, both fresh and dried. For winter bouquets the blossoms should be cut when they are fully opened and hung upside down in bunches in a cool, airy, shaded location until fully dried.

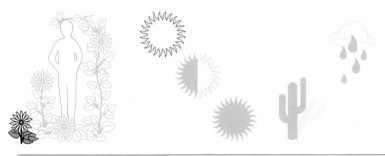

Xeranthemum annuum

Zea mays japonica
Rainbow Corn, Striped Maize

History: *Zea mays,* sweet corn, has never been found in its original wild state. Its origin is a matter of controversy. One theory is that it originated as a natural hybrid between grasses in Mexico; another theory claims that it is a species of plant kept in cultivation by the aboriginals of Mexico after its wild progenitors became extinct.

Description: Rainbow Corn is a novelty annual ornamental corn which grows about 60 to 70 in. (150 to 180 cm) tall with leaves that are striped green, pink, yellow, and white. It produces ears that are about 6 to 8 in. (15 to 20 cm) long but not edible by humans.

Propagation and Culture: Seeds should be sown where the plants are to develop in the garden after all danger of frost is past. Seeds should be spaced so that plants stand 8 to 12 in. (20 to 30 cm) apart. Rainbow Corn requires a fertile soil and full sun for maximum development. Seed is not commonly available.

Use: With its colorful and variegated foliage, Rainbow Corn can be used as a garden ornament (focal point) or as an interesting screen or hedge.

Zea mays japonica

Zinnia elegans 'Fantastic Light Pink'

Zinnia elegans 'Short Stuff'

Zinnia elegans 'Lilliput'

Zinnia elegans
Zinnia, Youth-and-Old-Age

History: *Zinnia* represents a group of Mexican annuals which belong to the Daisy family, *Asteraceae (Compositae).* Only the one species, *Zinnia elegans,* of which there are numerous strains and cultivars, is widely grown and has been given the common name of Youth-and-Old-Age.

Description: Zinnias come in many heights, flower forms, and sizes. Some are less than 12 in. (30 cm) tall with round flower heads less than 1 in. (2.5 cm) in diameter whereas others are up to 36 in. (90 cm) tall and bear 7 in. (18 cm) blossoms on strong, wiry stems. Zinnia "petals" are rather harsh and coarse to the touch, but their color range is fantastic including apricot, rose, cream, white, violet, pale yellow, and yellowish-green as well as the older familiar bright reds and oranges. There are also multicolored and striped cultivars as well.

Propagation and Culture: Zinnia seed may be germinated indoors 4 to 6 weeks before the last frost is expected and the plants put into the garden after all danger of frost has passed. Seeds germinate in 1 week at 68 to 86°F (20 to 30°C) and may respond to light. Zinnias grow best in hot weather and tend to go dormant or even deteriorate when temperatures remain cool. They should be planted at a spacing of 6 to 12 in. (15 to 30 cm) depending on the ultimate size of the cultivar being grown. In addition to warm weather, any good garden soil and full sun are all that Zinnias require .

Use: Zinnias are a good all-purpose garden annual for a hot summer season. They are decorative in beds, borders, or as an edging plant (dwarf types). They also make good cut flowers, both fresh and dried.

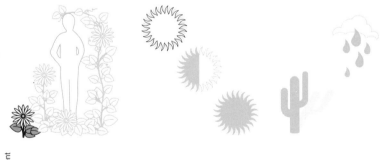

Reference
charts

Column groups: **CULTURE** spans Soil (soil type, Evenly Moist, Dry), Light (Full Sun, Partial Shade, Shade), and Propagation (Seed Start Date: Indoors – weeks before frost, Outdoors – early spring, Outdoors – after last frost; Tubers, Bulbs, Corms, Cuttings). **FLOWER** spans Color (Inconspicuous, White (Night Garden), Yellow, Orange, Red, Pink, Purple, Blue) and Cut (Fresh, Dried).

Botanical Name	Soil (O=ordinary; R=rich; S=sandy)	Evenly Moist	Dry	Full Sun	Partial Shade	Shade	Indoors – weeks before frost	Outdoors – early spring	Outdoors – after last frost	Tubers, Bulbs, Corms, Cuttings	Inconspicuous	White (Night Garden)	Yellow	Orange	Red	Pink	Purple	Blue	Fresh	Dried
Ageratum houstonianum	O			•			6-8					•				•		•	•	
Agrostis nebulosa	O			•				•				•							•	•
Alcea rosea (Althaea rosea)	O			•			6-8					•	•		•	•				
Amaranthus Group																				
Amaranthus caudatus	O	•		•			6		•						•		•			
Amaranthus hybridus var. erythrostachys (A. hypochondriacus)	O	•		•			6		•						•					
Amaranthus tricolor (A. melancholicus)	O	•		•			6		•		•									
Ammi majus	O			•			4-6	•				•							•	•
Ammobium alatum	S		•	•			6	•				•								•
Anagallis Group																				
Anagallis arvensis	S		•	•			6	•				•		•	•			•		
Anagallis monelli subsp. linifolia (A. linifolia, A. grandiflora)	S		•	•			6	•										•		
Anchusa capensis	R	•			•		6-8	•				•						•		
Antirrhinum majus	R			•			6-8					•	•	•	•	•			•	
Arctotis stoechadifolia (A. grandis)	S		•	•			6-8	•				•	•	•	•	•	•		•	
Argemone grandiflora and A. mexicana	S		•	•			6	•				•	•							
Asarina spp. (Maurandya spp.)	O			•	•		6-8					•	•			•	•	•		
Asclepias curassavica	R	•		•			6-8						•	•						•
Asperula orientalis (A.azurea setosa)	O	•			•	•		•									•	•	•	
Atriplex hortensis (A. hortensis astrosanguinea)	O	•		•			4-6	•							•		•			
Begonia Group																				
Begonia x semperflorens – cultorum and other hybrid cultivars	R	•		•	•	•	16-24			•		•				•	•			
Begonia x tuberhybrida	R	•			•	•	16-24			•		•	•	•	•	•				
Brachycome iberidifolia	R	•		•			4-6	•								•	•	•	•	
Brassica oleracea acephala and Brassica oleracea capitata	O			•			4-6	•											•	

	LANDSCAPE USE																					FAULTY HABITS			
Mat-like: below 6 in. (15 cm)	Edging: 6-9 in. (15-24 cm)	Foreground: 9-20 in. (24-50 cm)	Middle ground: 20-36 in. (50-90 cm)	Background: 36-48 in. (90-120 cm)	Middle background: 48-72 in. (120-180 cm)	Tall background: 72+ in. (180+ cm)	Spreading	Upright	Borders or Mass Plantings	Planters	Hanging Baskets	Groundcover/Understory	Hedges or Screens (climbers)	Rockery	Requires Sheltered Location	Foliage Prominent	Foliage or Flowers Fragrant	Prominent Seed Pods/Fruit	Native Plant (or Garden Escape)	Flowers Close at Night or on Cloudy Days	Aggressive or Weedy	Disease/Insect Susceptible	Poisonous	Page Number	Common Name
•	•	•					•		•	•		•												43	Ageratum, Flossflower
		•					•	•																44	Cloud Grass
				•			•	•				•												44	Annual Hollyhock
			•				•	•				•												45	Amaranth, Love-lies-bleeding, Tassle Flower
		•	•				•	•				•			•									46	Amaranth, Prince's Feather
	•	•					•	•							•									46	Amaranth, Joseph's Coat, Molten Fire, Summer Poinsettia
		•					•	•																47	Bishop's Flower, False Queen Anne's Lace
		•					•	•																48	Winged Everlasting
	•						•		•	•	•			•					•					48	Scarlet or Common Pimpernel, Shepherd's Clock
	•	•					•		•	•	•			•					•					49	Flaxleaf Pimpernel
		•							•			•												50	Summer Forget-me-not, Cape Forget-me-not, Alkanet, Bugloss
	•	•	•	•			•	•	•					•										50	Snapdragon
		•						•	•											•				52	Blue-eyed African Daisy, Arctotis
		•						•																52	Argemony, Prickly Poppy
			•	•	•						•	•												53	Chickabiddy
			•	•				•							•			•						54	Bloodflower, Bloodflower Milkweed
	•	•					•		•			•					•							54	Annual Woodruff
			•				•					•			•				•					55	Garden Atriplex, Orach, Sea Purslane
	•						•		•	•	•	•		•	•									56	Fibrous Begonia, Bedding Begonia, Wax Begonia
•	•						•		•	•	•	•			•									36/57	Hybrid Tuberous Begonia
	•	•					•		•	•							•							58	Swan River Daisy
		•					•	•							•									58	Ornamental Kale and Ornamental Cabbage

Botanical Name	Soil (O=ordinary; R=rich; S=sandy)	Evenly Moist	Dry	Full Sun	Partial Shade	Shade	Indoors – weeks before frost (Seed Start Date)	Outdoors – early spring	Outdoors – after last frost	Tubers, Bulbs, Corms, Cuttings	Inconspicuous	White (Night Garden)	Yellow	Orange	Red	Pink	Purple	Blue	Fresh	Dried
Briza Group																				
Briza maxima (B. major)	O		•	•				•												
Briza minor (B. gracilis, B. minima)	O		•	•				•												
Browallia speciosa and *Browallia viscosa*	O			•	•		6-8		•			•						•		
Calendula officinalis	R			•	•			•				•	•	•					•	
Callistephus chinensis	R			•			5-6					•	•			•	•	•	•		
Campanula Group																				
Campanula macrostyla	O			•				•				•				•	•			
Campanula medium (C. grandiflora)	R	•		•			8-10					•				•	•	•	•	
Canna Group																				
Canna x *generalis*	R	•		•					•				•	•	•	•				
Canna x *orchiodes*	R	•		•					•			•	•	•	•					
Cardiospermum halicacabum	O	•		•			6				•	•								
Carthamus tinctorius	O		•	•			6-8	•				•	•	•	•					
Catananche caerulea	O		•	•			6-8	•				•						•		•
Catharanthus roseus (Vinca rosea)	O	•		•	•							•				•				
Celosia cristata	O	•		•			4	•				•	•	•	•		•		•	•
Centaurea Group																				
Centaurea americana	O		•	•				•				•				•	•	•		
Centaurea cyanus	O		•	•			4	•				•			•	•	•	•		
Centaurea gymnocarpa and *Centaurea cineraria (C. candidissima)*	O		•	•			6-8													
Centaurea moschata (C. suaveolens, C. odorata, C. amberboii)	O		•	•				•				•	•		•	•		•		
Cerinthe aspera	O			•	•		8	•					•							
Charieis heterophylla	S		•	•			4-6	•									•	•		
Cheiranthus cheiri	O			•	•		8+						•	•	•		•			

LANDSCAPE USE / FAULTY HABITS

Mat-like: below 6 in. (15 cm)	Edging: 6-9 in. (15-24 cm)	Foreground: 9-20 in. (24-50 cm)	Middle ground: 20-36 in. (50-90 cm)	Background: 36-48 in. (90-120 cm)	Middle background: 48-72 in. (120-180 cm)	Tall background: 72+ in. (180+ cm)	Spreading	Upright	Borders or Mass Plantings	Planters	Hanging Baskets	Groundcover/Understory	Hedges or Screens (climbers)	Rockery	Requires Sheltered Location	Foliage Prominent	Foliage or Flowers Fragrant	Prominent Seed Pods/Fruit	Native Plant (or Garden Escape)	Flowers Close at Night or on Cloudy Days	Aggressive or Weedy	Disease/Insect Susceptible	Poisonous	Page Number	Common Name
		●					●	●	●									●						59	Large or Big Quaking Grass
	●						●		●									●						59	Lesser or Little Quaking Grass
	●								●	●	●													60	Browallia, Bush Violet
	●								●	●	●											●		61	Pot Marigold, Calendula
●	●	●							●	●	●											●		62	Annual Aster, China Aster
	●								●	●														63	Anatolian Bellflower
	●	●							●	●														63	Canterbury Bells
				●	●				●	●					●	●								37	Common Garden Canna
				●	●				●	●					●	●								37	Orchid-flowered Canna
					●								●					●						64	Balloon Vine, Heartseed, Love-in-a-puff
		●					●																	65	Safflower, Saffron Thistle
		●							●	●														65	Cupid's Dart, Blue Cupidone, Blue Succory
	●								●	●	●													66	Madagascar Periwinkle
●	●	●							●	●														67	Cockscomb, Woolflower
			●						●	●														68	Basket Flower
	●	●							●	●														68	Cornflower, Bachelor's Button
●	●	●							●	●						●								69	Dusty Miller
		●							●	●	●								●					70	Sweet Sultan
		●							●	●	●													70	Honeywort
●							●		●	●	●	●							●					71	Charieis
●	●						●		●	●	●	●							●					72	English Wallflower

CULTURE / **FLOWER**

Soil key: O = ordinary; R = rich; S = sandy

Botanical Name	Soil	Evenly Moist	Dry	Full Sun	Partial Shade	Shade	Indoors – weeks before frost	Outdoors – early spring	Outdoors – after last frost	Tubers, Bulbs, Corms, Cuttings	Inconspicuous	White (Night Garden)	Yellow	Orange	Red	Pink	Purple	Blue	Fresh	Dried
Chrysanthemum Group																				
Chrysanthemum carinatum, C. coronarium, and C. segetum Hybrids	O			•	•			•				•	•	•	•	•	•		•	
Chrysanthemum multicaule and Chrysanthemum paludosum	O			•	•		6-8	•				•	•							
Chrysanthemum parthenium (Matricaria capensis, Pyrethrum parthenium)	O	•		•	•		6-8	•				•	•						•	
Chrysanthemum ptarmiciflorum (Cineraria candicans)	O	•		•			6-8					•								
Cladanthus arabicus (C. proliferus, Anthemis arabica)	O	•		•			12-15						•							
Clarkia Group																				
Clarkia amoena (Godetia amoena)	S	•		•	•			•				•			•	•	•		•	
Clarkia unguiculata (C. elegans) and Clarkia pulchella	S	•		•	•			•				•		•	•	•	•		•	
Cleome hasslerana (C. spinosa, C. pungens) and Cleome lutea	O	•		•	•		4-6					•	•			•	•			
Cobaea scandens	R			•			6-8					•					•			
Coix lacryma-jobi	O	•		•			4-5		•		•									
Coleus x hybridus (Hybrids of C. blumei and C. pumilus)	O			•	•		10				•									
Collinsia heterophylla (C. bicolor)	O	•			•		3-4	•				•				•	•		•	
Consolida ambigua (Delphinium ajacis), C. regalis (D. consolida), & C. orientalis Hybrids	R	•		•	•			•				•				•	•	•	•	
Convolvulus tricolor	O	•		•			5-6	•				•			•	•	•	•		
Coreopsis basalis (C. drummondii) and Coreopsis tinctoria (C. bicolor)	O			•				•					•	•	•				•	
Cosmos bipinnatus and Cosmos sulphureus	O			•	•		5-6	•				•	•	•	•				•	
Craspedia spp. Hybrids	O	•		•			5-6		•				•						•	•
Crepis rubra (Barkhausia rubra)	O	•		•				•								•				
Cucurbita pepo ovifera and related species	O			•			2-3		•				•							
Cymbalaria muralis	O	•		•	•			•				•					•	•		
Cynoglossum amabile	O			•	•			•				•				•		•	•	
Dahlia coccinea and Dahlia pinnata Hybrids	R	•		•			6-8			•		•	•	•	•	•	•		•	
Datura metel and Datura inoxia	R	•		•			8-12					•	•			•	•			
Daucus carota carota	O			•			4-6	•				•								

Table: LANDSCAPE USE / FAULTY HABITS

Height Range							Form		Limitations and/or Special Adaptations							Special Features					Faulty Habits			Page Number	Common Name
Mat-like: below 6 in. (15 cm)	Edging: 6-9 in. (15-24 cm)	Foreground: 9-20 in. (24-50 cm)	Middle ground: 20-36 in. (50-90 cm)	Background: 36-48 in. (90-120 cm)	Middle background: 48-72 in. (120-180 cm)	Tall background: 72+ in. (180+ cm)	Spreading	Upright	Borders or Mass Plantings	Planters	Hanging Baskets	Groundcover/Understory	Hedges or Screens (climbers)	Rockery	Requires Sheltered Location	Foliage Prominent	Foliage or Flowers Fragrant	Prominent Seed Pods/Fruit	Native Plant (or Garden Escape)	Flowers Close at Night or on Cloudy Days	Aggressive or Weedy	Disease/Insect Susceptible	Poisonous	Page Number	Common Name
		●					●	●	●															73	Annual Chrysanthemums
	●						●	●	●	●		●		●					●					73	Annual Yellow or Butter Daisy, and Annual White Daisy
	●	●					●	●	●			●				●	●							74	Feverfew, Matricaria
		●					●	●								●								75	Silver Lace Dusty Miller
		●					●	●									●							76	Palm Springs Daisy, Cladanthus
		●					●	●	●															76	Godetia, Farewell-to-spring, Satin Flower
	●	●					●	●	●															77	Clarkia and Rocky Mountain Garland
				●			●	●	●			●					●							78	Cleome, Spider Flower and Yellow Spider Flower
						●							●											79	Cup-and-saucer Vine, Cathedral Bells, Mexican Ivy
		●	●				●	●										●						79	Job's Tears
	●	●	●				●	●	●							●								80	Coleus, Flame Nettle, Painted Leaves
		●	●				●	●						●										81	Collinsia, Chinese Houses, Pagoda Collinsia, Innocence
		●		●	●		●	●																81	Larkspur, Annual Delphinium
		●					●	●	●		●	●												82	Dwarf Morning Glory
		●	●				●	●	●										●					83	Calliopsis, Coreopsis, Tickseed
			●	●			●	●				●												84	Cosmos and Yellow Cosmos
		●					●	●																85	Drumstick Flower
	●						●	●						●										85	Hawk's Beard
				●			●						●					●		●				86	Ornamental Gourds
●							●				●	●		●							●			87	Kenilworth Ivy, Mother-of-thousands, Pennywort
		●					●	●													●			87	Chinese Forget-me-not, Hound's Tongue
		●	●	●			●	●																38/88	Dahlias
			●	●			●	●	●								●						●	89	Trumpet Flower, Angel's Trumpet, Downy Thorn Apple
		●					●	●																90	Queen Anne's Lace, White Lace Flower

Botanical Name	CULTURE — Soil (O = ordinary; R = rich; S = sandy)	Evenly Moist	Dry	Full Sun	Partial Shade	Shade	Indoors - weeks before frost (Seed Start Date)	Outdoors - early spring	Outdoors - after last frost	Tubers, Bulbs, Corms, Cuttings	Inconspicuous	White (Night Garden)	Yellow	Orange	Red	Pink	Purple	Blue	Fresh	Dried
Dianthus Group																				
Dianthus barbatus	O	•		•			6-8	•				•			•	•	•		•	
Dianthus caryophyllus	O	•		•			20					•	•		•	•			•	
Dianthus chinensis	O	•		•			6-8					•			•	•			•	
Diascia barberae	O	•		•			6-8	•								•				
Digitalis purpurea 'Foxy Strain'	O			•	•	•	20					•	•		•	•				
Dimorphotheca sinuata Hybrids	O	•		•			4-5		•			•	•	•	•	•			•	
Dyssodia tenuiloba (Thymophylla tenuifolia)	S	•		•			10-12						•						•	
Echinocystis lobata	O		•	•			4-5	•				•								
Echium lycopsis (E. plantagineum)		•		•			6-8	•				•				•	•	•		
Emilia javanica (E. coccinea, E. flammea, and E. sagittata)	O	•		•			4-6		•				•	•	•				•	
Eschscholzia californica	O	•		•				•				•	•	•	•	•				
Euphorbia Group																				
Euphorbia heterophylla	O	•		•			6-8				•								•	
Euphorbia marginata	O	•		•				•			•								•	
Eustoma grandiflorum (E. russellianum, Lisianthus russellianus)	O	•		•			20					•			•	•	•	•	•	
Fuchsia x hybrida	R			•	•					•		•			•	•	•			
Gaillardia pulchella picta	O		•	•			4-6	•				•	•	•	•				•	
Gazania ringens (G. splendens)	S	•		•			4-6						•	•	•	•				
Gilia capitata	O	•		•			4-5		•								•	•	•	
Gladiolus x hortulanus	O			•						•		•	•	•	•	•	•		•	
Gomphrena globosa	O	•		•			6-8					•	•			•	•		•	•
Gypsophila elegans	O	•		•			2-3	•				•			•	•			•	•
Helianthus Group																				
Helianthus annuus	O	•		•	•				•				•	•						
Helianthus debilis subsp. cucumerifolius	O	•		•	•			•				•	•	•	•	•			•	

Table — Landscape Use and Faulty Habits (• = applicable)

Mat-like: below 6 in. (15 cm)	Edging: 6-9 in. (15-24 cm)	Foreground: 9-20 in. (24-50 cm)	Middle ground: 20-36 in. (50-90 cm)	Background: 36-48 in. (90-120 cm)	Middle background: 48-72 in. (120-180 cm)	Tall background: 72+ in. (180+ cm)	Spreading	Upright	Borders or Mass Plantings	Planters	Hanging Baskets	Groundcover/Understory	Hedges or Screens (climbers)	Rockery	Requires Sheltered Location	Foliage Prominent	Foliage or Flowers Fragrant	Prominent Seed Pods/Fruit	Native Plant (or Garden Escape)	Flowers Close at Night or on Cloudy Days	Aggressive or Weedy	Disease/Insect Susceptible	Poisonous	Page Number	Common Name
	•	•					•		•	•	•								•					90	Annual Sweet William
	•															•	•							91	Annual Carnation
	•						•		•	•	•					•								92	Rainbow Pink, China Pink
	•							•	•	•														92	Twinspur
			•					•	•															93	Annual Foxglove
	•							•	•	•										•				94	Cape Marigold, Star-of-the-veldt
•								•	•	•	•													95	Dahlberg Daisy, Golden Fleece
					•								•					•	•					95	Wild Cucumber, Mock Cucumber, Balsam Apple
	•							•	•	•									•					96	Viper's Bugloss
		•						•	•															97	Tassel Flower, Flora's Paintbrush
	•						•		•	•	•	•			•					•				97	California Poppy
		•						•	•	•				•	•							•	98	Annual Poinsettia, Mexican Fire Plant, Fire-on-the-mountain
	•							•	•						•			•				•	99	Snow-on-the-mountain
•	•	•						•	•														100	Prairie Gentian
•	•									•	•												100	Fuchsia, Lady's-eardrops, Ladies'-eardrops
	•							•	•	•													101	Annual Gaillardia, Annual Blanket Flower
	•						•		•	•	•	•								•			102	Gazania, Treasure Flower
	•	•						•	•														103	Blue Thimble Flower
			•	•				•	•														39	Gladiolus, Gladiola, Sword Lily
•	•							•	•	•	•												103	Globe Amaranth
	•						•		•	•									•					104	Annual Baby's Breath
					•			•					•					•	•					105	Common Sunflower
			•	•				•					•					•						105	Cucumberleaf Sunflower

Annuals culture and flower chart.

Botanical Name	Soil (O=ordinary; R=rich; S=sandy)	Evenly Moist	Dry	Full Sun	Partial Shade	Shade	Indoors – weeks before frost	Outdoors – early spring	Outdoors – after last frost	Tubers, Bulbs, Corms, Cuttings	Inconspicuous	White (Night Garden)	Yellow	Orange	Red	Pink	Purple	Blue	Fresh	Dried
Helichrysum bracteatum	O			•			4-6	•				•	•		•	•	•		•	•
Heliotropium arborescens (H. peruvianum)	R			•	•		24					•						•		
Helipterum Group																				
Helipterum manglesii (Rhodanthe manglesii)	O		•	•				•				•			•	•	•		•	•
Helipterum roseum (Acrolinium roseum)	O		•	•				•				•			•	•			•	•
Helipterum humboldtiana (H. sanfordii)	O		•	•				•						•					•	•
Hesperis matronalis	O	•		•	•			•				•					•		•	
Humulus japonicus	O	•		•	•		4-6	•		•	•									
Hunnemannia fumariifolia	O		•	•			4-6						•						•	
Iberis amara (I. coronaria)	O		•	•				•				•							•	
Iberis umbellata	O		•	•				•				•			•	•	•		•	
Impatiens Group																				
Impatiens balsamina	R/S	•			•	•	4-6	•				•			•	•	•			
Impatiens 'New Guinea Hybrid'	R/S	•			•	•			•			•		•	•	•	•			
Impatiens wallerana (I. sultanii)	R/S	•			•	•	6-8	•				•	•	•	•	•	•	•		
Ipomea Group																				
Ipomea alba (Calonyction aculeatum, I. bona-nox)	O			•			8					•								
Ipomea purpurea and *Ipomea tricolor*	O		•	•			4-6	•				•			•	•	•	•		
Kochia scoparia trichophylla	O		•	•			4-6	•		•	•									
Lagurus ovatus	O		•	•				•		•	•									
Lantana camara and *Lantana montevidensis (L. sellowiana, L. delicatissima)*	R			•					•			•	•	•	•	•				
Lathyrus odoratus	O	•		•	•			•				•			•	•	•	•	•	
Lavatera trimestris	O			•				•				•				•			•	
Layia platyglossa	O		•	•				•						•					•	
Limnanthes douglasii	O			•			4-5	•						•						
Limonium sinuatum and *Limonium bonduellii superbum*	O		•	•			8	•				•	•			•	•	•	•	•

ANNUALS FOR THE PLAINS AND PRAIRIES

Mat-like: below 6 in. (15 cm)	Edging: 6-9 in. (15-24 cm)	Foreground: 9-20 in. (24-50 cm)	Middle ground: 20-36 in. (50-90 cm)	Background: 36-48 in. (90-120 cm)	Middle background: 48-72 in. (120-180 cm)	Tall background: 72+ in. (180+ cm)	Spreading	Upright	Borders or Mass Plantings	Planters	Hanging Baskets	Groundcover/Understory	Hedges or Screens (climbers)	Rockery	Requires Sheltered Location	Foliage Prominent	Foliage or Flowers Fragrant	Prominent Seed Pods/Fruit	Native Plant (or Garden Escape)	Flowers Close at Night or on Cloudy Days	Aggressive or Weedy	Disease/Insect Susceptible	Poisonous	Page Number	Common Name
		•	•				•	•																106	Strawflower, Everlasting Flower, Immortelle
		•	•				•	•	•						•		•							107	Common Heliotrope, Cherry Pie
•							•	•						•										107	Rhodanthe, Swan River Everlasting
		•	•				•	•																107	Acrolinium, Rose Everlasting, Rose Sunray
		•					•	•								•	•							107	Humboldt's Sunray, Yellow Everlasting
			•				•	•									•		•		•			108	Dame's Rocket, Sweet Rocket, Dame's Violet
					•		•						•		•	•					•			109	Japanese Hop Vine
		•	•				•	•	•															110	Mexican Tulip Poppy
	•	•					•	•																111	Rocket Candytuft, Hyacinth-flowered Candytuft
•	•						•	•	•					•										112	Fairy, Globe, or Common Annual Candytuft
•		•					•	•																112	Garden Balsam
	•							•	•	•	•				•									113	New Guinea Impatience
•	•						•	•	•	•	•	•												114	Patience Plant, Patient Lucy, Busy Lizzie
					•								•				•							115	Moonflower
					•		•				•	•	•	•										115	Morning Glory
			•				•		•			•				•			•		•			116	Summer Cypress, Burning Bush, Fire Bush
	•						•	•											•					117	Hare's-tail Grass, Rabbit-tail Grass
		•	•				•	•	•	•							•							118	Common Lantana and Trailing Lantana
	•	•	•	•	•			•					•				•							119	Sweet Pea
			•				•						•											120	Annual Rose Mallow, Tree Mallow
		•					•	•	•															120	Tidy Tips
	•							•																121	Meadow Foam, Fried Eggs
		•					•	•																122	Statice, Sea Lavender

Botanical Name	Soil (O=ordinary; R=rich; S=sandy)	Evenly Moist	Dry	Full Sun	Partial Shade	Shade	Indoors – weeks before frost	Outdoors – early spring	Outdoors – after last frost	Tubers, Bulbs, Corms, Cuttings	Inconspicuous	White (Night Garden)	Yellow	Orange	Red	Pink	Purple	Blue	Fresh	Dried
Linanthus androsaceus subsp. *micranthus* (*Gilia micrantha, Leptosiphon hybrida*)	O		•	•			4-5	•				•	•	•	•					
Linaria maroccana	O			•				•				•	•		•	•	•	•		
Linum grandiflorum	O		•	•				•				•			•	•	•	•		•
Lobelia erinus	R	•		•	•		12					•			•		•	•		
Lobularia maritima	O			•	•		4-6	•				•				•	•			
Lupinus Group																				
Lupinus Hybrids	R			•	•			•				•	•		•	•		•		
Lupinus subcarnosus and *Lupinus texensis*	R			•	•			•									•	•		
Machaeranthera tanacetifolia (*Aster tanacetifolius*)	O			•	•		6-8	•									•			
Malcolmia maritima (*Chieranthus maritimus*)	O			•	•			•				•	•		•	•	•			
Malope trifida	S			•			4-6	•				•			•	•	•		•	
Malva sylvestris zebrina and *Malva sylvestris mauritiana*	O			•	•			•				•				•	•			
Matricaria grandiflora (*Pentzia grandiflora, Pentzia* 'Gold Button')	O		•	•					•			•	•						•	•
Matthiola Group																				
Matthiola incana annua	R	•		•	•		5-6	•				•				•	•		•	•
Matthiola longipetala bicornis (*M. bicornis*)	R	•	•	•			5-6	•		•							•			
Mentzelia lindleyi (*Bartonia aurea*)	O		•	•				•					•							
Mesembryanthemum Group																				
Dorotheanthus bellidiformis (*Mesembryanthemum criniflorum*)	S		•	•			10-12					•		•	•	•				
Aptenia cordifolia 'Variegata' (*M. cordifolium* 'Variegatum')	S		•	•			10-12									•				
Mesembryanthemum crystallinum (*Cryophytum crystallinum*)	S		•	•			10-12					•				•				
Dorotheanthus tricolor (*Mesembryanthemum tricolor*)	S		•	•			10-12					•			•	•				
Mimulus x *hybridus* 'Grandiflorus'	O	•			•	•	10-12					•			•		•			
Mirabilis jalapa	O			•			4-6	•		•		•	•		•	•	•			
Moluccella laevis	O			•			10-12	•				•							•	•
Nemesia strumosa	R	•		•			4-6					•	•		•	•	•		•	

Mat-like: below 6 in. (15 cm)	Edging: 6-9 in. (15-24 cm)	Foreground: 9-20 in. (24-50 cm)	Middle ground: 20-36 in. (50-90 cm)	Background: 36-48 in. (90-120 cm)	Middle background: 48-72 in. (120-180 cm)	Tall background: 72+ in. (180+ cm)	Spreading	Upright	Borders or Mass Plantings	Planters	Hanging Baskets	Groundcover/Understory	Hedges or Screens (climbers)	Rockery	Requires Sheltered Location	Foliage Prominent	Foliage or Flowers Fragrant	Prominent Seed Pods/Fruit	Native Plant (or Garden Escape)	Flowers Close at Night or on Cloudy Days	Aggressive or Weedy	Disease/Insect Susceptible	Poisonous	Page Number	Common Name
	•						•	•	•															123	Stardust
		•					•	•	•	•				•					•					123	Annual Linaria, Morocco Toadflax
		•					•	•																124	Flowering Flax, Scarlet Flax
•							•	•	•	•	•	•												125	Bedding or Edging Lobelia
•	•						•		•	•	•			•					•			•		126	Sweet Alyssum
		•	•				•	•														•		127	Annual Lupine
		•					•	•														•		128	Texas Bluebonnet
		•	•				•	•																128	Tahoka Daisy
	•						•	•	•	•				•										129	Virginia Stock, Virginian Stock
			•					•																130	Malope, Mallow-wort
				•				•				•							•					130	High Mallow, Cheeses
		•	•					•								•	•							131	Gold Button, Gold Pompons, Pentzia
	•	•	•				•	•									•							132	Ten-weeks Stock, Common Stock
		•							•	•	•						•							133	Evening Stock, Grecian Stock
		•					•	•	•	•	•						•							133	Bartonia, Blazing Star
•							•		•	•	•													134	Livingstone Daisy
•							•			•	•	•				•								134	Variegated Heartleaf Mesembryanthemum
•							•			•	•	•				•								134	Ice Plant
•							•		•	•	•													134	Tricolor Mesembryanthemum
	•						•	•			•													135	Monkey Flower
		•	•				•	•												•				136	Four-o'clock, Marvel-of-Peru
			•				•	•																137	Bells of Ireland, Molucca Balm, Shellflower, Irish Bells
		•					•	•	•															138	Nemesia

CULTURE (Soil · Light · Propagation) — **FLOWER** (Color · Cut)

Soil key: O = ordinary; R = rich; S = sandy

Botanical Name	Soil	Evenly Moist	Dry	Full Sun	Partial Shade	Shade	Seed Start Date — Indoors (weeks before frost)	Outdoors - early spring	Outdoors - after last frost	Tubers, Bulbs, Corms, Cuttings	Inconspicuous	White (Night Garden)	Yellow	Orange	Red	Pink	Purple	Blue	Fresh	Dried
Nemophila menziesii	S		•	•	•			•										•		
Nicotiana alata (N. affinis)	O			•	•		4-6					•	•		•	•			•	
Nierembergia hippomanica var. violacea (N. caerulea)	R	•		•			8-10					•					•			
Nigella damascena	O			•			3-5	•				•				•	•	•	•	•
Nolana paradoxa (N. grandiflora)	O		•	•			8-10		•			•					•	•		
Ocimum basilicum	S			•			8-10				•	•								
Oenothera deltoides	O			•	•		6-8					•								
Papaver Group																				
Papaver alpinum	O			•				•				•	•	•	•	•			•	
Papaver commutatum	O			•				•							•				•	
Papaver glaucum	O			•				•							•				•	
Papaver rhoeas	O			•				•				•		•	•	•			•	
Pelargonium Group																				
Pelargonium x domesticum	O			•	•		20			•		•			•	•	•			
Pelargonium x hortorum	O			•	•		20			•		•			•	•	•			
Pelargonium peltatum	O			•	•		20			•		•				•	•			
Pelargonium spp.	O			•	•		20			•		•			•	•	•			
Pennisetum setaceum (P. ruppelii)	O			•			4-6		•						•	•				•
Perilla frutescens 'Crispa' (P. frutescens var. nankinensis)	O	•	•	•			4-6	•	•			•			•	•				
Petunia x hybrida	R	•		•	•		8-12					•	•	•	•	•	•			
Phacelia campanularia	S		•	•			4-6	•										•		
Phalaris canariensis	O			•	•			•												•
Phaseolus coccineus (P. multiflorus) and Phaseolus coccineus 'Albus'	R	•		•				•				•			•					
Phlox drummondii	O			•	•		4-6	•				•	•		•	•	•		•	
Polygonum capitatum	O			•	•		4-6									•				
Portulaca grandiflora	S		•	•			4-6	•				•	•	•	•	•				

LANDSCAPE USE / FAULTY HABITS

Mat-like: below 6 in. (15 cm)	Edging: 6-9 in. (15-24 cm)	Foreground: 9-20 in. (24-50 cm)	Middle ground: 20-36 in. (50-90 cm)	Background: 36-48 in. (90-120 cm)	Middle background: 48-72 in. (120-180 cm)	Tall background: 72+ in. (180+ cm)	Spreading	Upright	Borders or Mass Plantings	Planters	Hanging Baskets	Groundcover/Understory	Hedges or Screens (climbers)	Rockery	Requires Sheltered Location	Foliage Prominent	Foliage or Flowers Fragrant	Prominent Seed Pods/Fruit	Native Plant (or Garden Escape)	Flowers Close at Night or on Cloudy Days	Aggressive or Weedy	Disease/Insect Susceptible	Poisonous	Page Number	Common Name
	•						•		•	•				•										138	Baby Blue-eyes
		•	•	•			•	•																139	Flowering Tobacco, Jasmine Tobacco
	•						•		•	•				•										140	Cupflower, Nierembergia
	•	•					•	•	•									•	•					141	Love-in-a-mist, Devil-in-a-bush, Fennel Flower, Nigella
	•						•	•	•	•				•										141	Chilean Bellflower
		•					•	•	•	•		•				•								142	Dark Opal Basil, Sweet Basil
	•						•	•	•	•				•					•					143	Desert Evening Primrose, Hairy-calyx Sundrop
	•						•	•						•					•					143	Alpine Poppy
	•						•	•																144	Flanders Poppy
		•					•	•											•				•	144	Tulip Poppy
		•					•	•											•					144	Corn Poppy and Shirley Poppy
	•							•	•	•	•				•									145	Lady Washington Geranium; Royal, Fancy, Show Geranium
	•							•	•	•	•													146	Common Bedding Geranium, Zonal Geranium
		•					•			•	•	•												147	Ivy Geranium
	•						•	•									•							147	Scented Geranium
			•						•						•									148	Fountain Grass
	•	•	•				•	•	•							•	•							149	Perilla, Beefsteak Plant
	•	•					•	•	•	•							•							150	Petunia
	•						•	•						•					•				•	152	California Bluebell
		•	•	•			•	•				•			•			•	•					153	Canary Grass
					•		•						•					•						153	Scarlet Runner Bean and White Dutch Runner Bean
	•	•					•		•	•				•										154	Annual Phlox, Drummond Phlox
•							•		•	•		•		•										155	Polygonum, Knotweed
•							•		•	•		•		•						•				156	Portulaca, Rose Moss

Botanical Name	Soil (O = ordinary; R = rich; S = sandy)	Evenly Moist	Dry	Full Sun	Partial Shade	Shade	Seed Start Date	Indoors - weeks before frost	Outdoors - early spring	Outdoors - after last frost	Tubers, Bulbs, Corms, Cuttings	Inconspicuous	White (Night Garden)	Yellow	Orange	Red	Pink	Purple	Blue	Fresh	Dried
Probiscidea louisianica (Martynia proboscidea)	R	•		•			6-8						•								
Psylliostachys suworowii (Limonium suworowii)	O		•	•			8	•									•	•		•	
Reseda odorata	R		•	•	•		3-4		•				•		•					•	
Ricinus communis	R	•		•			6-8			•											
Rudbeckia hirta	O			•	•		6-8	•						•	•	•				•	
Salpiglossis sinuata	R			•			8-10							•	•	•			•	•	
Salvia Group																					
Salvia farinacea	R		•	•	•		8-10											•		•	
Salvia splendens	R		•	•	•		4-6						•			•	•	•			
Salvia viridis (S. horminum)	R		•	•	•		4-6						•				•	•	•		•
Sanvitalia procumbens	S		•	•			3	•						•							
Scabiosa Group																					
Scabiosa atropurpurea	R			•			5-6		•				•			•	•	•	•	•	
Scabiosa stellata	R			•			5-6		•									•			•
Scaevola aemula	O		•	•	•		12-16						•					•	•		
Schizanthus x wisetonensis	O	•		•	•		6-8						•			•	•	•			
Senecio Group																					
Senecio cineraria (Cineraria maritima)	O		•	•			10-12														
Senecio elegans (Jacobaea elegans)	S		•	•			8-10						•			•		•		•	
Silene armeria and Silene pendula	O			•					•				•			•	•				
Tagetes Group																					
Tagetes erecta	O			•			4-6						•	•	•					•	
Tagetes patula	O			•			4-6							•	•	•				•	
Tagetes tenuifolia (T.signata)	O			•			4-6							•	•					•	
Thunbergia alata	R	•		•	•		4-6						•	•	•						
Torenia fournieri		◦			•		10-12						•	•				•			

Height Range							Form		Limitations and/or Special Adaptations							Special Features					Faulty Habits				
Mat-like: below 6 in. (15 cm)	Edging: 6-9 in. (15-24 cm)	Foreground: 9-20 in. (24-50 cm)	Middle ground: 20-36 in. (50-90 cm)	Background: 36-48 in. (90-120 cm)	Middle background: 48-72 in. (120-180 cm)	Tall background: 72+ in. (180+ cm)	Spreading	Upright	Borders or Mass Plantings	Planters	Hanging Baskets	Groundcover/Understory	Hedges or Screens (climbers)	Rockery	Requires Sheltered Location	Foliage Prominent	Foliage or Flowers Fragrant	Prominent Seed Pods/Fruit	Native Plant (or Garden Escape)	Flowers Close at Night or on Cloudy Days	Aggressive or Weedy	Disease/Insect Susceptible	Poisonous	Page Number	Common Name
		•					•		•							•	•							157	Unicorn Plant, Proboscis Flower, Ram's Horn
	•						•	•																158	Pink Poker Statice, Russian Statice, Rat-tail Statice
	•						•	•	•								•							158	Mignonette
					•		•					•			•								•	159	Castor Bean, Castor Oil Plant
			•				•	•											•					160	Gloriosa Daisy, Black-eyed Susan
	•	•					•	•						•										161	Salpiglossis, Painted Tongue
		•					•	•																162	Mealycup Sage
•	•	•					•	•																162	Scarlet Sage, Salvia
	•	•					•	•																163	Clary Sage
•							•	•	•					•										164	Creeping Zinnia
	•	•					•	•																164	Pincushion Flower, Sweet Scabious, Mourning Bride
	•	•					•	•										•						165	Papermoon, Starflower
	•	•					•	•			•	•												166	Australian Blue Fan-flower, Fairy Fan-flower
	•	•					•		•	•	•													166	Butterfly Flower, Poor Man's Orchid, Schizanthus
	•	•					•	•	•						•									167	Dusty Miller
		•					•	•																168	Purple Groundsel, Purple Ragwort
	•	•					•	•	•					•										168	None-so-pretty, Sweet William Catchfly and Nodding Catchfly
			•				•	•																169	African Marigold or Aztec Marigold
•	•						•	•	•	•	•													169	French Marigold
		•					•	•	•	•	•													169	Dwarf Signet Marigold
			•	•			•		•	•	•		•											170	Black-eyed Susan Vine, Thunbergia
	•	•					•	•	•	•														171	Wishbone Flower, Torenia

Botanical Name	Soil: O = ordinary; R = rich; S = sandy	Evenly Moist	Dry	Full Sun	Partial Shade	Shade	Indoors – weeks before frost (Seed Start Date)	Outdoors – early spring	Outdoors – after last frost	Tubers, Bulbs, Corms, Cuttings	Inconspicuous	White (Night Garden)	Yellow	Orange	Red	Pink	Purple	Blue	Fresh	Dried
Trachymene caerulea (Didiscus caeruleus)	S			•			6-8	•									•	•		
Tricholaena rosea (Rhynchelytrum repens)	S	•	•					•						•		•				•
Tropaeolum Group																				
Tropaeolum majus	S	•		•	•			•				•	•	•	•	•		•		
Tropaeolum peregrinum	S	•		•	•			•					•							
Ursinia anethoides	O	•		•			4-6						•	•					•	
Venidium fastuosum	S	•		•			6-8					•	•	•					•	
Verbena Group																				
Verbena x *hybrida (V.* x *hortensis)*	R			•			10-12					•			•	•	•	•		
Verbena peruviana (V. chamaedriyolia)	R			•			10-12								•					
Verbena rigida (V. venosa)	R			•			10-12								•		•		•	
Verbesina encelioides	O		•	•				•					•						•	
Vinca major 'Variegata'	O				•					•							•	•		
Viola x *wittrockiana* and *Viola* x *williamsii*	R	•		•	•		10-12					•	•	•	•	•	•	•		
Xanthisma texana	O		•	•				•					•						•	
Xeranthemum annuum	S			•			4-6		•			•				•	•		•	•
Zea mays japonica	R			•					•		•									
Zinnia elegans	O			•			4-6					•	•	•	•	•	•		•	•

Mat-like: below 6 in. (15 cm)	Edging: 6-9 in. (15-24 cm)	Foreground: 9-20 in. (24-50 cm)	Middle ground: 20-36 in. (50-90 cm)	Background: 36-48 in. (90-120 cm)	Middle background: 48-72 in. (120-180 cm)	Tall background: 72+ in. (180+ cm)	Spreading	Upright	Borders or Mass Plantings	Planters	Hanging Baskets	Groundcover/Understory	Hedges or Screens (climbers)	Rockery	Requires Sheltered Location	Foliage Prominent	Foliage or Flowers Fragrant	Prominent Seed Pods/Fruit	Native Plant (or Garden Escape)	Flowers Close at Night or on Cloudy Days	Aggressive or Weedy	Disease/Insect Susceptible	Poisonous	Page Number	Common Name
		•					•	•																172	Blue Lace Flower
			•					•	•															173	Ruby Grass, Natal Grass
	•	•		•			•		•	•	•	•	•				•				•			173	Common Nasturtium, Garden Nasturtium
				•			•						•								•			174	Canary-bird Flower, Canary-bird Vine, Canary Creeper
		•					•	•	•								•			•				175	Dill-leaf Ursinia
		•					•	•							•					•				176	Cape Daisy, Monarch-of-the-veldt
•	•	•					•	•	•	•	•			•			•							176	Verbena, Vervain
•								•	•					•										176	Scarlet Verbena, Creeping Verbena
		•	•					•									•							176	Brazilian Verbena, Tall Verbena
		•					•	•						•										177	Butter Daisy, Golden Crownbeard
•							•				•	•				•								178	Variegated Periwinkle
	•							•	•	•	•						•							179	Pansy, Heartsease and Viola, Tufted Pansy
		•						•	•			•								•				180	Sleepy Daisy, Star-of-Texas
		•					•	•																180	Common Immortelle
					•		•	•				•				•								181	Rainbow Corn, Striped Maize
	•	•	•				•	•	•															182	Zinnia, Youth-and-Old-Age

Glossary

Acidity: the amount of acid present (associated with high hydrogen ion concentration). See pH.

Adventitious: occurring in unusual or abnormal places, e.g., roots growing from leaves.

Alkalinity: the amount of hydroxides present (associated with low hydrogen ion concentration). See pH.

Ambient: surrounding on all sides; encompassing.

Analogous colors: similar or comparable colors. Analogous colors are beside each other on the color wheel: one color has to be present in all, e.g., yellow, yellow-orange, orange.

Annual: a plant that completes its life cycle within one year. During this time it grows, flowers, produces seeds, and dies.

Apothecary: a pharmacist or druggist.

Asexual reproduction: any form of reproduction not involving the union of gametes (egg and sperm).

Axil: the angle formed between a stem and the base of the petiole of a leaf; normally the site of a lateral bud.

Basal rosette: a cluster or whorl of leaves at ground level, typical of the first season vegetative growth of a biennial; a cluster of leaves at the base of a flower stalk.

Biennial: a plant that completes its life cycle within two years, the first season's growth being strictly vegetative.

Birren System: a scheme for outdoor color which uses six primaries listed in a descending order of the amount of light reflected from each: white 80%, yellow 55%, green 35%, red 25%, blue 20%, and black 0%.

Botrytis: a genus of pathogenic fungi that causes disease in various kinds of plants.

Bracts: modified leaves which may occur immediately below a flower or flower head and appear to be part of the flower.

Bud sport: a mutation which occurs within a bud causing the shoot which develops from that bud to be genetically different from the rest of the plant.

Bulb: a bud-like plant storage structure, generally globe shaped, composed of fleshy leaf bases attached to a disk-shaped stem plate.

Chemical fertilizer: a commercial fertilizer containing various percentages of nitrogen – phosphorus – potassium.

Chroma: strength or parity of color.

Complementary colors: any two colors that combine well to produce perfection (wholeness or completeness). Complementary colors are opposite on the color wheel; i.e., red-green, orange-blue, purple-yellow.

Compound leaves: leaves which have the usual blade portion divided into individual leaflets.

Corm: an underground storage organ similar to a bulb but consisting of swollen stem tissue covered with dry membranous leaf bases.

Crown: the place where stems and roots meet, usually at ground level.

Culinary: suitable for or used in cooking.

Cultivar: a uniform group of cultivated plants obtained by breeding or selection, and propagated as a pure line; a horticultural or agricultural variety.

Cuttings: leaves, roots, or stems of a plant removed to form roots and other missing parts to propagate a new plant.

Damping-off: a disease of seedlings causing them to wither and die.

Dioecious: refers to individual plants of a given kind having either male (staminate) or female (pistilate) flowers but not both.

Dormancy: lack of growth of seeds, buds, bulbs, etc. due to unfavorable environmental conditions (external dormancy) or to factors within the organ itself (internal dormancy or rest).

Dormant: in a state of inactivity or apparent inactivity.

Drifts: refers to mounds of color of irregular shape and size produced in a flower border as a result of careful planning; informal or natural looking placement of plants within a bed or border.

Embryo: a miniature plant within a seed, normally produced from a zygote as the result of the union of gametes (sperm and egg).

Escape from cultivation: a domesticated plant that has become naturalized in a particular area and is capable of thriving and multiplying on its own (a non-native wild plant).

Essential elements: all the nutrients required, both mineral and non-mineral, for healthy plant growth.

Etymology: the branch of linguistics that deals with the origin and development of words.

Everlasting: flowers of various plants which retain their shape and color when air dried and are useful for winter bouquets and arrangements, e.g., Statice (*Limonium* spp.).

Fibrous roots: a root system composed of relatively thin roots that branch and rebranch to form an expanding network.

Floret: a small flower; the individual flowers that make up a flower head or inflorescence.

Foundation planting: plants placed to hide the foundation of a house or other building; a planting along a foundation.

Genus (genera): the usual major subdivision(s) of a family in the classification of plants or animals; usually consists of more than one species.

Germination: the process whereby the embryo in a seed grows and emerges from the seed to become a seedling.

Ground cover: refers to low-growing plants that spread readily to cover the ground with vegetation.

Grow-on: to grow or develop so as to fit or be suited to.

Hardening: the treatment of plants in such a way as to increase their resistance to low temperatures and drought.

Hardy: refers to plants adapted to cold temperatures or other adverse climatic conditions of an area.

Herbaceous perennial: a plant which lives for three or more growing seasons and does not develop woody tissues.

Hue: color; the colors of the rainbow or refracted white light, e.g., red, yellow, orange, etc.

Hybrid: the offspring of two plants of different genetic makeup.

Inflorescence: a collective term for a group of flowers attached to a common axis (stem).

Internodal: referring to the parts of a stem between nodes.

Interplant: to plant one kind of plant in between (an)other kind(s) of plant(s).

Layering: a form of vegetative propagation in which an intact stem develops roots as the result of contact with the soil (or another rooting medium).

Legume: a plant belonging to the pulse or pea family (Leguminosae).

Linear leaf: a leaf that is long and narrow with parallel margins.

Loam: refers to a soil in which the proportion of sand, silt, and clay are approximately equal.

Lobed: having rounded projections or divisions; in reference to leaves, having lobes or divisions extending less than half way to the middle of the blade.

Luminosity: the quality or condition of radiating or reflecting light.

Macronutrients: those nutrients required by plants in relatively large amounts, e.g., nitrogen, phosphorus, potassium.

Marginally hardy: on the borderline of being hardy enough to survive in a given climatic zone.

Massed: plants of one kind grouped in quantity close together to produce a strong visual effect.

Microclimate: atmospheric environmental conditions in the immediate vicinity of a plant. It includes interchanges of energy, gases, and water between atmosphere and soil.

Midrib: the central vein of a leaf blade.

Monochromatic: different values or intensities of one color.

Mulch: a material such as straw, leaves, peat, compost, etc., that is spread upon the surface of the soil to protect the soil and plant roots and crowns from the effects of rain, soil crusting, freezing, or evaporation.

Naturalize: to introduce a plant from one environment to another to which the plant becomes established and more or less adapted by surviving for many generations.

Night garden: a garden that is visibly attractive in very low light (night-time conditions) containing white or luminous colored flowers and/or highly reflective foliage (grey or bright green).

Nodes: the regions of stems where leaves are attached and buds are located.

Nomenclature: a set or system of names or terms such as those used in the classification of plants.

Off-shoots: short, horizontal stems which occur in whorls or near whorls in plant crowns.

Opposite leaves: refers to plants which produce two leaves at each node; used as a trait for identification and classification.

Organic matter: carbon containing materials of either plant or animal origin, which exist in all stages of decomposition in soils.

Organic soil: a soil containing a high percentage of organic matter.

Ornamental: refers to a plant grown for its aesthetic properties.

Palmate: refers to a compound leaf with all the leaflets arising from one point at the end of the petiole. May also refer to the pattern of veins in the blade of a simple leaf.

Panicle: a type of inflorescence similar to a raceme, but with a branched cluster of flowers in place of each single flower.

Pasteurization: heating to a prescribed temperature for a specific period of time in order to destroy or check activity of micro-organisms (after French chemist Louis Pasteur); used to destroy bacterial and fungal pathogens in soil.

Perennial: a plant which does not die after flowering but lives from year to year.

pH: a measure of acidity or alkalinity expressed as the negative log of the hydrogen ion concentration. A pH of 7 is neutral; less than 7 is acidic; more than 7 is basic or alkaline.

Pinnate: refers to a compound leaf with the leaflets arranged along both sides of a common axis. May also refer to the pattern of veins in a simple leaf where secondary veins extend laterally from a single midrib.

Prick-out: to transplant seedlings from seed pans to shallow pots or trays.

Propagation: the act of propagating or multiplying by any process of natural reproduction from the parent stock.

Prostrate: a plant or stem of a plant which lies flat on the ground.

Pubescent: covered with short hairs, usually fine or down-like.

Raceme: a type of inflorescence in which stalked flowers are borne on a single, unbranched main axis.

Rhizome: a horizontal stem that grows partly or entirely underground, often thickened and serving as a storage organ.

Ribbon planting: a narrow bed or planting of flowers along a walkway, wall, fence, or other such structure.

Rosette: a dense cluster of leaves on a very short stem or axis.

Saline soil: an alkali soil with more than 2000 ppm soluble salts, but relatively low sodium content. Such soils can often be reclaimed by leaching.

Scarification: the chemical or physical treatment used on some kinds of seeds in order to break or weaken the seed coat sufficiently for germination to occur.

Seed leaves: the cotyledons or embryo leaves which store or absorb food and may also function as true leaves after germination.

Self-sow: plants which propagate themselves from seed once established.

Senescence: growing old, aging; the deterioration of plant tissues and their final death.

Separation: the use of bulbs and corms in propagation utilizing the naturally detachable parts.

Sessile: without a petiole (as in some leaves), or without a pedicel (as in some flowers).

Softwood cuttings: cuttings taken from soft, succulent, new spring growth of deciduous or evergreen species of woody plants.

Species: a group of similar distinct plants capable of interbreeding to produce offspring like themselves. One or more species make up a genus.

Specimen plant: a plant placed by itself in the landscape as a focal point or point of interest.

Spike: a type of inflorescence similar to a raceme but having sessile (stalkless) flowers or florets attached directly to the central axis with the oldest flowers at the base.

Stamen: the male reproductive organ of a plant.

Sterile: infertile; not capable of producing viable seeds; free of micro organisms, particularly pathogens.

Stolon: a runner, or any basal branch or above-ground stem that is inclined to root at the nodes when they come into contact with the ground.

Stratification: the storing of seeds at low temperature (35 to 39°F (2 to 4°C) usually) under moist conditions in order to break physiological dormancy or rest.

Stratified: placed in strata or layers, seed that has been stored between layers of moist earth or peat moss in order to break dormancy.

Succulent: a plant having fleshy and juicy tissues; non-woody.

Sun scald: high temperature injury to plant tissue due to exposure to intense sunlight.

Systemic: describes a pesticide that acts through a plant's tissues, poisoning a pest that attacks the plant.

Taproot: an elongated, deeply growing primary root.

Terminal: used in reference to stem cuttings in which only the upper end portion of a plant shoot is used to make the cutting.

Tilth: well cultivated soil

Tuber: an enlarged underground stem tip serving as a storage organ of starch or related materials.

Tuberous root: a thick, tuber-like root which serves as a storage organ.

Umbel: a type of inflorescence in which the individual flower stalks (pedicels) all arise from the tip of the main stalk (peduncle).

Value: refers to the reflectiveness of flower colors. White and yellow are considered high value colors, whereas red and blue are considered low value (see Birren System).

Variegated: patterned with two distinct colors or shades of color. Mostly applied to yellow and green or white and green leaves, but can also apply to flowers.

Vegetative: referring to asexual (stem, leaf, root) development in plants in contrast to sexual (flower, seed) development.

White garden: a garden containing only plants with white flowers and/or plants with grey or silvery foliage.

Whorled cluster: a group of three or more flowers, fruits, leaves, etc., arising from a common point of attachment.

Whorled leaves: a group of three or more leaves arising from the same node.

Cross-Reference Index

English-Latin

Acrolinium
Helipterum roseum (Acrolinium roseum)
African Marigold
Tagetes erecta
Ageratum
Ageratum houstonianum
Alkanet
Archusa capensis
Alpine Poppy
Papaver alpinum
Alyssum, Sweet
Lobularia maritima
Amaranth
Amaranthus caudatus, Amaranthus hybridus var. *erythrostachys (A. hypochondriacus), Amaranthus tricolor (A. melancholicus)*
Amaranth, Globe
Gomphrena globosa
Anatolian Bellflower
Campanula macrostyla
Angel's Trumpet
Datura metel and *Datura inoxia*
Annual Aster
Callistephus chinensis
Annual Baby's Breath
Gypsophila elegans

Annual Blanket Flower
Gaillardia pulchella picta
Annual Butter Daisy
Chrysanthemum multicaule
Annual Carnation
Dianthus caryophyllus
Annual Chrysanthemum
Hybrids of *Chrysanthemum carinatum, Chrysanthemum coronarium,* and *Chrysanthemum segetum*
Annual Delphinium
Consolida ambigua (Delphinium ajacis) , Consolida regalis (Delphinium consolida) and *Consolida orientalis*
Annual Foxglove
Digitalis purpurea 'Foxy Strain'
Annual Gaillardia
Gaillardia pulchella picta
Annual Hollyhock
Alcea rosea (Althaea rosea)
Annual Linaria
Linaria maroccana
Annual Lupine
Lupinus Hybrids
Annual Phlox
Phlox drummondii
Annual Poinsettia
Euphorbia heterophylla

Annual Rose Mallow
Lavatera trimestris
Annual Sweet William
Dianthus barbatus
Annual White Daisy
Chrysanthemum paludosum
Annual Woodruff
Asperula orientalis (Asperula azurea setosa)
Annual Yellow Daisy
Chrysanthemum multicaule
Apple, Balsam
Echinocystis lobata
Apple, Downy Thorn
Datura metel and *Datura inoxia*
Arctotis
Arctotis stoechadifolia (A. grandis)
Argemony
Argemone grandiflora and *Argemone mexicana*
Aster, Annual
Callistephus chinensis
Aster, China
Callistephus chinensis
Australian Blue Fan-flower
Scaevola aemula
Aztec Marigold
Tagetes erecta

Baby Blue-eyes
  Nemophila menziesii
Baby's Breath, Annual
  Gypsophila elegans
Bachelor's Button
  Centaurea cyanus
Balloon Vine
  Cardiospermum halicacabum
Balsam Apple
  Echinocystis lobata
Balsam, Garden
  Impatiens balsamina
Bartonia
  Mentzelia lindleyi (Bartonia aurea)
Basil, Dark Opal
  Ocimum basilicum
Basil, Sweet
  Ocimum basilicum
Basket Flower
  Centaurea americana
Bedding Begonia
  Begonia x *semperflorens – cultorum* and
  other hybrid cultivars
Bedding Geranium, Common
  Pelargonium x *hortorum*
Bedding Lobelia
  Lobelia erinus
Beefsteak Plant
  Perilla frutescens 'Crispa' *(P. frutescens*
  var. *nankinensis)*
Begonia, Bedding
  Begonia x *semperflorens – cultorum* and
  other hybrid cultivars
Begonia, Fibrous
  Begonia x *semperflorens – cultorum* and
  other hybrid cultivars
Begonia, Hybrid Tuberous
  Begonia x *tuberhybrida*
Begonia, Wax
  Begonia x *semperflorens – cultorum* and
  other hybrid cultivars
Bellflower, Anatolian
  Campanula macrostyla
Bellflower, Chilean
  Nolana paradoxa (N. grandiflora)
Bells of Ireland
  Moluccella laevis
Big Quaking Grass
  Briza maxima (B. major)
Bishop's Flower
  Ammi majus
Black-eyed Susan
  Rudbeckia hirta
Black-eyed Susan Vine
  Thunbergia alata
Blanket Flower, Annual
  Gaillardia pulchella picta
Blazing Star
  Mentzelia lindleyi (Bartonia aurea)
Bloodflower
  Asclepias curassavica
Bloodflower Milkweed
  Asclepias curassavica
Bluebell, California
  Phacelia campanularia
Blue Cupidone
  Catananche caerulea
Blue Fan-flower, Australian
  Scaevola aemula

Blue Lace Flower
  Trachymene caerulea (Didiscus caeruleus)
Blue Succory
  Catananche caerulea
Blue Thimble Flower
  Gilia capitata
Blue-eyed African Daisy
  Arctotis stoechadifolia (A. grandis)
Bluebonnet, Texas
  Lupinus subcarnosus and *Lupinus
  texensis*
Brazilian Verbena
  Verbena rigida (V. venosa)
Browallia
  Browallia speciosa and *Browallia viscosa*
Bugloss
  Archusa capensis
Bugloss, Viper's
  Echium lycopsis (E. plantagineum)
Burning Bush
  Kochia scoparia trichophylla
Bush Violet
  Browallia speciosa and *Browallia viscosa*
Busy Lizzie
  Impatiens wallerana (I. sultanii)
Butter Daisy
  Verbesina encelioides
Butterfly Flower
  Schizanthus x *wisetonensis*

Calendula
  Calendula officinalis
California Bluebell
  Phacelia campanularia
California Poppy
  Eschscholzia californica
Calliopsis
  Coreopsis basalis (C. drummondii) and
  Coreopsis tinctoria (C. bi-color)
Canary Creeper
  Tropaeolum peregrinum
Canary Grass
  Phalaris canariensis
Canary-bird Flower
  Tropaeolum peregrinum
Canary-bird Vine
  Tropaeolum peregrinum
Candytuft, Common Annual
  Iberis umbellata
Candytuft, Fairy
  Iberis umbellata
Candytuft, Globe
  Iberis umbellata
Candytuft, Hyacinth-flowered
  Iberis amara (I. coronaria)
Candytuft, Rocket
  Iberis amara (I. coronaria)
Canna, Common Garden
  Canna x *generalis*
Canna, Orchid-flowered
  Canna x *orchiodes*
Canterbury Bells
  Campanula medium (C. grandiflora)
Cape Daisy
  Venidium fastuosum
Cape Forget-me-not,
  Archusa capensis
Cape Marigold
  Hybrids of *Dimorphotheca sinuata*

Carnation, Annual
  Dianthus caryophyllus
Castor Bean
  Ricinus communis
Castor Oil Plant
  Ricinus communis
Catchfly, Nodding
  Silene armeria and *Silene pendula*
Catchfly, Sweet William
  Silene armeria and *Silene pendula*
Cathedral Bells
  Cobaea scandens
Charieis
  Charieis heterophylla
Cheeses
  Malva sylvestris zebrina and *Malva
  sylvestris mauritiana*
Cherry Pie
  Heliotropium arborescens (H. peruvianum)
Chickabiddy
  Asarina spp. *(Maurandya* spp.)
Chilean Bellflower
  Nolana paradoxa (N. grandiflora)
China Aster
  Callistephus chinensis
China Pink
  Dianthus chinensis
Chinese Forget-me-not
  Cynoglossum amabile
Chinese Houses
  Collinsia heterophylla (C. bi-color)
Chrysanthemum, Annual
  Hybrids of *Chrysanthemum carinatum,
  Chrysanthemum coronarium,* and
  Chrysanthemum segetum
Cladanthus
  *Cladanthus arabicus (C. proliferus,
  Anthemis arabica)*
Clarkia
  Clarkia unguiculata (C. elegans)
Clary Sage
  Salvia viridis (S. horminum)
Cleome
  Cleome hasslerana (C. spinosa, C. pungens)
Cloud Grass
  Agrostis nebulosa
Cockscomb
  Celosia cristata
Coleus
  Coleus x *hybridus (C. blumei* and *C.
  pumilus)*
Collinsia
  Collinsia heterophylla (C. bi-color)
Collinsia, Pagoda
  Collinsia heterophylla (C. bi-color)
Common Annual Candytuft
  Iberis umbellata
Common Bedding Geranium
  Pelargonium x *hortorum*
Common Garden Canna
  Canna x *generalis*
Common Heliotrope
  Heliotropium arborescens (H. peruvianum)
Common Immortelle
  Xeranthemum annuum
Common Lantana
  Lantana camara
Common Nasturtium
  Tropaeolum majus

Common Pimpernel
Anagallis arvensis
Common Stock
Matthiola incana annua
Common Sunflower
Helianthus annuus
Coreopsis
Coreopsis basalis (C. drummondii) and
Coreopsis tinctoria (C. bicolor)
Corn Poppy
Papaver rhoeas
Corn, Rainbow
Zea mays japonica
Cornflower
Centaurea cyanus
Cosmos
Cosmos bipinnatus
Cosmos, Yellow
Cosmos sulphureus
Creeping Verbena
Verbena peruviana (V. chamaedriyolia)
Creeping Zinnia
Sanvitalia procumbens
Cucumber, Mock
Echinocystis lobata
Cucumber, Wild
Echinocystis lobata
Cucumberleaf Sunflower
Helianthus debilis subsp. *cucumerifolius*
Cup-and-saucer Vine
Cobaea scandens
Cupflower
Nierembergia hippomanica var. *violacea*
(N. caerulea)
Cupid's Dart
Catananche caerulea
Cypress, Summer
Kochia scoparia trichophylla

Dahlberg Daisy
Dyssodia tenuiloba (Thymophylla
tenuiloba)
Dahlia
Hybrids of *Dahlia coccinea* and *Dahlia*
pinnata
Daisy, Annual Butter
Chrysanthemum multicaule
Daisy, Annual White
Chrysanthemum paludosum
Daisy, Annual Yellow
Chrysanthemum multicaule
Daisy, Blue-eyed African
Arctotis stoechadifolia (A. grandis)
Daisy, Butter
Verbesina encelioides
Daisy, Cape
Venidium fastuosum
Daisy, Dahlberg
Dyssodia tenuiloba (Thymophylla
tenuiloba)
Daisy, Gloriosa
Rudbeckia hirta
Daisy, Livingstone
Dorotheanthus bellidiformis
(Mesembryanthemum criniflorum)
Daisy, Palm Springs
Cladanthus arabicus (C. proliferus,
Anthemis arabica)

Daisy, Sleepy
Xanthisma texana
Daisy, Swan River
Brachycome iberidifolia
Daisy, Tahoka
Machaeranthera tanacetifolia (Aster
tanacetifolius)
Dame's Rocket
Hesperis matronalis
Dame's Violet
Hesperis matronalis
Dark Opal Basil
Ocimum basilicum
Delphinium, Annual
Consolida ambigua (Delphinium ajacis) ,
Consolida regalis (Delphinium consolida)
and *Consolida orientalis*
Desert Evening Primrose
Oenothera deltoides
Devil-in-a-bush
Nigella damascena
Dill-leaf Ursinia
Ursinia anethoides
Downy Thorn Apple
Datura metel and *Datura inoxia*
Drummond Phlox
Phlox drummondii
Drumstick Flower
Craspedia spp.
Dusty Miller
Centaurea gymnocarpa and *Centaurea*
cineraria (C. candidissima), Senecio
cineraria (Cineraria maritima)
Dusty Miller, Silver Lace
Chrysanthemum ptarmiciflorum (Cineraria
candicans)
Dwarf Morning Glory
Convolvulus tricolor
Dwarf Signet Marigold
Tagetes tenuifolia (T. signata)

Edging Lobelia
Lobelia erinus
English Wallflower
Cheiranthus cheiri
Evening Primrose, Desert
Oenothera deltoides
Evening Stock
Matthiola longipetala bicornis (M.
bicornis)
Everlasting Flower
Helichrysum bracteatum
Everlasting, Rose
Helipterum roseum (Acrolinium roseum)
Everlasting, Swan River
Helipterum manglesii (Rhodanthe
manglesii)
Everlasting, Winged
Ammobium alatum
Everlasting, Yellow
Helipterum humboldtiana (H. sanfordii)

Fairy Candytuft
Iberis umbellata
Fairy Fan-flower
Scaevola aemula
False Queen Anne's Lace
Ammi majus
Fan-flower, Australian Blue
Scaevola aemula

Fan-flower, Fairy
Scaevola aemula
Fancy Geranium
Pelargonium x *domesticum*
Farewell-to-spring
Clarkia amoena (Godetia amoena)
Fennel Flower
Nigella damascena
Feverfew
Chrysanthemum parthenium (Matricaria
capensis, Pyrethrum parthenium)
Fibrous Begonia
Begonia x *semperflorens – cultorum* and
other hybrid cultivars
Fire Bush
Kochia scoparia trichophylla
Fire-on-the-mountain
Euphorbia heterophylla
Flame Nettle
Coleus x *hybridus (C. blumei* and *C.*
pumilus)
Flanders Poppy
Papaver commutatum
Flax, Flowering
Linum grandiflorum
Flax, Scarlet
Linum grandiflorum
Flaxleaf Pimpernel
Anagallis monelli subsp. *linifolia (A.*
linifolia, A. grandiflora)
Flora's Paintbrush
Emilia javanica (E. coccinea, E. flammea,
and *E. sagittata)*
Flossflower
Ageratum houstonianum
Flowering Flax
Linum grandiflorum
Flowering Tobacco
Nicotiana alata (N. affinis)
Forget-me-not, Cape
Archusa capensis
Forget-me-not, Chinese
Cynoglossum amabile
Forget-me-not, Summer
Archusa capensis
Fountain Grass
Pennisetum setaceum (P. ruppelii)
Four-o'clock
Mirabilis jalapa
Foxglove, Annual
Digitalis purpurea 'Foxy Strain'
French Marigold
Tagetes patula
Fried Eggs
Limnanthes douglasii
Fuchsia
Fuchsia x *hybrida*

Gaillardia, Annual
Gaillardia pulchella picta
Garden Atriplex
Atriplex hortensis (A. hortensis
astrosanguinea)
Garden Balsam
Impatiens balsamina
Garden Nasturtium
Tropaeolum majus
Garland, Rocky Mountain
Clarkia pulchella

Gazania
Gazania ringens (G. splendens)
Gentian, Prairie
Eustoma grandiflorum (E. russellianum,
Lisianthus russellianus)
Geranium, Common Bedding
Pelargonium x hortorum
Geranium, Fancy
Pelargonium x domesticum
Geranium, Ivy
Pelargonium peltatum
Geranium, Lady Washington
Pelargonium x domesticum
Geranium, Royal
Pelargonium x domesticum
Geranium, Scented
Pelargonium spp.
Geranium, Show
Pelargonium x domesticum
Geranium, Zonal
Pelargonium x hortorum
Gladiola, Gladiolus
Gladiolus x hortulanus
Globe Amaranth
Gomphrena globosa
Globe Candytuft
Iberis umbellata
Gloriosa Daisy
Rudbeckia hirta
Godetia
Clarkia amoena (Godetia amoena)
Gold Button
Matricaria grandiflora (Pentzia grandiflora,
Pentzia 'Gold Button')
Gold Pompons
Matricaria grandiflora (Pentzia grandiflora,
Pentzia 'Gold Button')
Golden Crownbeard
Verbesina encelioides
Golden Fleece
Dyssodia tenuiloba (Thymophylla
tenuiloba)
Gourds, Ornamental
Cucurbita pepo ovifera and related species
Grass, Canary
Phalaris canariensis
Grass, Cloud
Agrostis nebulosa
Grass, Fountain
Pennisetum setaceum (P. ruppelii)
Grass, Hare's-tail
Lagurus ovatus
Grass, Large or Big Quaking
Briza maxima (B. major)
Grass, Lesser or Little Quaking
Briza minor (B. gracilis, B. minima)
Grass, Natal
Tricholaena rosea (Rhynchelytrum repens)
Grass, Rabbit-tail
Lagurus ovatus
Grass, Ruby
Tricholaena rosea (Rhynchelytrum repens)
Grecian Stock
Matthiola longipetala bicornis (M.
bicornis)
Groundsel, Purple
Senecio elegans (Jacobaea elegans)

Hairy-calyx Sundrop
Oenothera deltoides
Hare's-tail Grass
Lagurus ovatus
Hawk's Beard
Crepis rubra (Barkhausia rubra)
Heartleaf Mesembryanthemum, Variegated
Aptenia cordifolia 'Variegata'
(Mesembryanthemum cordifolium
'Variegatum')
Heartsease
Viola x wittrockiana
Heartseed
Cardiospermum halicacabum
Heliotrope, Common
Heliotropium arborescens (H. peruvianum)
High Mallow
Malva sylvestris zebrina and Malva
sylvestris mauritiana
Hollyhock, Annual
Alcea rosea (Althaea rosea)
Honeywort
Cerinthe aspera
Hop Vine, Japanese
Humulus japonicus
Hound's Tongue
Cynoglossum amabile
Humboldt's Sunray
Helipterum humboldtiana (H. sanfordii)
Hyacinth-flowered Candytuft
Iberis amara (I. coronaria)
Hybrid Tuberous Begonia
Begonia x tuberhybrida

Ice Plant
Mesembryanthemum crystallinum
(Cryophytum crystallinum)
Immortelle
Helichrysum bracteatum
Immortelle, Common
Xeranthemum annuum
Impatience, New Guinea
Impatiens 'New Guinea Hybrid'
Innocence
Collinsia heterophylla (C. bi-color)
Irish Bells
Moluccella laevis
Ivy Geranium
Pelargonium peltatum
Ivy, Mexican
Cobaea scandens
Ivy, Kennilworth
Cymbalaria muralis
Japanese Hop Vine
Humulus japonicus
Jasmine Tobacco
Nicotiana alata (N. affinis)
Job's Tears
Coix lacryma-jobi
Joseph's Coat
Amaranthus tricolor (A. melancholicus)

Kenilworth Ivy
Cymbalaria muralis
Knotweed
Polygonum capitatum

Lace Flower, Blue
Trachymene caerulea (Didiscus caeruleus)
Lady's-eardrops, Ladies'-eardrops
Fuchsia x hybrida
Lady Washington Geranium
Pelargonium x domesticum
Lantana, Common
Lantana camara
Lantana, Trailing
Lantana montevidensis (L. sellowiana, L.
delicatissima)
Large Quaking Grass
Briza maxima (B. major)
Larkspur
Consolida ambigua (Delphinium ajacis) ,
Consolida regalis (Delphinium consolida)
and Consolida orientalis
Lesser Quaking Grass
Briza minor (B. gracilis, B. minima)
Little Quaking Grass
Briza minor (B. gracilis, B. minima)
Linaria, Annual
Linaria maroccana
Livingstone Daisy
Dorotheanthus bellidiformis
(Mesembryanthemum criniflorum)
Lobelia, Bedding
Lobelia erinus
Lobelia, Edging
Lobelia erinus
Love-in-a-mist
Nigella damascena
Love-in-a-puff
Cardiospermum halicacabum
Love-lies-bleeding
Amaranthus caudatus
Lupine, Annual
Lupinus Hybrids

Madagascar Periwinkle
Catharanthus roseus (Vinca rosea)
Maize, Striped
Zea mays japonica
Mallow, Annual Rose
Lavatera trimestris
Mallow, High
Malva sylvestris zebrina and Malva
syvestris mauritiana
Mallow, Tree
Lavatera trimestris
Mallow-wort
Malope trifida
Malope
Malope trifida
Marigold, African
Tagetes erecta
Marigold, Aztec
Tagetes erecta
Marigold, Cape
Hybrids of Dimorphotheca sinuata
Marigold, Dwarf Signet
Tagetes tenuifolia (T. signata)
Marigold, French
Tagetes patula
Marigold, Pot
Calendula officinalis
Marvel-of-Peru
Mirabilis jalapa

Matricaria
Chrysanthemum parthenium (Matricaria
capensis, Pyrethrum parthenium)
Meadow Foam
Limnanthes douglasii
Mealycup Sage
Salvia farinacea
Mesembryanthemum, Tricolor
Dorotheanthus tricolor
(Mesembryanthemum tricolor)
Mesembryanthemum, Variegated Heartleaf
Aptenia cordifolia 'Variegata'
(Mesembryanthemum cordifolium
'Variegatum')
Mexican Fire Plant
Euphorbia heterophylla
Mexican Ivy
Cobaea scandens
Mexican Tulip Poppy
Hunnemannia fumariifolia
Mignonette
Reseda odorata
Milkweed, Bloodflower
Asclepias curassavica
Mock Cucumber
Echinocystis lobata
Molten Fire
Amaranthus tricolor (A. melancholicus)
Molucca Balm
Moluccella laevis
Monarch-of-the-veldt
Venidium fastuosum
Monkey Flower
Mimulus x hybridus 'Grandiflorus'
Moonflower
Ipomea alba (Calonyction aculeatum, I.
bona-nox)
Morning Glory
Ipomea purpurea and Ipomea tricolor
Morning Glory, Dwarf
Convolvulus tricolor
Morocco Toadflax
Linaria maroccana
Mother-of-thousands
Cymbalaria muralis
Mourning Bride
Scabiosa atropurpurea

Nasturtium, Common
Tropaeolum majus
Nasturtium, Garden
Tropaeolum majus
Natal Grass
Tricholaena rosea (Rhynchelytrum repens)
Nemesia
Nemesia strumosa
New Guinea Impatience
Impatiens 'New Guinea Hybrid'
Nierembergia
Nierembergia hippomanica var. violacea
(N. caerulea)
Nigella
Nigella damascena
Nodding Catchfly
Silene armeria and Silene pendula
None-so-pretty
Silene armeria and Silene pendula

Orach
Atriplex hortensis (A. hortensis
astrosanguinea)
Orchid, Poor Man's
Schizanthus x wisetonensis
Orchid-flowered Canna
Canna x orchiodes
Ornamental Cabbage
Brassica oleracea capitata
Ornamental Gourds
Cucurbita pepo ovifera and related species
Ornamental Kale
Brassica oleracea acephala

Pagoda Collinsia
Collinsia heterophylla (C. bi-color)
Paintbrush, Flora's
Emilia javanica (E. coccinea, E. flammea,
and E. sagittata)
Painted Leaves
Coleus x hybridus (C. blumei and C.
pumilus)
Painted Tongue
Salpiglossis sinuata
Palm Springs Daisy
Cladanthus arabicus (C. proliferus,
Anthemis arabica)
Pansy
Viola x wittrockiana
Pansy, Tufted
Viola x williamsii
Papermoon
Scabiosa stellata
Patience Plant
Impatiens wallerana (I. sultanii)
Patient Lucy
Impatiens wallerana (I. sultanii)
Pennywort
Cymbalaria muralis
Pentzia
Matricaria grandiflora (Pentzia grandiflora,
Pentzia 'Gold Button')
Perilla
Perilla frutescens 'Crispa' (P. frutescens
var. nankinensis)
Periwinkle, Madagascar
Catharanthus roseus (Vinca rosea)
Periwinkle, Variegated
Vinca major 'Variegata'
Petunia
Petunia x hybrida
Phlox, Annual
Phlox drummondii
Phlox, Drummond
Phlox drummondii
Pimpernel, Common
Anagallis arvensis
Pimpernel, Flaxleaf
Anagallis monelli subsp. linifolia (A.
linifolia, A. grandiflora)
Pimpernel, Scarlet
Anagallis arvensis
Pincushion Flower
Scabiosa atropurpurea
Pink(s)
See Rainbow Pink or China Pink
Pink Poker Statice
Psylliostachys suworowii (Limonium
suworowii)

Poinsettia, Annual
Euphorbia heterophylla
Poinsettia. Summer
Amaranthus tricolor (A. melancholicus)
Polygonum
Polygonum capitatum
Poor Man's Weather Glass
Anagallis arvensis
Poor Man's Orchid
Schizanthus x wisetonensis
Poppy, Alpine
Papaver alpinum
Poppy, California
Eschscholzia californica
Poppy, Corn
Papaver rhoeas
Poppy, Flanders
Papaver commutatum
Poppy, Mexican Tulip
Hunnemannia fumariifolia
Poppy, Prickly
Argemone grandiflora and Argemone
mexicana
Poppy, Shirley
Papaver rhoeas
Poppy, Tulip
Papaver glaucum
Portulaca
Portulaca grandiflora
Pot Marigold
Calendula officinalis
Prairie Gentian
Eustoma grandiflorum (E. russellianum,
Lisianthus russellianus)
Prickly Poppy
Argemone grandiflora and Argemone
mexicana
Primrose, Desert Evening
Oenothera deltoides
Prince's Feather
Amaranthus hybridus var. Erythrostachys
(A. hypochondriacus)
Proboscis Flower
Probiscidea louisianica (Martynia
proboscidea)
Purple Groundsel
Senecio elegans (Jacobaea elegans)
Purple Ragwort
Senecio elegans (Jacobaea elegans)
Purslane, Sea
Atriplex hortensis (A. hortensis
astrosanguinea)

Quaking Grass, Large or Big
Briza maxima (B. major)
Quaking Grass, Lesser or Little
Briza minor (B. gracilis, B. minima)
Queen Anne's Lace
Daucus carota carota

Rabbit-tail Grass
Lagurus ovatus
Ragwort, Purple
Senecio elegans (Jacobaea elegans)
Rainbow Corn
Zea mays japonica
Rainbow Pink
Dianthus chinensis

Ram's Horn
  Probiscidea louisianica (Martynia proboscidea)
Rat-tail Statice
  Psylliostachys suworowii (Limonium suworowii)
Rhodanthe
  Helipterum manglesii (Rhodanthe manglesii)
Rocket Candytuft
  Iberis amara (I. coronaria)
Rocket, Dame's
  Hesperis matronalis
Rocket, Sweet
  Hesperis matronalis
Rocky Mountain Garland
  Clarkia pulchella
Rose Everlasting
  Helipterum roseum (Acrolinium roseum)
Rose Mallow, Annual
  Lavatera trimestris
Rose Moss
  Portulaca grandiflora
Rose Sunray
  Helipterum roseum (Acrolinium roseum)
Royal Geranium
  Pelargonium x domesticum
Ruby Grass
  Tricholaena rosea (Rhynchelytrum repens)
Runner Bean, Scarlet
  Phaseolus coccineus (Phaseolus multiflorus)
Runner Bean, White Dutch
  Phaseolus coccineus 'Albus'
Russian Statice
  Psylliostachys suworowii (Limonium suworowii)

Safflower
  Carthamus tinctorius
Saffron Thistle
  Carthamus tinctorius
Sage, Clary
  Salvia viridis (S. horminum)
Sage, Mealycup
  Salvia farinacea
Sage, Scarlet
  Salvia splendens
Salpiglossis
  Salpiglossis sinuata
Salvia
  Salvia splendens
Satin Flower
  Clarkia amoena (Godetia amoena)
Scarlet Flax
  Linum grandiflorum
Scabious, Sweet
  Scabiosa atropurpurea
Scarlet Pimpernel
  Anagallis arvensis
Scarlet Runner Bean
  Phaseolus coccineus (Phaseolus multiflorus)
Scarlet Sage
  Salvia splendens
Scarlet Verbena
  Verbena peruvianum (V. chamaedriyolia)
Scented Geranium
  Pelargonium spp.
Schizanthus
  Schizanthus x wisetonensis

Sea Lavender
  Limonium sinuatum and *Limonium bonduellii superbum*
Sea Purslane
  Atriplex hortensis (A. hortensis astrosanguinea)
Shellflower
  Moluccella laevis
Shepherd's Clock
  Anagallis arvensis
Shirley Poppy
  Papaver rhoeas
Show Geranium
  Pelargonium x domesticum
Silver Lace Dusty Miller
  Chrysanthemum ptarmiciflorum (Cineraria candicans)
Sleepy Daisy
  Xanthisma texana
Snapdragon
  Antirrhinum majus
Snow-on-the-mountain
  Euphorbia marginata
Spider Flower
  Cleome hasslerana (C. spinosa, C. pungens)
Spider Flower, Yellow
  Cleome lutea
Star-of-Texas
  Xanthisma texana
Star-of-the-veldt
  Hybrids of *Dimorphotheca sinuata*
Stardust
  Linanthus androsaceus subsp. *micranthus (Gilia micrantha, Leptosiphon hybrida)*
Starflower
  Scabiosa stellata
Statice
  Limonium sinuatum and *Limonium bonduellii superbum*
Statice, Pink Poker
  Psylliostachys suworowii (Limonium suworowii)
Statice, Rat-tail
  Psylliostachys suworowii (Limonium suworowii)
Statice, Russian
  Psylliostachys suworowii (Limonium suworowii)
Stock, Common
  Matthiola incana annua
Stock, Evening
  Matthiola longipetala bicornis (M. bicornis)
Stock, Grecian
  Matthiola longipetala bicornis (M. bicornis)
Stock, Ten-weeks
  Matthiola incana annua
Stock, Virginian or Virginia Stock
  Malcolmia maritima (Chieranthus maritimus)
Strawflower
  Helichrysum bracteatum
Striped Maize
  Zea mays japonica
Summer Cypress
  Kochia scoparia trichophylla
Summer Forget-me-not
  Archusa capensis

Summer Poinsettia
  Amaranthus tricolor (A. melancholicus)
Sundrop, Hairy-calyx
  Oenothera deltoides
Sunflower, Common
  Helianthus annuus
Sunflower, Cucumberleaf
  Helianthus debilis subsp. *cucumerifolius*
Sunray, Humboldt's
  Helipterum humboldtiana (H. sanfordii)
Sunray, Rose
  Helipterum roseum (Acrolinium roseum)
Swan River Daisy
  Brachycome iberidifolia
Swan River Everlasting
  Helipterum manglesii (Rhodanthe manglesii)
Sweet Alyssum
  Lobularia maritima
Sweet Basil
  Ocimum basilicum
Sweet Pea
  Lathyrus odoratus
Sweet Rocket
  Hesperis matronalis
Sweet Scabious
  Scabiosa atropurpurea
Sweet Sultan
  Centaurea moschata (C. suaveolens, C. odorata, C. amberboii)
Sweet William Catchfly
  Silene armeria and *Silene pendula*
Sweet William, Annual
  Dianthus barbatus
Sword Lily
  Gladiolus x hortulanus

Tahoka Daisy
  Machaeranthera tanacetifolia (Aster tanacetifolius)
Tall Verbena
  Verbena rigida (V. venosa)
Tassel Flower
  Amaranthus caudatus, Emilia javanica (E. coccinea, E. flammea, and *E. sagittata)*
Ten-weeks Stock
  Matthiola incana annua
Texas Bluebonnet
  Lupinus subcarnosus and *Lupinus texensis*
Thimble Flower, Blue
  Gilia capitata
Thistle, Saffron
  Carthamus tinctorius
Thorn Apple, Downy
  Datura metel and *Datura inoxia*
Thunbergia
  Thunbergia alata
Tickseed
  Coreopsis basalis (C. drummondii) and *Coreopsis tinctoria (C. bi-color)*
Tidy Tips
  Layia platyglossa
Toadflax, Morocco
  Linaria maroccana
Toadflax, Wall
  Cymbalaria muralis
Tobacco, Flowering
  Nicotiana alata (N. affinis)

Tobacco, Jasmine
  Nicotiana alata (N. affinis)
Torenia
  Torenia fournieri
Trailing Lantana
  Lantana montevidensis (L. sellowiana, L. delicatissima)
Treasure Flower
  Gazania ringens (G. splendens)
Tree Mallow
  Lavatera trimestris
Tricolor Mesembryanthemum
  Dorotheanthus tricolor (Mesembryanthemum tricolor)
Trumpet Flower
  Datura metel and *Datura inoxia*
Tufted Pansy
  Viola x *williamsii*
Tulip Poppy
  Papaver glaucum
Twinspur
  Diascia barberae

Unicorn Plant
  Probiscidea louisianica (Martynia proboscidea)
Ursinia, Dill-leaf
  Ursinia anethoides

Variegated Heartleaf Mesembryanthemum
  Aptenia cordifolia 'Variegata' (Mesembryanthemum cordifolium 'Variegatum')
Variegated Periwinkle
  Vinca major 'Variegata'
Verbena
  Verbena x *hybrida (V.* x *hortensis)*
Verbena, Brazilian
  Verbena rigida (V. venosa)
Verbena, Creeping
  Verbena peruviana (V. chamaedriyolia)
Verbena, Scarlet
  Verbena peruviana (V. chamaedriyolia)
Verbena, Tall
  Verbena rigida (V. venosa)
Vervain
  Verbena x *hybrida (V.* x *hortensis)*
Viola
  Viola x *williamsii*
Violet, Bush
  Browallia speciosa and *Browallia viscosa*
Violet, Dame's
  Hesperis matronalis
Viper's Bugloss
  Echium lycopsis (E. plantagineum)
Virginia Stock
  Malcolmia maritima (Chieranthus maritimus)
Virginian Stock
  Malcolmia maritima (Chieranthus maritimus)

Wall Toadflax
  Cymbalaria muralis
Wallflower, English
  Cheiranthus cheiri
Wax Begonia
  Begonia x *semperflorens – cultorum* and other hybrid cultivars
White Buttons
  Chrysanthemum paludosum
White Dutch Runner Bean
  Phaseolus coccineus 'Albus'
White Lace Flower
  Daucus carota carota
Wild Cucumber
  Echinocystis lobata
Winged Everlasting
  Ammobium alatum
Wishbone Flower
  Torenia fournieri
Woodruff, Annual
  Asperula orientalis (Asperula azurea setosa)
Woolflower
  Celosia cristata

Yellow Buttons
  Chrysanthemum multicaule
Yellow Cosmos
  Cosmos sulphureus
Yellow Everlasting
  Helipterum humboldtiana (H. sanfordii)
Yellow Spider Flower
  Cleome lutea
Youth-and-Old-Age
  Zinnia elegans

Zinnia
  Zinnia elegans
Zinnia, Creeping
  Sanvitalia procumbens
Zonal Geranium
  Pelargonium x *hortorum*

References

Bailey, L.H. *The Standard Cyclopedia of Horticulture.* Macmillan Company, New York. 1941

Blombery, R M. *A Guide to Native Australian Plants.* Angus and Robertson Ltd. 1967.

Crockett, James Underwood. *Annuals.* Time-Life Books, New York. 1971.

Everett, T H (editor). *New Illustrated Encyclopedia of Gardening.* Greystone Press, New York. 1964.

Friends of the University of Alberta Devonian Botanic Garden. 1991 and 1992 Members' Seed List.

Galbraith, Jean. *A Field Guide to the Wild Flowers of South and East Australia.* William Collin Sons & Co. Ltd. 1977.

Godwin, B J. *Alberta Supernaturals.* Instructional Design, Olds College, Olds, Alberta. 1986.

Graf, Alfred Byrd. *Exotica Series 4.* Roehrs Company Publishers, N.J. (12th ed). 1985.

Hartmann, H T and D E Kester. *Plant Propagation: Principles and Practices.* Prentice-Hall Inc, N.J. (4th ed). 1983.

Hortus Third. *A Concise Dictionary of Plants Cultivated in the United States and Canada.* Macmillan Publishing Co Inc. 1976.

Huxley, Anthony. *An Illustrated History of Gardening.* Padding Press Ltd, New York and London (in association with the Royal Horticultural Society). 1978.

Hyams, Edward. *A History of Gardens and Gardening.* Praeger Publishers, New York. 1971.

Looman, J and K F Best. *Budd's Flora of the Canadian Prairie Provinces.* Publication 1662 of the Research Branch, Agriculture Canada. 1979.

Porter, C L. *Taxonomy of Flowering Plants.* W H Freeman and Company (2nd ed). 1967.

Taylor's Guide to Annuals (several authors), Houghton Mifflin Company, Boston 1986 (first edition).

Toop, Edgar W and Sara Williams. *Perennials for the Prairies.* University of Alberta and University of Saskatchewan. 1991.

Williams, S. *Starting Seeds Indoors* (Short Course Manual). University of Saskatchewan, Saskatoon, Sask.

About the Author

Edgar Toop is a graduate of Ohio State University having received his Master of Science in 1957 (Floriculture) and Doctorate in 1960 (Plant Pathology). After completion of his formal education, he taught general botany at Ohio State University before going to the University of Alberta, Canada, as a horticulture professor. He is currently a professor emeritus from the University of Alberta, having retired in 1987 after 25 years of service to its Faculty of Agriculture, Forestry and Home Economics.

Over the years, he has served on the executive of various agricultural and horticultural organizations, including the Canadian Society for Horticultural Science and the Western Canadian Society for Horticulture, an organization that included members from the Great Plains States and Alaska. He is a member of both the International Society for Horticultural Science and the Sigma Xi.

Edgar was recognized by the Alberta Horticultural Association in 1987 when he was awarded the Centennial Gold Medal (the Association's highest award for horticultural achievement). In 1990 he was the recipient of the Alberta Greenhouse Growers Association's Meritorious Service Award. He has also been awarded an honorary life membership in the Western Canadian Society for Horticulture and the Canadian Society for Horticultural Science.